Caryl Churchill
Plays: 2

Softcops, Top Girls, Fen, Serious Money

The plays in this volume include some of the finest work seen in British theatre in recent years, including the international hit *Serious Money* which established Churchill as one of the most powerful and innovative satirists of her time.

Softcops 'is Foucault rendered as a music-hall turn and Victorian freak show . . . I can remember few evenings when theatre and history combined to give such intelligent fun.' *Times Literary Supplement*

'*Top Girls* has a combination of directness and complexity which keeps you both emotionally and intellectually alert. You can smell life, and at the same time feel locked in an argument with an agile and passionate mind.' *Sunday Times*

Fen scrutinises the lives of the low-paid women potato pickers of the Fen: 'The playwright pins down her poetic subject matter in dialogue of impressive vigour and economy.' *Financial Times*

Serious Money is a satirical study of the effects of the Big Bang: 'Pure genius . . . the first play about the City to capture the authentic atmosphere of the place.' *Daily Telegraph*

Caryl Churchill has written for the stage, television and radio. Her stage plays include *Owners* (Royal Court Theatre Upstairs, 1972); *Objections to Sex and Violence* (Royal Court, 1975); *Light Shining in Buckinghamshire* (for Joint Stock, Theatre Upstairs, 1976); *Vinegar Tom* (for Monstrous Regiment, Half Moon and ICA, London, and on tour, 1976); *Traps* (Theatre Upstairs, 1977); *Cloud Nine* (Joint Stock at the Royal Court and on tour, 1979, De Lys Theatre, New York, 1981); *Three More Sleepless Nights* (Soho Poly and Theatre Upstairs, 1980); *Top Girls* (Royal Court, London and Public Theatre, New York, 1982); *Fen* (Joint Stock, Almeida Theatre and Royal Court, London, and on tour, and Public Theatre, New York, 1983); *Softcops* (RSC at the Pit, 1984); *A Mouthful of Birds*, with David Lan (for Joint Stock at the Royal Court and on tour, 1986); *Serious Money* (Royal Court and Wyndhams Theatre, London, 1987); *Icecream* (Royal Court, London, 1989); *Mad Forest* (Central School of Speech and Drama, London, 1990); *Lives of the Great Poisoners* (Arnolfini, Bristol, 1991); *The Skriker* (Royal National Theatre, 1994); and a translation of Seneca's *Thyestes* (Royal Court Theatre Upstairs, 1994).

CARYL CHURCHILL

Plays: 2

Softcops
Top Girls
Fen
Serious Money

Methuen Drama

METHUEN DRAMA CONTEMPORARY DRAMATISTS

13 15 17 19 20 18 16 14

This collection first published in Great Britain in 1990
by Methuen Drama
Reissued in this series in 1996
This collection copyright © 1990 by Caryl Churchill
Introduction copyright © 1990 by Caryl Churchill

Methuen Drama
A & C Black Publishers Ltd
38 Soho Square, London W1D 3HB

Softcops first published in Great Britain as a Methuen Paperback original by
Methuen London. Copyright © 1983, 1986 by Caryl Churchill

Fen first published in Great Britain as a Methuen Paperback original in
1983 by Methuen London in association with Joint Stock Theatre Group
Copyright © 1983, 1986 by Caryl Churchill
'Girls' Song' copyright © 1983, 1986 by Ilona Sekacz

Top Girls first published in Great Britain as a Methuen Paperback original
by Methuen London. Copyright © 1982, 1984 by Caryl Churchill

Serious Money first published in Great Britain as a Methuen Paperback
original in 1987 by Methuen London Ltd.
This edition is fully revised, post-production. Copyright © 1987, 1989 by
Caryl Churchill
'Future's Song' © Ian Dury and Mickey Gallagher
'Five More Glorious Years' song © Ian Dury and Chaz Jankel

The author has asserted her moral rights

A CIP Catalogue record for this book is available from the British Library
ISBN 9-780413-622709

In *Softcops* Caryl Churchill has reflected some ideas from *Surveiller et punir*
by Michel Foucault, published by Gallimard, Paris, for which she is most grateful.

In *Fen* 'Girls' Song' is based on quotations from *Fen Women* by Mary
Chamberlain (Virago, 1977). The pitchfork murder story in Scene Ten is
based on material in an unpublished work by Charles Hansford.

The author gratefully acknowledges use of the following books as background
research for *Top Girls*: *The Confessions of Lady Nijo*, translated from the Japanese
by Karen Brazell, and published by Peter Owen Ltd, London; *A Curious Life for
a Lady* (about Isabella Bird) by Pat Barr, originally published by Macmillan,
London.

Printed and bound in Great Britain by Cox & Wyman Ltd, Reading, Berkshire.

Contents

A Chronology of Performed Plays

PLAY	WRITTEN	PERFORMED [s=stage, r=radio tv=television]
Downstairs	1958	1958 *s*
You've No Need to be Frightened	1959?	1961 *r*
Having a Wonderful Time	1959	1960 *s*
Easy Death	1960	1961 *s*
The Ants	1961	1962 *r*
Lovesick	1965	1966 *r*
Identical Twins	?	1968 *r*
Abortive	1968?	1971 *r*
Not . . .not . . .not . . .not . . .not enough oxygen	?	1971 *r*
Schreber's Nervous Illness	?	1972 *r*
Henry's Past	1971	1972 *r*
The Judge's Wife	1971?	1972 *r*
Owners	1972	1972 *s*
Moving Clocks Go Slow	1973	1975 *s*
Turkish Delight	1973	1974 *tv*
Perfect Happiness	1973	1973 *r*
Objections to Sex and Violence	1974	1975 *s*
Traps	1976	1977 *s*
Vinegar Tom	1976	1976 *s*
Light Shining in Buckinghamshire	1976	1976 *s*
Floorshow (contributor to)	1977	1977 *s*
The After Dinner Joke	1977	1978 *tv*
The Legion Hall Bombing	1978	1979 *tv*
Softcops	1978	1983 *s*
Cloud Nine	1978	1979 *s*
Three More Sleepless Nights	1979	1980 *s*
Crimes	1981	1981 *tv*
Top Girls	1980–2	1982 *s*
Fen	1982	1983 *s*
Midday Sun (with Geraldine Pilgrim and Pete Brooks)	1984	1984 *s*

INTRODUCTION

Softcops was written in 1978, after reading Foucault's *Surveiller et Punir*. It fitted so well with what I was thinking about that I abandoned the play I was groping towards and quickly wrote something that used Foucault's examples as well as his ideas. I put it aside and years later showed it to Howard Davies, who encouraged me to both cut and expand it, and it was done by the RSC in 1984.

After *Softcops*, *Cloud Nine* (Plays: One) and then *Top Girls*, which came slowly. I recently found a reference to Dull Gret in a notebook from years before, and in 1979 I started thinking about a play that would have a lot of women characters doing various jobs and of course the same year Thatcher got in for the first time. It took '80 and '81 to work it out. Meanwhile I wrote *Three More Sleepless Nights* for Les Waters, which he directed at the Soho Poly in '80, and used overlapping dialogue in a quarrel; it seemed the answer for the dinner scene too.

Top Girls was directed by Max Stafford-Clark at the Royal Court in '82, and immediately after it opened I went to the fens with Joint Stock. *Fen* is a play with more direct quotes of things people said to us than any other I've written – 'I wouldn't want my mother to think she'd bred a gibber', 'Jarvis, come and make my coffin', – almost everything Ivy says was said to us but by several different people. The murder story of Frank and Val was taken from a newspaper cutting and the murder story of the man in the coffin from the unpublished memoirs of farmworker Charles Hansford. Most of what the ghost says is taken from a threatening letter written at the time of the Littleport riots. It's a play where I have a particularly lively sense of how much it owes to other people, those who talked to us of course, the actors and Les Waters, and it will always be inseparable in my mind from Annie Smart's set of a field in a room.

In '86 another Joint Stock show with Les Waters and Annie Smart, *A Mouthful of Birds*, co-written with David Lan and choreographed by Ian Spink. Our starting point was possession – Euripides' *Bacchae* and David's work with spirit mediums in Zimbabwe. As soon as it opened I joined Max Stafford-Clark for a two-week workshop on the City – the Joint Stock way

of working but set up by the Royal Court. The idea to do a
show about the City came from Max, and I'd done no
preparation at all before we started. As usual the group opened
the subject up in a way one person couldn't possibly have done
in the time or in many times the time, and gave me a sense of
that appalling and exciting world that carried me through
weeks of reading and researching alone during Big Bang, the
Guinness scandal, Boesky, all of which, with extraordinary
timing, happened between the workshop and the beginning of
rehearsal. With so much to learn I put off writing the play till
the last minute, till, almost submerged with documentary
material, I got the idea of writing the play in verse and was
able to move. The play was still very ungainly by the first day
of rehearsal, and we all owed a lot to Max's clarity and
optimism, as I came and went with new versions of scenes
which the actors took on with dazzling flexibility. British
Telecom refused to provide telephones for the Wyndham's
production, writing to say 'This is a production with which no
public company would wish to be associated.'

SOFTCOPS

Softcops was first presented by the Royal Shakespeare Company at the Barbican Pit on 2 January 1984, with the following cast:

DUVAL	Christopher Bowen
MINISTER	John Carlisle
VIDOCQ	Geoffrey Freshwater
ELOQUENT RICH MAN	Hepburn Graham
LAFAYETTE	Tom Mannion
MAGISTRATE	
BENTHAM	
CONSPIRATOR	Pip Miller
SCHOOLBOY	
OLDER BROTHER	David Shaw-Parker
WARDER	
BOY	Brian Parr
HEADMASTER	Bill Stewart
HOLIDAYMAKER	
LACENAIRE	Malcolm Storry
CONSPIRATOR	
PIERRE	Ian Talbot
MAN ON RACK	Philip Walsh
WARDER	

Other parts: WORKERS, SCHOOL CHILDREN, RICH MEN, CHAIN GANG etc., played by members of the cast.
The Medici String Quartet: Paul Robertson *violin*, David Matthews *violin*, Ivo van der Werff *viola*, Anthony Lewis *cello*

Directed by Howard Davies
Designed by Bob Crowley
Music by Nigel Hess
Lighting by Michael Colf
Movement by Stuart Hopps
Sound by John A. Leonard
Stage Manager Michael Dembowicz
Deputy Stage Manager Jill Macfarlane
Assistant Stage Manager Stephen Dobbin

The play takes place in Paris in the nineteenth century, mainly in the 1830s.

Author's Note

Vidocq and Lacenaire are the original cop and robber, Vidocq, the criminal who became chief of police using the same skills of disguise and cunning, and Lacenaire, the glamorous and ineffectual murderer and petty thief, who was briefly a romantic hero. They both wrote their memoirs, and from the London Library you can take home the original edition of Vidocq's, each volume signed firmly with his name.

I read them after reading Michel Foucault's *Discipline and Punish*, which fascinatingly analyses the change in methods of control and punishment from tearing the victim apart with horses to simply watching him. Jeremy Bentham comes in here, the inventor of the panopticon, the tower from which one person can watch and control many, an idea that goes right through the way society is organised.

I had had an idea for a play called *Softcops*, which was to be about the soft methods of control, schools, hospitals, social workers, when I came across the Foucault book, and was so thrilled with it that I set the play not here and now but in nineteenth century France, where Vidocq puts on half a dozen disguises and Lacenaire is feted by the rich in his cell, while the king's assassin is quietly disposed of. There is a constant attempt by governments to depoliticise illegal acts, to make criminals a separate class from the rest of society so that subversion will not be general, and part of this process is the invention of the detective and the criminal, the cop and the robber.

Caryl Churchill (First published in *RSC News*, Winter 1983)

Further note

Softcops was originally written in 1978, under a Labour Government, when the question of soft controls seemed more relevant than in 1984, the year of its first production, when Thatcher was dismantling the welfare state. That year, audiences were particularly alive to the connection between Bentham's panopticon and Orwell's Big Brother. In 1985, as this edition goes to press, the Government are attempting to depoliticise the miners and the rioters by emphasising a 'criminal element'.

Caryl Churchill *1985*

Production note
The production was developed by the director, designer, composer, choreographer, actors, musicians and myself in a way that I have not attempted to describe — I have for instance kept the original stage direction I wrote for the rescue of Lafayette from the scaffold rather than try to convey the choreography by which it was done. Nor have I stipulated that the set is a neglected room in a great house, that the actors are in evening dress, or that there is a string quartet on stage throughout. These things come from Howard Davies' production and it does not seem right to appropriate them as part of the play.

Caryl Churchill *1985*

A high scaffold is being erected. PIERRE *is anxiously supervising and helping drape it in black cloth and put up posters and placards. A crocodile of young* BOYS *in uniform crosses the stage with their* HEADMASTER, *circles and stops in front of the scaffold.*

PIERRE. Ah, you've brought them for me. I need children with their soft minds to take the impression. More folds this side. Yes, the minister will see them learning. More, more, it hardly reaches the ground. Not long now. It's worth waiting for.

HEADMASTER. They can stand as long as necessary. They have stood three hours.

PIERRE. I can't hold the nail steady. Thank you. My hands are shaking. I want it to be perfect.

HEADMASTER. While you're waiting, examine your consciences.

PEOPLE *go by, stop, go on, come back, gather some distance from the scaffold. The* CHILDREN *stand motionless.*

PIERRE. I hope the rain keeps off. The dye isn't fast.

HEADMASTER. The design is excellent.

PIERRE. There is a balance if I can get it. Terror, but also information. Information, but also terror. But I dream of something covering several acres and completely transforming – as you know. I won't bore you. But if the minister is impressed today I hope for a park.

HEADMASTER. I'm sure it strikes terror.

CHILDREN. Yes, sir.

HEADMASTER. And makes us love our duty.

CHILDREN. Yes, sir.

HEADMASTER. It's a better lesson than talk. Saves the throat.

PIERRE. Help them with the balance. The event will be horrible but the moral is there. Learn while you're young to worship Reason. Reason is my goddess. Fall at her feet. Unfortunately the minister has happy memories of sheer horror. That sign is crooked. Would it be better lower down? Can the children read it?

The HEADMASTER *indicates a* CHILD, *who reads.*

CHILD. 'Jean Lafayette murdered his employer by strangling and will himself be strangled by hanging by the neck.'

PIERRE. Good, leave it there. Where are the red ribbons? Look, children, red is a symbol of blood and passion, the blood shed by passion and the blood shed by Reason in justice and grief. Grief is symbolised of course by the black.

The WORKMEN *are putting red ribbons on the scaffold.*

Or does it look more striking without the ribbons? Should grief be the dominant theme? Blood can be represented by itself. The procession comes down the hill so the crowd can watch its approach. Doleful music specially composed. I've written a speech for the magistrate and one for each of the condemned men. There are three, I hope you can stay. No, take the ribbons off.

The WORKMEN *start taking the ribbons off.*

When the minister sees the children it will help him grasp the educational —

Music: wind and drums.

They're coming. They're early. Get the ribbons off. Stand back.

The WORKMEN *go. One ribbon is left on.* PIERRE *is watching the procession approach.*

See, see the effect. Where's the minister? We can't start. It's fine in the sunlight, the pigeons fly up. The minister is missing the procession.

The procession comes in: the MAGISTRATE *in black; the* EXECUTIONER *in red; the* MUSICIANS *and* GUARDS *in black and red; black-draped cart; the* PRISONER *in the cart in black except for his right hand in a red glove which he holds up. A placard round his neck: Jacques Duval, thief.*

PIERRE (*to the* MAGISTRATE). Welcome, welcome, sir. It's very good of you to take part in this experimental — Excuse me, there's something wrong here. We have the wrong placard I think. (*He takes down the notice about Lafayette and hunts for one about Duval.*) Thief, thief, leg of lamb. (*To* MAGISTRATE:) I hope the walk hasn't tired you, sir. Slight problem, nothing to worry about, I'm afraid the minister has been detained. It's not quite time, I think. I wonder if you could just go round again. You could wait here, sir, if you'd rather and the rest of the procession could just go round the square. No need to go back up the hill. That's right, people will move aside, music again too, it's very moving, well done, music, music.

The procession slowly circles. PIERRE *puts up the correct notice.*

HEADMASTER. That gentleman is the magistrate. See his wise face, kind and stern. Here comes the cart, see the villain. You can see the weakness and evil. His right hand which did the evil deed is clad in red. One of these men is the executioner — ah, that one in red. He carries an instrument of justice. What does red symbolise?

CHILD. Blood, sir.

HEADMASTER. And?

CHILD. Passion, sir.

PIERRE. Get that ribbon off, off.

PIERRE *realises the* WORKMEN *have gone and gets the ribbon off himself.*

HEADMASTER. What will he do with the wicked man?

CHILD. Hang him, sir.

HEADMASTER. Wrong.

CHILD. Hurt him, sir.

HEADMASTER. Hurt him, yes, can somebody be more precise?

CHILD. Cut his hand off, sir.

HEADMASTER. Yes, you can see it written on the notice. He will cut off the hand that stole the leg of lamb.

CHILD. Please, sir, shouldn't they cut his leg off, sir?

Meanwhile the MINISTER *has arrived and is greeted by* PIERRE.

PIERRE. They came down the hill, a moment of great solemnity, the power of the law struck home to the heart and mind, the pigeons flew up. You see the notices, sir, explaining, so everyone understands what is happening and isn't carried away by emotion.

MINISTER. They can't read.

PIERRE. The magistrate also makes a speech, sir. And each condemned man makes a speech. Some of them can read, sir. A few of them. Maybe not.

HEADMASTER. Your country loves its children like a father. And when the children are bad the country grieves like a father. And punishes like a father.

The procession stops by the scaffold.

MAGISTRATE. There's a word here not very clearly written.

PIERRE. I can't read my own writing. Whatever you think.

MAGISTRATE. Execution?

PIERRE. Very likely. (*To* MINISTER:) A headmaster has brought his pupils. The use of punishment as education —

MAGISTRATE. 'This is a day of mourning.'

PIERRE. Ah, ah, excuse me, execration.

MAGISTRATE. 'Day of mourning.'

PIERRE. No, the word, here, execration.

MAGISTRATE. Very good, I would never have thought of that. Execration. Let me make a note. 'This is a day of mourning.

We are, you see, in black. We mourn that one of our citizens has broken the law. We mourn that we must separate ourselves from this citizen and inflict this penalty upon him. Black symbolises our grief and our — ha — execration of his crime. This man has with his right hand —'

PIERRE. Hold it up, hold it up.

MAGISTRATE. — 'committed an act against his fellow men. And it is with grief that his right hand will be taken from him. We do not rejoice in vengeance. There will be no singing and dancing, no cursing and fighting. It is a sad necessity for him and for us. Our social order —'

Meanwhile one of the CHILDREN *fidgets, is taken out of line by the* HEADMASTER, *caned on the hand and returned to his place. The rest of the* CHILDREN *stand motionless.*

MINISTER. Can't we get on with the punishment?

PIERRE. This is the general introduction to the whole —

MINISTER. Never bore a mob.

PIERRE. We're about half-way.

MINISTER. Where's the executioner?

PIERRE (*to* MAGISTRATE). Thank you, we'll stop there, thank you.

PIERRE *claps;* HEADMASTER *joins in;* CHILDREN *join in. By then* PIERRE *has stopped.*

Now the condemned man will speak. Listen and learn. Music.

Music. The prisoner, DUVAL, *climbs on to the scaffold. Cheers and jeers from the* CROWD.

Wait till the music stops. Now.

DUVAL. I, Jacques Duval.

PIERRE. Go on.

DUVAL. I, Jacques Duval.

PIERRE. Don't cry, speak up. (*To the* MINISTER:) Tears of repentance.

DUVAL. I, Jacques Duval. Under sentence of having my right hand cut off —

PIERRE. Hold it up. Good.

DUVAL. Call out. Call out . . .

PIERRE. Theft, crime of theft, cut off for the crime —

DUVAL. Theft, crime of theft, cut off. Fellow citizens. Call out to my fellow citizens.

PIERRE. Learn —

DUVAL. Learn by my terrible example. Never steal even if you're hungry because . . .

PIERRE. Because it is against the laws —

DUVAL. Laws of our beloved country. And your hand will be cut off.

PIERRE. Up, up, that's right.

DUVAL. I'm very sorry what I done.

PIERRE. Good.

DUVAL. And submit, is it? Submit the punishment the judge give me. Gladly. Gladly submit. Judge give me. And . . .

PIERRE. I am happy —

DUVAL. — I am happy —

PIERRE. — to be an example —

DUVAL. — example

PIERRE. — to you all.

DUVAL. — all.

PIERRE. Watch —

DUVAL. Watch what is done to me today and remember it tomorrow.

PIERRE. If you are sorry for me —

DUVAL. Yes, that's it.

PIERRE. Keep the law. Go on.

DUVAL. Go on.

PIERRE. No, keep the law.

DUVAL. Yes.

PIERRE. And then I'll know my pain did some good.

DUVAL. I don't know what comes after.

PIERRE. That's all.

MINISTER. Where's the executioner?

HEADMASTER. Are all your eyes open?

MAN IN CROWD. Jacques! I'm here. Jacques!

DUVAL. Don't look!

> DUVAL's *hand is cut off and displayed to the* CROWD *by the* EXECUTIONER. *He faints and is put in the cart.* PIERRE *indicates to the* MUSICIANS *that they should play. The* GUARDS *take the cart out,* DUVAL's FRIEND *running after. The* MUSICIANS *play. One of the children,* LUC, *turns aside to be sick. The others stand motionless.*

MINISTER. It's over very quickly. I don't count the talking. When I was a boy one punishment would last from noon till sunset. You could buy food and drink. I remember one time they lit a fire to throw the corpse on in the late afternoon and he held on and held on and they had to build the fire up again in the evening. It was still glowing at midnight, and people still standing. That was the wheel, of course, you don't see it now. People don't want to read, they don't want speeches. You'll drive them away, and what's the use of a punishment if nobody sees it? What brings a crowd, it's very simple, is agony, I'm not saying they don't appreciate something fine. They like an executioner who's good at his job. They like fine instruments. Nothing upsets a crowd more than hacking. But they like something unusual and they like a man to stay conscious so he doesn't miss it.

PIERRE. There's a good crowd here today.

MINISTER. That's the novelty. They don't want a school, they want a festival.

PIERRE. A festival means riots. People attack the executioner.

MINISTER. And the soldiers shoot them down.

The HEADMASTER *has got the sick child,* LUC, *and made him stand with his arms over his head.*

HEADMASTER. Now control yourself. Stand with your arms up till I tell you.

MINISTER. Listen, my boy. People have vile dreams. The man who dares cut a throat while he's awake is their hero. But then justice dares cut and burn and tear that man's body, far beyond what he did and beyond their dreams. So they worship us. That's why it's a festival.

PIERRE. But I don't want them to be caught up. Their hearts may beat a little faster but all the time they must be thinking.

The music starts again for the approach of the procession — the return of the GUARDS *and the cart.*

MINISTER. While the fire burned and long after it died down there was considerable fornication. Not only among the poor.

PIERRE. Ah look, sir, excuse me, down the hill.

MINISTER. I found my way to a lady who had never been more than civil to me and my hand under her skirt found her ready for hours of ingenuity beyond my dreams. Next day she received me for tea as usual. The people went about their work quite silently.

PIERRE. I want them to look at the illegal act in the perspective of the operation of society and the light of Reason.

The cart comes in with LAFAYETTE, *a murderer. He is already speaking in the cart and continues when he is transferred to the scaffold.* PIERRE *suddenly remembers that the placard must be changed and hurries to do it.*

LAFAYETTE. Lafayette. Look at me. Remember the name. Lafayette. Murderer. Murderer. Want to know what I did? Killed my boss. Killed old daddy Anatole right in his office. He was shouting like he does, know how he shouts. And I was on him, hands round his neck, would he stop shouting, would he hell. So I kept hanging on, didn't I. I'm meant to say sorry for that. Sorry sorry sorry sorry sorry. Do you think I am? I shit on the judges. I shit on my boss. I shit on you. I really did shit on my boss. Do you shit on your boss? You didn't kill him though, did you, I'm the killer. And I'm the one going to die. Want to die instead? You can if you like. I don't want to. You do it. You kill him instead, all right? He goes a horrible colour, wait and see. I'm not sorry, I'm glad. It wasn't easy but I did it. Lafayette did it.

Meanwhile:

PIERRE. This isn't what we arranged he would say.

MINISTER. Just hang him.

PIERRE. I wrote a speech.

MINISTER. Where's the executioner?

PIERRE (*to* LAFAYETTE). Look, you agreed what you were going to say.

LAFAYETTE *strikes him. Instant brawl.* LAFAYETTE *is seized by the* EXECUTIONER *and* GUARDS, *a hood put over his head and a noose round his neck. The* CROWD *throws stones, shouts, climbs on to the scaffold. The* CHILDREN *scatter.* LAFAYETTE *is hoisted up. The* EXECUTIONER *is hit by a stone. The* MINISTER *and* MAGISTRATE *escape from the scaffold.* PIERRE *tries to defend the scaffold and is knocked down, pulling the black cloth with him. The rope hanging* LAFAYETTE *is cut by one of the* CROWD. *He gets down and tries to run but is pulled down by someone else. The scaffold is broken. The* CROWD *has formed into two groups, one beats up* LAFAYETTE *and one beats up the* EXECUTIONER. *The* DIGNITARIES *and* MUSICIANS *are standing aside in a huddle. The* CHILDREN *are watching what is done to* LAFAYETTE *and the* EXECUTIONER. *A line of* SOLDIERS *comes on with fixed bayonets and advances. The* CROWD *scatters and disappears.* LAFAYETTE *and the* EXECUTIONER *are lying on the ground.* LAFAYETTE *sits up, still with the hood and noose on, and collapses again. One of the* MUSICIANS *blows a few wild notes, a* DRUMMER *joins in. One of the* SOLDIERS *turns towards them. Silence.*

The SOLDIERS *go. The* MAGISTRATE *and* MINISTER *go.*
The CHILDREN *get back into a crocodile and* LUC *lifts his*
arms again. PIERRE *gets out from under the black cloth,*
blood on his face. The GUARDS *and* MUSICIANS *put the*
pieces of broken scaffold in the cart, put LAFAYETTE *and*
the EXECUTIONER *on top, and go out. Just* PIERRE *and the*
HEADMASTER *and the* CHILDREN *are left.*

What I visualise you see. Is a Garden of Laws. Where, over
several acres, with flowering bushes, families would stroll on
a Sunday. And there would be displayed every kind of crime
and punishment. Different coloured hats. Different coloured
posters. Guides to give lectures on civic duty and moral
feeling. And people would walk gravely and soberly and
reflect. And for the worst crime. Parricide. An iron cage
hanging high up in the sky. Symbolic of the rejection by
heaven and earth. From anywhere in the city you could look
up. And see him hanging there, in the sun, in the snow. Year
after year. Quietly take it to heart. A daily lesson.

The HEADMASTER *wipes blood off* PIERRE's *face.*

HEADMASTER (*to* LUC). You may put your arms down now.

The HEADMASTER *and* CHILDREN *go out.* PIERRE *is left*
alone. The MINISTER *and* VIDOCQ *approach from opposite*
sides.

MINISTER. The best informer we have is Vidocq. He's a villain
but he catches villains. I've a good mind to persuade him to
change his way of life and make him Chief of Police.

VIDOCQ. Here comes the minister. He can't do without me. But
everyone treats informers like dirt. I've a good mind to
persuade him to trust me and make me Chief of Police.

MINISTER. Is that you, Vidocq?

VIDOCQ. What is the real colour of Vidocq's hair? I don't know
myself. Grey by now. Do I really wear spectacles? Is this
moustache real or stuck on? If it's real, did I grow it as a
disguise? Or will it be a disguise when I shave it off? Who have
you come to see, sir? And do you see him?

MINISTER. I see someone useful.

VIDOCQ. Always that, sir. I'm twenty men and all of them at your service.

MINISTER. I have a special job for you, Vidocq.

VIDOCQ. I'll be glad to do it, sir, whatever it is.

MINISTER (*aside*). This is going too fast. He'll never accept if I ask him point blank.

VIDOCQ (*aside*). I'm being too eager. He won't believe I'm not tricking him.

MINISTER. We'll talk about it later. You may not be the right person for this particular enterprise.

VIDOCQ. Yes, I'm not that interested in sneaking.

MINISTER. I can manage without your services.

VIDOCQ. I can do without you an all.

MINISTER (*aside*). This is terrible.

VIDOCQ (*aside*). This is terrible. Sir, I hear you've had a great success in arresting the notorious regicide, Fieschi.

MINISTER. It's not generally known but I don't mind telling you. He was discovered yesterday drunk in an attic.

VIDOCQ. The police don't often have such luck.

MINISTER. It takes skill to catch a man like that.

VIDOCQ. Yes, I'm quite surprised they managed it.

MINISTER. The police force is a force to be reckoned with.

VIDOCQ. I've nothing against the police force as such.

MINISTER. It's not as efficient as it might be.

VIDOCQ. That's exactly what I think myself.

MINISTER. Ah.

PIERRE *approaches*.

PIERRE. Excuse me, sir, did you say Fieschi? Fieschi who tried to murder the king with an infernal machine? That will count as regicide, sir, parricide, even though the king wasn't hurt. Might it not be the occasion, sir, for the use of the iron cage I mentioned to you which would hang above the Garden of Laws and —

MINISTER. Aren't you ashamed?

PIERRE. It didn't go quite according to plan, sir.

MINISTER. I should have told the soldiers to shoot.

PIERRE. Next time —

MINISTER. Next time I will have the prisoners flogged. And ten men taken from the crowd.

PIERRE. If the prepared speeches —

MINISTER. They will all be gagged.

PIERRE. My idea, sir, is that in the park —

MINISTER. Never. Tell him, Vidocq. You were a boy when pain was seen to be necessary. We are dealing with a wild animal and we keep it off us with raw meat and whips. We don't teach it to sit up and beg and feed it sugar lumps. It bit you this morning and I'm glad.

PIERRE. Reason is my goddess.

MINISTER. Reason uses whips. The minister has no further use for your services.

PIERRE. Thank you, sir.

PIERRE *starts to leave.*

MINISTER. I'd have Fieschi ten days dying but that has all been abolished. But you and I, Vidocq, know what it is to live in fear.

VIDOCQ. Come back here. Not a rich man?

PIERRE. No.

VIDOCQ. Poor but honest?

PIERRE. And not stupid.

VIDOCQ. Idealist? Visionary? Reformer?

PIERRE. It will happen. If not me, someone else.

VIDOCQ. No, never someone else. Me. Me. If you think of a good idea get the credit. My slightest whim I go for like a life's ambition. Here's some money for you.

VIDOCQ *throws a gold coin on the ground.*

All you've got to do is pick it up. But if you don't do it before I count a hundred, I'll shoot you in the leg. I count in ones. The gun is loaded. The coin is real gold. It's not tied to a string. Well?

PIERRE *looks from one to the other and laughs nervously.*

Neither of us will touch you. You have a hundred seconds to pick up the coin. But of course you might get cramp and fall down. There might be an earthquake. Someone else might run up and get the coin first. And then I will shoot you in the leg. Never mind what I'm after.

PIERRE. All right.

VIDOCQ *starts to count.* PIERRE *stands still till ten then walks very slowly and picks up the coin.*

VIDOCQ. Again?

PIERRE. Wouldn't mind.

VIDOCQ. No, this time we're going to do it different. Come here. Hands behind your back. You can have another coin just for asking. But if you do I'll hit you in the face.

PIERRE. No you won't.

VIDOCQ. It's not so bad as being shot in the leg. Want a coin?

PIERRE. No.

VIDOCQ. Real gold.

PIERRE. No.

VIDOCQ. Off you go then. There you are. It's not what the punishment is, sir, it's knowing you're going to get it. You could take a whole year to kill a man and nobody cares because nobody expects to get caught. You can cover the whole town with posters and nobody reads them because nobody expects to get caught. I've never been caught.

PIERRE. I never thought of that.

MINISTER. It's not true. Vidocq has convictions for theft, blackmail —

VIDOCQ. But I never did any of that. It was always a mistake. I happened to look like the man that done it. I was walking past at the time. Somebody had it in for me. I have done some jobs, I will admit, but you couldn't tell me one of them.

MINISTER. You're saying the police make mistakes?

VIDOCQ. Say you divided the country into ten areas, then into ten divisions, ten subdivisions, ten branches, ten sections, where are we getting, ten policemen in each section.

MINISTER. A million policemen?

VIDOCQ. It's not the number so much as the shape. And at the top a strong man.

MINISTER. A strong man at the top.

VIDOCQ. Do you know what a card index is, sir?

MINISTER. Little boxes.

VIDOCQ. With cards in them, with names on, in the order of the alphabet.

MINISTER. A friend of mine is a naturalist and I believe he —

VIDOCQ. You want a box with all the criminals. And another box with all the kinds of crime. You get a blackmail, b, look it up, who's done blackmail before, Vidocq, V, look him up, how he operates, where you find him, you've got me.

MINISTER. You don't want me to get you.

VIDOCQ. No, sir, if you took my advice I'd have to change my way of life.

MINISTER (*aside*). He said he'd have to change his way of life.

VIDOCQ (*aside*). Dare I suggest it now?

MINISTER (*aside*). Is this the moment to make the offer?

VIDOCQ. Of course I am a professional where crime is concerned. I couldn't lead a life completely cut off from it.

MINISTER (*aside*). Is he saying he won't go straight?

I have known you a long time and I know what you are.

VIDOCQ (*aside*). Is he saying he can't ever trust me?

PIERRE. I've had an idea. I think Monsieur Vidocq would make an excellent Chief of Police. I know you both think my ideas never work out.

MINISTER. But you know Monsieur Vidocq would never want to be a policeman.

VIDOCQ. You know the minister would never trust me.

PIERRE. The card index box appeals to Reason.

VIDOCQ. The boy's not stupid, you know.

MINISTER. Not at all. He's one of the brightest in my department.

VIDOCQ. You should listen to what he says.

MINISTER. I value his opinion very highly. I didn't really dismiss him just now.

VIDOCQ *gives* PIERRE *a gold coin.*

VIDOCQ. You can think of this coin as the perfect crime, no trouble, from the days before Vidocq was Chief of Police.

PIERRE (*to the* MINISTER). Sir, about the park —

MINISTER. Chief of Police.

The MINISTER *and* VIDOCQ *embrace.*

Crimes against property is an area of concern. I have land. I have warehouses. In the bad old days the peasants used to take liberties, chop down trees for firewood, that sort of thing, perfectly understandable, the old feudal landlords were monsters. But you can't have that now the land's owned by respectable citizens. You can't have that in warehouses. I lose thousands.

VIDOCQ. Wherever you get a lot of workers, sir, you'll get a lot of bad characters.

MINISTER. I sometimes think you see that if I took one of them as an example and set up a wheel by the factory gate —

VIDOCQ. Not a wheel, sir, a card index box. We'll have the bad characters in a box. You'll see. You can trust the rest. And the police will live so close to that criminal class, take informers from it, know it like itself, so every time someone reaches for a gold coin, wham, he's hit in the face.

MINISTER. I regret the disappearance of the thumbscrew. But that's the nostalgia of an old man.

PIERRE. A golden age. Crime will be eliminated.

VIDOCQ. Not entirely eliminated, no. It is my profession.

MINISTER. Vidocq, can I trust you?

VIDOCQ. I'm going to be famous.

PIERRE *takes out a book and reads.*

PIERRE. The memoirs of Vidocq.

VIDOCQ. Every night a new crime against property. I want to catch the gang redhanded. I get drinking with their leader. I seem to be from the provinces. I seem not to want him to guess I've escaped from prison. I seem to let him get me drunk.

ANTIN *and* VIDOCQ 2, *who looks nothing like* VIDOCQ.

ANTIN. Stick with me and you'll be all right. I'll settle Vidocq one of these days.

VIDOCQ 2. Everyone says that.

ANTIN. Right then, we'll settle him tonight.

VIDOCQ 2. You know where he lives?

ANTIN. Coming?

VIDOCQ. So we wait for me outside my door. But I don't show up all night.

ANTIN. I'll get him tomorrow. Now then, you interested in a job?

VIDOCQ. So we plan a robbery for the next night. And to his surprise the police turn up.

ANTIN. Here, what's this?

VIDOCQ 2. I'm Vidocq.

Tableau of VIDOCQ 2 *arresting* ANTIN.

PIERRE (*reads*). A butcher was robbed and murdered on the road.

VIDOCQ. I get two of them, Court and Raoul. The third's a retired customs officer. I go to his village. He's mending a road with thirty other men. If I try to arrest him, they'll kill me.

VIDOCQ 3, *quite different again, and* PONS GERARD, VIDOCQ *embraces* PONS.

VIDOCQ 3. How's the family?

PONS. What? what?

VIDOCQ 3. Have I changed so much?

PONS. I can't quite —

VIDOCQ 3 (*whispers*). Friend of Court and Raoul.

PONS (*for the benefit of the other men*). Ah ah, my dear old friend.

VIDOCQ. So I get him alone.

PONS. Who was it got them?

VIDOCQ 3. Who do you think?

PONS. I'd like to see that Vidocq. What I'd do to him.

PONS *gives* VIDOCQ *a drink.*

VIDOCQ 3. What you'd do to Vidocq is give him a drink.

PONS. Don't make me laugh.

VIDOCQ 3. I'm Vidocq.

Tableau — VIDOCQ 3 *arrests* PONS GERARD.

PIERRE (*reads*). There was cholera in Paris. Three hundred people died every day. Riots broke out. The army was having trouble. It was thought Louis-Philippe might lose his throne.

VIDOCQ. There's a group building a barricade so I go up behind them with a few men in plain clothes. I'm carrying a red flag, which makes it easier to get about. They're looking in front where the soldiers are coming. I take hold of their leader, Colombat. I say, Come along now, I'm Vidocq.

What VIDOCQ *describes is happening.* VIDOCQ 4 *with a red flag arrests* COLOMBAT.

VIDOCQ 4. Come along now, I'm Vidocq.

Tableau — VIDOCQ 4 *arrests* COLOMBAT.

VIDOCQ. We cleared five barricades so the army had freedom of movement. The revolt was suppressed. It was a matter of public order. More than half the people on the street were villains. I've welcomed every kind of government, always hoping for order. Better my way than the army shooting. Which they still did of course. One young man couldn't get the bloodshed out of his mind and subsequently tried to kill the king. I disguised myself as a duchess one day and shook the king's hand.

PIERRE. Speaking of killing the king, sir, the regicide, the one with the infernal machine, sir, I was wondering if we could make a display —

VIDOCQ. Make a display? of a regicide?

MINISTER. The rack? — no.

PIERRE. The iron cage — everyone stares up — amazing spectacle —

VIDOCQ. A regicide? You want to take people's attention off. You don't want to make an example of a regicide, people follow an example. What you want for a spectacle is someone good-looking and a bit out of the ordinary. Lacenaire.

MINISTER. Who's Lacenaire?

VIDOCQ. Second-rate little villain. Bungles half his jobs.

MINISTER. Then what's the point?

PIERRE. I've heard of Lacenaire.

VIDOCQ. He's writing his memoirs. People pass them round on little bits of paper.

PIERRE. That could be a wonderful means of education if he was warning young people against — is he? I suppose not.

VIDOCQ. He's pretty. He writes verses. He'll do.

LACENAIRE *is brought on between two* POLICEMEN.

LACENAIRE (*recites*).
What is life? What is death? What is virtue? What is
philosophy?
Science? Honour? Gold? Friendship's not much either.
If there's a God, he only loves himself.
Why are you frightened of death? Ah, nothingness.
Curse me – I laugh. Curse me – I'm firm in my frenzy.
But if I'd believed in goodness I would have been good.

VIDOCQ. Perfect.

LACENAIRE. I didn't commit murder for money, I did it for
blood. I decided to become the scourge of society. Father said
I would end on the guillotine.

MINISTER. Isn't this dangerous?

VIDOCQ. Marvellous, isn't it, and he's not even good at his job.
His famous robberies only got him a few hundred. He makes a
noise, he trips over, he faints. He quarrels with all his friends,
he betrays them, he blackmails, he gets blackmailed. He
doesn't plan. Or he makes plans and tells everyone what he's
going to do so it's all over Paris before he's done it. The other
villains despise him. He's a complete failure.

LACENAIRE. I can't live out there. I'd rather be in prison with
my brothers. There's a society of the rich and a society of the
wretched. I identify with the wretched. I too have been
rejected. I too seek vengeance. Murder is an example to others.
I am an example, a man of good birth, a poetic genius, who
has deliberately made himself a murderer. With these hands.

RICH MEN *are arriving for a feast in* LACENAIRE's *cell. They
cheer and clap as* LACENAIRE *talks.* LACENAIRE *is sat
down, his face wiped, hair combed, drink poured for him,
food put before him. The* MINISTER, VIDOCQ, PIERRE *and
the* HEADMASTER *are all there. A* PHRENOLOGIST *feels*
LACENAIRE's *head and a* WRITER *takes down every word
he says.*

RICH MEN. He's so young.
All he's been through.

Yes but you can see in his eyes.
Never trust eyes like that.
It's the shape of his skull.
No, it's his free will.
His pure self-interest.
I conduct my business like that.

MINISTER. He looks like a success.

VIDOCQ. Do you trust me?

MINISTER. I think I have to.

LACENAIRE. My mother never loved me. That may be the
explanation you're looking for. If I'd been born forty years
earlier I would have been a hero of the revolution. I would like
to pull the city down.

RICH MAN. I pulled down six of my houses yesterday and the
tenants ran out like rats.

LACENAIRE. I'll save a fine chair, a painting of Napoleon and a
silk scarf, and the rest can go. I don't like ugliness.

ANOTHER RICH MAN. Nor do I, have nothing in my house but
beautiful things.

LACENAIRE. I hate beauty worse.

Applause.

PHRENOLOGIST. The bumps on his head indicate that he is not
aggressive. He is rather of a timid disposition.

LACENAIRE. Timid? Timid? With this hand — Yes, of course, go
on. Write down every word I say. Feel my bumps. Cut me up
when I'm dead. It's still not me. You'll never know. I am a
secret.

WRITER. What? What?

ANOTHER RICH MAN. 'You'll never know. I am a secret.'

PIERRE. But he shouldn't be a secret if he's a spectacle.

HEADMASTER. My pupils have no time for secrets.

PIERRE. If Lacenaire had been properly educated he'd feel the
right things for people to see. There's something new here, I

can't quite —

LACENAIRE. Why do you kill animals?

ANOTHER RICH MAN. Me? I don't think —

LACENAIRE. Don't you eat meat? Don't you hunt? You have designed ways of torturing animals as delicate as your furnishings. And you call me a murderer.

ANOTHER RICH MAN (*to* PIERRE). He killed his kitten by hitting it against the wall and he cried for hours.

LACENAIRE. I have a horror of all suffering. But you only understand if it happens to someone like you. So you murder every day. I have sacrificed myself to prove it. You can't understand love, but you understand fear. I'm going to die tomorrow. And when I die, everything I've ever seen will come to an end. The city will fall. Your chandeliers are down. That's my vengeance.

ANOTHER RICH MAN. Wear this for me tomorrow.

ANOTHER RICH MAN. Wear this for me.

LACENAIRE *spits at him. Laughter and clapping.*

LACENAIRE. I won't wear your jewels because you'll take them off my corpse and say 'Lacenaire wore this for me'. And the glory of my death is not yours.

MINISTER. Half an hour on the rack and he wouldn't talk so much.

VIDOCQ. He couldn't be better if I'd invented him. Lacenaire, do you know who I am?

LACENAIRE. A fat idiot like the rest.

VIDOCQ. Vidocq, Chief of Police.

LACENAIRE. A fat idiot worse than the rest.

Laughter and clapping.

PIERRE. I think you er believe in Reason?

LACENAIRE. I believe in necessity.

PIERRE. Ah. I believe in Reason. I don't think either of us believes in God.

LACENAIRE. Don't try to make friends with me.

PIERRE. No, of course. Sorry.

LACENAIRE. No, I don't believe in God. I tried for a moment
yesterday afternoon. My only virtue is sensibility. No one has
ever had such a prodigious facility for writing verse. Good
verse. And bad verse.

RICH MEN. Recite a poem.
Sing a song.
Oh please.

LACENAIRE. I never like showing my compositions.

RICH MEN. Yes yes.

LACENAIRE. *The Thief Asks the King for a Job.*

RICH MEN. This song is banned.
Oh wonderful.

LACENAIRE *stands and sings.*

LACENAIRE. I'm such a thief your Majesty,
I'm such a villain you'll agree
I'd make a great policeman.

I spend cash that's not my own,
Never hear the victim groan —
I'd make a great minister.

I'm cunning, greedy, really bad,
A lot of people think I'm mad —
I'd make a great king.

Laughter, applause, cheers.

I could just as well have written the opposite. I happened to
meet some republicans in prison one day, that's all. We've
never had liberty yet, not for one day. Is it worth all the
blood? And you tell me to respect human life. I'm
committing suicide, that's all. A very spectacular suicide with
a very big knife. Does anyone dare say I'm not committing
suicide?

RICH MEN *sing in imitation of* LACENAIRE.

RICH MEN. What a brilliant demonstration,
  Symbol of his generation —
  You'll make a great martyr.

  All your friends will thrill to see you,
  How we wish that we could be you —

LACENAIRE. Friends? What friends? My friends don't like me. I am their leader to overthrow the world and they won't see it. They're jealous. I miss them.

RICH MEN. They're just villains and they hate you,
  Only we appreciate you —
  Murder is Art!

Further shouts from the RICH MEN.

  The metaphysics!
  Lacenaire, I share your soul!

LACENAIRE. They are gods. And you are little lice on their bodies. Pop. Little specks of blood.

RICH MAN. Lacenaire, I can imagine you robbing me. I'd wake up in the night. Is someone there? I get out of bed my heart beating. Was it a cat? Someone is breathing. I stop breathing. Yes, someone is breathing. I strike a light. It's knocked out of my hand. My arm is forced up behind my back. I'm tied to a chair. My eyes are getting used to the dark. I see you moving about my room. You throw my clothes on the floor. You find my jewels and fill your pockets. You slash the mattress and find the gold. You pull down the velvet curtains and throw them over my head and force them into my mouth, the chair falls over, I'm suffocating inside the curtains. You kick free of them, you're leaving. Lacenaire! You pity me. You pull the curtains off. You pick the chair up and me on it. Oh Lacenaire. You slap my face. The taste of blood in my mouth. You put your knife deep into my chest. Lacenaire, Lacenaire. Let me give you this ring. Put it on your finger. Ah. You would ruin me if you were free.

LACENAIRE *is by now quite passive, lets the ring be put on his finger.*

RICH MEN. Lacenaire, you would kill me.

You would rape my wife on the table.

You would rape me.

You would rape the little schoolchildren.

You would burn my house, I would run through the hall with my hair on fire screaming Lacenaire, Lacenaire.

They are all giving him jewellery and money, embracing him, snatching off his shoe as a souvenior. One of them pulls down his own trousers.

Stand on me, Lacenaire, stand on me. On me, on me. Stand on me, I'm so rich. Stand on me, Lacenaire, I'm so boring.

Two of them with their trousers down bend over and the others help LACENAIRE *up. Others take their trousers down or dance on the table, pour drinks on their heads, rub cake in each other's faces.* LACENAIRE *stands unsteadily, balanced on two bottoms.*

VIDOCQ. You are the greatest living criminal. And in me you have met your match because I am the greatest living detective. I hear you have written your memoirs. After your death I will have them published.

Cheers.

LACENAIRE. No one else could have caught me, so he's got to be a genius. I'll drink to you, Vidocq.

VIDOCQ. Your health, Lacenaire.

Shouts of 'Vidocq', 'Lacenaire'. VIDOCQ *is in London with his exhibition: large Dutch painting of a battle, quantity of wax fruit, reaping hook, chopper, thumbscrews etc, manacles and chains, weighted boots, braces, a pen, a black box.* VIDOCQ *speaks in a French accent as he is speaking English to the public.*

VIDOCQ. Ladies and gentlemen, here for the first time in London you can see the great exhibition of the great Vidocq, for many years chief of the sûreté in Paris, that is the detective force. I have here many marvels for you and also I will astound you by my skill at disguises which made me able to catch so many criminals of Paris. First we have here many paintings, very fine, by Dutch masters, Langendyk, Van der Veldes, and other works of the Italian, Dutch, Flemish and French schools. While you are looking excuse me one moment.

He goes out and simultaneously appears, a different VIDOCQ, *from the other side, acknowledging applause.*

Thank you, thank you. This is how I catch them you see. The next exhibit is a collection perfectly unique of tropical fruits, modelled from wax by a special process now lost so it can never be repeated. See the pineapple, mango, pomegranate, guava, in their natural colours, excuse me —

And as before he instantly reappears, transformed.

Thank you. Very kind. Now here we have many souvenirs of the dark side of Paris life. This reaping hook was an instrument by which a young man killed his mother. This chopper also has been soaked in blood. Here is some very old thing, the thumbscrew, from times not long ago, but also very long ago I am glad to say. Also these chains, chains of the chain gang, of prisoners going to the galleys. Now ladies and gentlemen, regard. These manacles and boots with heavy weights I myself, Vidocq, wore these in my youth. Yes I myself, Vidocq, was led astray and falsely accused when a young man, I had some of the wild spirits of the young, and in spite of these very heavy chains I escaped, as I tell in my memoirs which are on sale here today. I escape and offer my services to my country to work here for the police. Now excuse me while you examine these things.

He reappears as before.

And now ladies and gentlemen we come to the most exciting souvenirs of the exhibition. What have we here? We have the braces, yes the braces that held up the trousers of — Fieschi! the notorious cowardly regicide, who made an attempt on the life of King Louis Philippe with an infernal machine. And here we have a pen. Just a pen? What a pen! It is the pen with which in his prison cell, under sentence of death for a foul murder, that most celebrated criminal Lacenaire, the poet-murderer Lacenaire, wrote his memoirs. With this very pen. And now ladies and gentlemen, I beg you not to tell anyone when you leave this place what I am going to show you now. Yes, it would bring more people here. But it would spoil the surprise for them. Surprise? No, the shock. Tell your friends there is something very special, very horrible, very unique, they must come themselves to see what it is. Ladies and gentlemen —

VIDOCQ *opens the black box and takes from it a black velvet cushion with an embalmed hand on it.*

— the hand that held the pen. The hand that held the knife. The hand of Lacenaire! The hand of a man put to death on the guillotine of France! The hand of glory! Thank you, thank you.

PIERRE. Lacenaire should have been in the centre of the garden. And overhead in a cage I would have put Fieschi, who tried to kill His Majesty. It would have had such educational value. And now everyone's in the street watching Lacenaire, not knowing what to think of him because nobody's telling them, all dancing and screaming, complete confusion. What I love in people is their reason, but they will leap about. I've decided to be a teacher. I despair of my Garden of Laws. It will never happen. I see it so clearly but I'll never walk down those paths and see among the flowers all those little theatres of punishment. I must give it up.

HEADMASTER. You'll make an excellent teacher.

PIERRE. Vidocq is bringing some order into crime. He knows who the criminals are and he will catch them. But then what? What do you do with them? If you don't use their bodies to demonstrate the power of the law — Never mind. Let someone else solve it. Show me your class.

The HEADMASTER *rings a bell.* SCHOOLCHILDREN *run to their benches. Some of them are wearing harnesses to correct their posture.*

HEADMASTER. Enter

CHILDREN *put one leg over bench.*

your benches.

CHILDREN *put second leg over and sit down.*

Take

CHILDREN *put one hand to their slates.*

your slates.

CHILDREN *take the slates.*

The HEADMASTER *has a wooden clapper with which he signals instructions to the* CHILDREN. *He gives a book to a* CHILD, *signals once, and the* CHILD *starts to read in Latin. The* CHILD *makes a mistake, the* HEADMASTER *signals twice. The* CHILD *goes back, makes the same mistake, the* HEADMASTER *signals twice. The* CHILD *goes back, makes the same mistake, the* HEADMASTER *signals three times. The* CHILD *goes back to the beginning of the passage. Soon the* HEADMASTER *signals for the* CHILD *to stop, one signal. He makes a gesture and signals once. The* CHILDREN *start writing.*

HEADMASTER. The very good, the good, the mediocre, the bad. Four classes. Different badges of different colours. A completely separate group, the shameful, who can join the others when they deserve to. Children can be promoted or demoted so all are under equal pressure to behave well. Everyone has a place on the benches according to how they are classified.

The HEADMASTER *moves among the* CHILDREN, *correcting their positions while they write.*

The body turned slightly to the left. The left foot slightly forward of the right. The distance of the right arm from the body should be two fingers. The thumb should be parallel to the table. The forefinger —

Distant outcry of CROWD.

LUC. Lacenaire!

The CHILDREN *all stop writing. The* HEADMASTER *looks at* LUC. LUC *steps out of his place. The* HEADMASTER *signals once. The* CHILDREN *write.*

PIERRE. Lacenaire should have been in my garden. And Fieschi, who was put to death yesterday before dawn, nobody even came, what a waste. You have heard of him? He —

HEADMASTER. Ugly little fellow like hundreds of others, suddenly gets it into his head to kill the king. Shameful behaviour. Better not to think about it and it disappears. But Lacenaire carries himself well, he has a gift. Not a great poet, but a definite gift. I write occasional hexameters myself. We don't want to do what he did, of course, but boys have a hero for a day. But it doesn't mean you can shout out in class.

The HEADMASTER *canes* LUC *on the hand.* LUC *goes back to his place.*

I rarely have to raise my voice. I rarely have to speak. Two fingers remember. Don't let the forefinger slip down the page.

PIERRE. I see now. They've kept Fieschi a secret because he's dangerous and made a circus out of Lacenaire. Things are changing and I'm not part of them. There must be a new idea I haven't thought of.

The HEADMASTER *corrects the* CHILDREN *while they write.* PIERRE *also walks up and down among the* CHILDREN. *He stops by one in harness.*

PIERRE. Is this a punishment?

HEADMASTER. Good heavens no, it helps his back grow straight. And this boy, you see, was inclined to poke his chin. They will all be normal in time.

PIERRE. Yes of course. I saw it in my garden. It helps the boy. I must learn to be a teacher.

HEADMASTER. You have to know what you want from them every moment of the day.

The distant cry again. LUC *jerks but controls himself. Everyone stops writing for a split second then continues.*

I use the cane very rarely now I have perfected the timetable.

I enjoy my work. I see the results of it. Their bodies can be helped by harnesses. And their minds are fastened every moment of the day to a fine rigid frame.

PIERRE. Thank you, but I can't work in a school. I must go and see what's happening. If I could fasten the prisoner to a frame. Without over-exciting the public. If I could fasten the public to a frame. I think I'm on the brink —

Several PRISONERS *stand together with iron collars round their necks, joined by a chain to a central chain. The last prisoner, a* BOY, *is dragged screaming by a* WARDER *to where another* WARDER *is waiting with a hammer and anvil to put on his collar.* PIERRE *watches with interest.*

BOY. No no no. I'd rather die. Do anything with me but don't put me in the chain gang.

PIERRE. You'd rather die? That's very interesting. Could you tell me why?

BOY. Sir, kind sir, help me, I'm innocent. Don't let them put me in the chain gang. I never done it. No no no.

PIERRE. Does death seem more glorious?

WARDER. Excuse me, sir, we have got a job to do here.

PIERRE. Of course, I'm sorry, don't let me get in the way.

BOY. No no no! Not the chain! No!

PIERRE. Is it the degradation? Are you upset by the prospect of being a spectacle? You will cross the whole country with people jeering at you, is that the problem?

2ND WARDER. Get the bastard over here, will you.

He comes to help.

PIERRE. I understand there is considerable sexual abuse of younger prisoners. Is that something that disgusts you? Would solitary confinement —

BOY. Not the chain, help, I never done it, no. I don't want to go in the chain gang. No no no no no no no.

The BOY *is firmly seized and held down.*

WARDER. Lowest of the low, sir, that's what it is. You can't get no lower than the chain gang.

2ND WARDER. If you don't keep still I might miss.

BOY. No no no.

2ND WARDER. Now.

BOY is suddenly absolutely silent and still. 2ND WARDER bangs the collar shut. BOY gets up and totters to the others.

WARDER. There you are, lads. That's the lot.

PIERRE. So would you say this is the worst punishment we have in terms of deterrent effect on the prisoners and also on the public who see them pass? Who wouldn't weep to see them. The man will put back his master's hen, the child will put back the biscuit. The crowd gazes in silent awe. They turn back thankful to their honest toil. So would you agree their journey across France is a national education? And could be reinforced with placards and lectures? Perhaps I should travel with the chain gang and give a seminar in every village.

A sudden outburst. The WARDERS are leaving and the CHAIN GANG are alone, they embrace, cheer, laugh, stamp, swear. The BOY laughs and cheers loudest of all.

BOY. Free free free.

PIERRE. I beg your pardon.

WARDER. Not what I'd call an education, sir. I should stand further over here if I was you. No, it teaches bad men how to be worse and it teaches them pride in it.

PIERRE. But what does it teach the crowd who sees them?

WARDER. Teaches the crowd to riot.

PIERRE. Oh dear.

WARDER. Teaches hate of the rich. Scorn of the obedient. Defiance of fate.

PIERRE. Oh but surely —

WARDER. Whole country's in an uproar, sir, when the chain gang's gone through.

PIERRE. That's because there are no placards.

WARDER. Lowest of the low, the chain. Don't have to behave.

Not like you and me with jobs to lose.

PIERRE. You don't envy them, surely?

WARDER. Want to try it, sir? You might enjoy it. I've got a spare collar here.

PIERRE. Well, no, ha ha.

WARDER. I shouldn't stand there, sir, if I was you.

The CHAIN GANG *have taken from their pockets ribbons, plaited straws and flowers, and are decorating themselves and each other.* PIERRE *approaches them.*

PIERRE. Excuse me. Now you have your chains on, are they very heavy?

BOY. Out of my way, shitface.

PIERRE. Do you feel your guilt brought home to you? No of course, you're the poor wretch who's innocent.

BOY. Course I'm not fucking innocent. What you take me for? I done a murder they never found out. I done two. I done six. I done a landlord! I done a banker! I done a policeman!

Cheers from the CHAIN GANG. *They start to stamp, dance and sing. The* WARDERS *go.*

WARDER. I shouldn't stay here, sir, if I was you.

The CHAIN GANG *stamp and dance round singing to the tune of 'The Marseillaise'.*

CHAIN GANG. What do these people want with us,
Do they think they'll see us cry?
We rejoice in what is done to us
And our judges will die.

PIERRE hesitates, then approaches them again.

PIERRE. Supposing I was to write a placard, would you wear it round your neck?

He is caught in the circle, tripped and dragged, disappearing among them as they rush on, singing.

CHAIN GANG. Pleasure has betrayed you,
She loves us instead.

She'd rather dance along the street
Than die with you in bed.
Pleasure is in chains,
She loves to share our pains,
She follows where the song goes,
Chains chains chains.

Your scorn, your hate, your fear,
All belongs to us.
Your gold you hold so dear
All belongs to us.
We've bought it with our lives,
We'll give it to your wives
    for a kiss
    for a fuck.
When we're free when we're free
Who would you rather be
    you or us?
    Try your luck.
    You or us.
    Try your luck.

Far from home, far from home,
Sometimes we moan and groan and moan.
Look in our eyes, what a surprise,
The black judge dies when he sees our eyes.

Children bear your chains,
They're beating on a drum,
They're blowing on a trumpet
When they see us come.

Children bear your chains,
It's not for very long.
The king and queen will carry them
When they hear our song.

Children break your chains,
They're beating on a drum.
Our star is shining in the sky
And our day will come.

Children break your chains
Beating on a drum
Children break their laws
Our day will come.

Children break your chains
Children break your chains
Children break your chains

The CHAIN GANG *rush off.* PIERRE *is left, battered.*

An OLD MAN *approaches. It is* JEREMY BENTHAM.

BENTHAM. You seem to be suffering, my boy.

PIERRE. Never mind, sir, it's only me. Greatest happiness of the greatest number, sir.

BENTHAM. That's all right then.

PIERRE. Mr Bentham, I know you have advocated solemn executions with black clothing and religious music, and that is why I presume to intrude on your time. I have a small demonstration.

BENTHAM. The death penalty should be abolished.

PIERRE. There's no question of death here. It would take place in a garden. An English garden would be ideal, with roses.

BENTHAM. Roses last from early summer right into the winter. They provide a considerable pleasure of long duration. An act of sexual intercourse is a hundred times more intense a pleasure than the smell of a rose. But the roses last many hundred times longer. So multiplying the degree of pleasure by the duration, the ratio of the pleasure of roses to that of sex is approximately 500 to 1, a comfort to us in our old age.

PIERRE *meanwhile wheels on a stand covered with a black curtain.*

PIERRE. Sir, I too would like to live according to reason and mathematics. If you could support my scheme my garden might become a reality. May I show you?

PIERRE *pulls aside the black curtain. Inside there is a* MAN *on the rack. Posters.*

BENTHAM. I hope this has not been arranged for me.

PIERRE. There's little to see in France now except the chain gang and that seems to cause riots. I've had to accept that what my garden lacks is the ancient extreme punishments. Here you have the shock and at the same time the reasonable explanation of how the crime came about and how to resist any such tendencies in one's own life.

BENTHAM. But this sight is not giving us a pleasure greater than the man's suffering. I've seen enough. Release the man at once.

PIERRE. I must devise punishments that will continue to be a novelty and a real attraction to the public.

BENTHAM. Stop stop. It goes on and on.

PIERRE. That's the perfection. It can go on all day and every day. Don't worry, Mr Bentham, come closer. He doesn't feel a thing. Can you see now? The wheels turn but he is not stretched. It's an optical illusion.

BENTHAM. He's not suffering?

PIERRE. That's my new discovery. There's no need for him to suffer. What matters is that he's seen to suffer. That's what will deter people from crime.

BENTHAM (*to the* MAN *on the rack*). Are you all right?

MAN. I wouldn't mind a cup of tea.

PIERRE. You can get down now, thank you.

PIERRE *gives the* MAN *some money and he goes.*

BENTHAM. Well I'm most relieved. You must want your garden very much. I spent years on a scheme of my own. Talking to architects, looking at land. I spent thousands of pounds of my own money. My brother thought of it first in Russia to supervise the workers in the dockyards. It's an iron cage, glazed, a glass lantern —

PIERRE. An iron cage?

BENTHAM. A central tower. The workers are not naturally obedient or industrious. But they became so.

PIERRE. The workers gaze up at the iron cage?

BENTHAM. No no, your idea has to be reversed. Let me show you. Imagine for once that you're the prisoner. This is your cell, you can't leave it. This is the central tower and I'm the guard. I'll watch whatever you do day and night.

PIERRE. I just have to sit here?

BENTHAM. Of course in Russia they were doing work.

BENTHAM *goes behind the curtain, which is the central tower.* PIERRE *goes on sitting. Time goes by. He fidgets.*

PIERRE. Mr Bentham?

Am I doing it properly?

Do you want me to draw some conclusions? It's not comfortable being watched when you can't see the person watching you. You can see all of us prisoners and we can't see each other. We can't communicate by tapping on the walls because you're watching us. Is that right? Mr Bentham? I understand how it works. Can I get up now?

BENTHAM *comes out of the back of the stand unseen by* PIERRE. *He creeps round so that he's behind him while he talks.* BENTHAM *giggles silently.*

The prisoners can't get strength from each other, is that what you want me to observe?

The darkness of a dungeon is some protection, to be always in the light is pitiless.

I begin to feel you must know what I'm like. I find it quite hard to sit still, I'm energetic by nature, I feel quite nervous.

You get to know each prisoner and you can compare him with the others. But I don't know how the others are behaving. You know everything that's going on and I don't know at all.

I think it's most ingenious, Mr Bentham, an excellent means of control. Without chains, without pain. Can I get up now?

Really, Mr Bentham, I think I have appreciated your idea. Am I supposed to sit here all afternoon?

I'm getting a little bored. I must admit I'd wander off and look at the roses if you weren't keeping an eye on me because I really think I've got everything out of this I can and it's wasting my time to keep me sitting here. Instead of thousands of people watching one prisoner, one person can watch thousands of prisoners. I've always wanted to affect the spectators. You're affecting the person who is seen. This is a complete reversal for me. I think I've learnt everything, Mr Bentham. Is there anything else?

BENTHAM. That you don't need to be watched all the time. What matters is that you think you're watched. The guards can come and go. It is, like your display, an optical illusion.

BENTHAM *goes.*

PIERRE. It's hard to give up my garden. I do have a weakness for a spectacle. But this way is far more reasonable. It's nothing like a theatre. More like a machine. It's a form of power like the steam engine. I just have to apply it.

BOYS *in bleached uniforms walk in in single file and line up silently. A* NEW BOY *arrives.* PIERRE *and the* MINISTER *look on.*

MINISTER. Where are the placards?

PIERRE. Here we have a model reformatory, sir, modern educational methods, the application of Mr Bentham's panopticon —

MINISTER. Don't you hang notices round their necks?

PIERRE. No sir, it's an entirely new —

MINISTER. I was beginning to like the placards.

PIERRE. No sir, you'll find this —

MINISTER. Well I hope they don't knock you down. There's always flogging.

An OLDER BOY *brings the* BOY *to* PIERRE.

PIERRE. You have been sent here because you don't sleep at home.

BOY. I stay awake.

PIERRE. You're a vagabond.

BOY. You're not.

PIERRE. What's your station in life?

BOY. I'm an army officer, forty-two years old.

PIERRE. You're not more than fourteen.

BOY. Write it down.

PIERRE. You will work here. A reformatory is not a prison.
There are workshops and there are fields. You have no father?

BOY. My father's got no son.

PIERRE. Nor mother either?

BOY. I'm a miracle.

PIERRE. Here you will live in a group called a family. The other
boys are your brothers. Each family has a head, whom you
will obey, and is divided into two sections, each with a second
in command. You will have a number. You will answer to it at
roll call three times a day. Your number is 321. This is your
elder brother. He will stay with you all the time. And I will
pay constant attention to your case.

MINISTER. Not one of you will be torn apart by horses. And I
hope you're grateful. (*To* PIERRE:) You may be on to
something this time, my boy. Congratulations.

The MINISTER *and* PIERRE *go off.*

BOY. Do they beat you?

BROTHER. Not any more. If you do wrong they put you in a
cell by yourself. And on the wall there's big black letters, God
Sees You.

BOY. That's all right. I don't believe in God.

BROTHER. You will though.

BOY. Don't mind what they do if they don't beat me.

BROTHER. We preferred the beatings. But the cell is better for
us.

BOY. What sort of thing gets you into trouble?

BROTHER. Speaking when you shouldn't. Walking out of step. Looking up when you should look down.

BOY. But what about stealing? And swearing? And hitting someone in the stomach? And setting fire?

BROTHER. There's no time.

BOY. I do what I like.

BROTHER. But we like to do what we ought.

BOY. I don't.

The line walks round once in single file. The BOY *at the back steps backward leaving a space. The* BROTHER *puts the* BOY *in the space.*

BROTHER. This is your place. We're going to the courtyard now and the monitor inspects our clothes. Then we go to where we sleep. At the first drumroll you get undressed and stand by your hammock. At the second drumroll all the boys on the left on a count of one two three get into their hammocks and lie down. It's quite easy. Then the boys on the right do it. Then we go to sleep. You go to sleep lying on your back with your hands outside the cover. You always go to sleep straight away because you've been working hard all day and then there's military exercise and gymnastics. We'll teach you. You can't talk now.

The BROTHER *takes his place at the head of the line.*

BOY. What if you stay awake?

BROTHER. You don't.

BOY. What if you do?

BROTHER. If you stay awake, don't open your eyes.

The line starts to walk off. The BOY *steps out of his place and watches them. They stop, still leaving his space. They turn and look at him. Suddenly he runs and gets into place, gets into step as they go out.*

The stage is empty. Two CONSPIRATORS *enter.*

CONSPIRATOR A. There's one way that can't fail.

CONSPIRATOR B. What's that?

CONSPIRATOR A. Throw myself under the horses' hooves with the bomb. Either it explodes straight off, or anyway the horses shy and there's a delay and at that moment you go into action with the second bomb, so either way the whole thing goes up.

CONSPIRATOR B. Either way you go up.

CONSPIRATOR A. It can't fail.

CONSPIRATOR B. You'd go that far?

CONSPIRATOR A. Wouldn't you?

CONSPIRATOR B. We can't afford to lose you. Too many of us are dead already.

CONSPIRATOR A. Someone's betraying us, that's why.

CONSPIRATOR B. Yes, someone's playing a double game.

CONSPIRATOR A. It's hard to think one of your friends is a spy.

CONSPIRATOR B. It's impossible. Everyone would give his life.

CONSPIRATOR A. So everyone's equally under suspicion.

CONSPIRATOR B. Even me. Even you.

CONSPIRATOR A. Do you ever feel you can't go on?

CONSPIRATOR B. You stop sleeping.

CONSPIRATOR A. My stomach's water, my eyes itch. I'll be glad when it's over.

CONSPIRATOR B. When you throw the bomb?

CONSPIRATOR A. That or . . .

CONSPIRATOR B. What? What?

CONSPIRATOR A. I sometimes think there's more spies than conspirators. Who plans the assassinations, us or them? Do we only murder so they can arrest us?

CONSPIRATOR B. Listen, listen, what you've always said. However far control goes, subversion —

CONSPIRATOR A. We think we're subversive. They allow us.

CONSPIRATOR B. They kill one of us, two more —

CONSPIRATOR A. Do you believe it?

CONSPIRATOR B. It's what you've always said.

CONSPIRATOR A. I don't know.

CONSPIRATOR B. You're overtired. Let's get some coffee.

CONSPIRATOR A. It's me.

CONSPIRATOR B. What is? What?

CONSPIRATOR A. I can't go on. I'm the spy.

CONSPIRATOR B. Not you.

CONSPIRATOR A. Everyone's under suspicion.

CONSPIRATOR B. But not you. Not really you.

CONSPIRATOR A. Yes.

CONSPIRATOR B. Always?

CONSPIRATOR A. Yes.

CONSPIRATOR B. When you recruited me?

CONSPIRATOR A. Yes.

CONSPIRATOR B. When you assassinated the duke?

CONSPIRATOR A. Yes.

CONSPIRATOR B. But you're the one we all depend on.

CONSPIRATOR A. Yes.

CONSPIRATOR B. I was just an ordinary villain. You explained. You said I could be a hero. And now what? What? All along? A spy all along? Michel's death? And Marc, not Marc? And Louis arrested last week, all you? But I'll tell the others. We'll kill you. Why did you tell me?

CONSPIRATOR A. I was tired.

CONSPIRATOR B. We'll kill you.

CONSPIRATOR A. You won't tell the others. I feel better now. Everyone has moments of weakness.

CONSPIRATOR B. Of course I'll tell. I can't protect you.

CONSPIRATOR A. I'm sorry I told you but it means I have to kill you. (*He has a gun.*)

CONSPIRATOR B. It doesn't.

CONSPIRATOR A. Yes.

CONSPIRATOR B. I won't tell.

CONSPIRATOR A. Sorry.

CONSPIRATOR B. Wait.

CONSPIRATOR A. Yes?

CONSPIRATOR B. Wait.

CONSPIRATOR A. Hurry.

CONSPIRATOR B. You'll laugh.

CONSPIRATOR A. What?

CONSPIRATOR B. You'll laugh. It's all right, old friend, it's all right. The police are as full of secrets as we are. To think I never knew. And you never knew.

CONSPIRATOR A. What?

CONSPIRATOR B. It's me too. I'm a police spy too. So you needn't kill me, all right? We just have to go on keeping each other's secret and doing our job. My dear old friend. I thought Michel and Marc and Louis were all my own work, and all the time it was you too. It is tiring, isn't it, the double life, twice as exhausting. What a relief to know. We'll never say another word about it, but we have each other now. We were always comrades, I always loved you, and how much more comrades now. How I love you now. Truth at last.

CONSPIRATOR A. But I was lying, you see.

CONSPIRATOR B. What?

CONSPIRATOR A. I'm not a spy.

CONSPIRATOR B. What?

CONSPIRATOR A. You are.

CONSPIRATOR B. What?

CONSPIRATOR A. Sorry. (*He raises the gun.*)

CONSPIRATOR B. What?

A beach. A group of MEN *are paddling in the sea, their trousers rolled up round their knees.* PIERRE *is sitting on the sand reading some files. He has a handkerchief on his head and is drinking a bottle of wine. The* MEN *in the sea chat and play.*

MEN. It's cold.
No it's not cold.
Mind the crab
Ooh where?
Don't splash
Is that a jellyfish?

A HOLIDAYMAKER *approaches, carrying a book.*

HOLIDAYMAKER. Lovely day.

PIERRE. Lovely.

HOLIDAYMAKER. They're having fun.

PIERRE. Oh yes, they're good lads.

HOLIDAYMAKER. Nice picnic.

PIERRE. Care to join me?

HOLIDAYMAKER. Oh I didn't mean — well thank you very much.

He sits with PIERRE *and shares the wine.* PIERRE *is already slightly drunk and gets more so.*

Workers from the factory are they, having an outing?

PIERRE. I do bring workers to the seaside, yes. I also bring convicts.

HOLIDAYMAKER. Convicts are they? Now I come to look at them they have got sinister faces. You don't want to get convicts mixed up with ordinary people on a beach. I'm a respectable working man.

PIERRE. I do bring convicts, as part of their rehabilitation you see, and I also bring patients from the hospital.

HOLIDAYMAKER. Oh patients are they? Salt water do them good. Nothing contagious of course. More convalescent?

PIERRE. I do bring physically ill patients to the beach but I also
bring mentally disturbed —

HOLIDAYMAKER. Oh, mental cases. That accounts for it. Very
well behaved I must say for loonies.

PIERRE. I do bring —

HOLIDAYMAKER. Quite safe I suppose?

PIERRE. I know them all by name. I've turned a mob into
individuals.

HOLIDAYMAKER. Come when they're called do they?

PIERRE. It's nice for them to have a day off out of the workshop.
Don't worry, I keep an eye on them.

HOLIDAYMAKER. That's the thing. Keep an eye on them.

PIERRE. Very interesting cases some of them.

HOLIDAYMAKER. I like a good story.

PIERRE. That one over there with a long nose and close-set eyes.

HOLIDAYMAKER. Close-set eyes is a sure sign. And if your
eyebrows meet.

PIERRE. He stirred up trouble at his place of work. Something
about an association of workers. He resisted the police to such
an extent the army had to be called in. Extremely violent
criminal type, psychopath, paranoid fantasies, unhappy
childhood, alcoholic father, inadequate mother —

HOLIDAYMAKER. Ah, that's often the way.

PIERRE. Extremely disorganised personality, with high blood
pressure and low intelligence, a weak heart, anarchist
literature, abnormal sexual proclivities, and cold feet due to
inadequate circulation.

HOLIDAYMAKER. Responding to treatment is he?

PIERRE. Cries a good deal. Unemployable.

HOLIDAYMAKER. You must be a great comfort.

PIERRE. I do my best to understand him.

HOLIDAYMAKER (shows his book). I'm fascinated by criminal

literature. Ever read Arsène Lupin? High-class burglar in white gloves and a detective who's always after him. Takes your mind off things.

PIERRE. I used to want a garden you see.

HOLIDAYMAKER. I've got a small garden.

PIERRE. Flowering bushes. Where families would stroll on a Sunday. Iron cages high in the sky.

HOLIDAYMAKER. I like a garden.

PIERRE. Instead I've got a city. Whole city. All on the great panoptic principle.

One of the MEN *suddenly gives a cry and leaps to attack* PIERRE. *Before he reaches him there is a shot and the* MAN *falls.* PIERRE *jumps at the sound of the shot but is otherwise unperturbed. The other* MEN *stand frozen. Two* GUARDS *come and carry the dead* MAN *off.*

HOLIDAYMAKER. Good heavens!

PIERRE. Poor fellow. There's always a few. Fascinating case, I'm sorry to lose him. Never very happy.

HOLIDAYMAKER. Good heavens! Well. Was that a guard I suppose was it? Armed guard?

PIERRE. Very rarely necessary. I regard it as a failure.

HOLIDAYMAKER. Stands by does he, in case of trouble?

PIERRE *goes over to the* MEN, *who are still standing still.*

PIERRE. I'm sorry about that. Very inconsiderate of Legrand to spoil the afternoon for the rest of us. Did it startle you? It startled me. This is not what I — This is not what you — Isn't the sea pretty today? We've still another thirty-five minutes to enjoy ourselves.

The MEN *start to paddle and splash again.* PIERRE *slowly goes back and sits down with the* HOLIDAYMAKER.

HOLIDAYMAKER. Nasty shock for you.

PIERRE. I don't like loud noises.

HOLIDAYMAKER. Still it is a comfort to have that kind of protection.

PIERRE. I think so. Yes, I think so. Ultimately of course I hope — I'd like to see — well afternoons like this are so inspiring. Afternoons like this one was. The guard is inclined to over-react, he's only young. I must speak to the minister.

The HOLIDAYMAKER *takes a hipflask from his pocket.*

HOLIDAYMAKER. Here.

PIERRE *drinks. The* HOLIDAYMAKER *drinks. They sit in silence. The* HOLIDAYMAKER *passes the flask again.*

PIERRE. Mustn't have too much.

HOLIDAYMAKER. Bit of a shock.

PIERRE. Yes, but I —

PIERRE *takes the flask and drinks.*

The trouble is I have to make a speech. Later on. In front of the minister. He's going to lay the foundation stone. I'm always a little nervous at these official — I shall just explain quite simply how the criminals are punished, the sick are cured, the workers are supervised, the ignorant are educated, the unemployed are registered, the insane are normalised, the criminals — No, wait a minute. The criminals are supervised. The insane are cured. The sick are normalised. The workers are registered. The unemployed are educated. The ignorant are punished. No. I'll need to rehearse this a little. The ignorant are normalised. Right. The sick are punished. The insane are educated. The workers are cured. The criminals are cured. The unemployed are punished. The criminals are normalised. Something along those lines.

HOLIDAYMAKER. Lovely day out for them. Nice treat.

PIERRE *and the* HOLIDAYMAKER *drink. The* MEN *look at* PIERRE.

TOP GIRLS

Note on characters

ISABELLA BIRD (1831-1904) lived in Edinburgh, travelled extensively between the ages of 40 and 70.

LADY NIJO (b.1258) Japanese, was an Emperor's courtesan and later a Buddhist nun who travelled on foot through Japan.

DULL GRET is the subject of the Brueghel painting, Dulle Griet, in which a woman in an apron and armour leads a crowd of women charging through hell and fighting the devils.

POPE JOAN, disguised as a man, is thought to have been Pope between 854-856.

PATIENT GRISELDA is the obedient wife whose story is told by Chaucer in The Clerk's Tale of *The Canterbury Tales*.

Note on layout

A speech usually follows the one immediately before it BUT:
1: when one character starts speaking before the other has finished, the point of interruption is marked / .

eg. ISABELLA: This is the Emperor of Japan? / I once met the
                Emperor of Morocco.
    NIJO: In fact he was the ex-Emperor.

2: a character sometimes continues speaking right through another's speech:

eg. ISABELLA: When I was forty I thought my life was over. /
                Oh I was pitiful. I was
    NIJO: I didn't say I felt it for twenty years. Not
                every minute.
    ISABELLA: sent on a cruise for my health and I felt even
                worse. Pains in my bones, pins and needles . . .
                etc.

3: sometimes a speech follows on from a speech earlier than the one immediately before it, and continuity is marked*.

eg. GRISELDA: I'd seen him riding by, we all had. And he'd
                seen me in the fields with the sheep*.
    ISABELLA: I would have been well suited to minding sheep.
    NIJO: And Mr Nugent riding by.
    ISABELLA: Of course not, Nijo, I mean a healthy life in
                the open air.
    JOAN: *He just rode up while you were minding the
                sheep and asked you to marry him?

where 'in the fields with the sheep' is the cue to both 'I would have been' and 'He just rode up'.

Top Girls was first performed at the Royal Court Theatre, London on 28 August 1982 with the following cast:

MARLENE	Gwen Taylor
ISABELLA BIRD JOYCE MRS KIDD	Deborah Findlay
LADY NIJO WIN	Lindsay Duncan
DULL GRET ANGIE	Carole Hayman
POPE JOAN LOUISE	Selina Cadell
PATIENT GRISELDA NELL JEANINE	Lesley Manville
WAITRESS KIT SHONA	Lou Wakefield

Directed by Max Stafford Clark
Designed by Peter Hartwell

This production transferred to Joe Papp's Public Theatre, New York, later the same year, and returned to the Royal Court early in 1983.

ACT ONE	Restaurant. Saturday night.
ACT TWO	
Scene One:	'Top Girls' Employment agency. Monday morning.
Scene Two:	Joyce's back yard. Sunday afternoon.
Scene Three:	Employment agency. Monday morning.
ACT THREE	Joyce's kitchen. Sunday evening, a year earlier.

Production note
Top Girls was originally written in three acts and I still find that structure clearer: Act One, the dinner; Act Two, Angie's story; Act Three, the year before. But two intervals do hold things up, so in the original production we made it two acts with the interval after what is here Act Two, scene two. Do whichever you prefer.

Caryl Churchill *1985*

ACT ONE

Restaurant. Table set for dinner with white tablecloth. Six places.
   MARLENE *and* WAITRESS.

MARLENE. Excellent, yes, table for six. One of them's going to
   be late but we won't wait. I'd like a bottle of Frascati straight
   away if you've got one really cold.

The WAITRESS *goes.*

ISABELLA BIRD *arrives.*

Here we are. Isabella.

ISABELLA. Congratulations, my dear.

MARLENE. Well, it's a step. It makes for a party. I haven't time
   for a holiday. I'd like to go somewhere exotic like you but I
   can't get away. I don't know how you could bear to leave
   Hawaii. / I'd like to lie in the sun forever, except of course I

ISABELLA. I did think of settling.

MARLENE. can't bear sitting still.

ISABELLA. I sent for my sister Hennie to come and join me. I
   said, Hennie we'll live here forever and help the natives. You
   can buy two sirloins of beef for what a pound of chops costs
   in Edinburgh. And Hennie wrote back, the dear, that yes, she
   would come to Hawaii if I wished, but I said she had far better
   stay where she was. Hennie was suited to life in Tobermory.

MARLENE. Poor Hennie.

ISABELLA. Do you have a sister?

MARLENE. Yes in fact.

ISABELLA. Hennie was happy. She was good. I did miss its face, my own pet. But I couldn't stay in Scotland. I loathed the constant murk.

MARLENE. Ah! Nijo!

She sees LADY NIJO *arrive.*

The WAITRESS *enters with wine.*

NIJO. Marlene!

MARLENE. I think a drink while we wait for the others. I think a drink anyway. What a week.

The WAITRESS *pours wine.*

NIJO. It was always the men who used to get so drunk. I'd be one of the maidens, passing the sake.

ISABELLA. I've had sake. Small hot drink. Quite fortifying after a day in the wet.

NIJO. One night my father proposed three rounds of three cups, which was normal, and then the Emperor should have said three rounds of three cups, but he said three rounds of nine cups, so you can imagine. Then the Emperor passed his sake cup to my father and said, 'Let the wild goose come to me this spring.'

MARLENE. Let the what?

NIJO. It's a literary allusion to a tenth-century epic, / His Majesty was very cultured.

ISABELLA: This is the Emperor of Japan? / I once met the Emperor of Morocco.

NIJO. In fact he was the ex-Emperor.

MARLENE. But he wasn't old? / Did you, Isabella?

NIJO. Twenty-nine.

ISABELLA. Oh it's a long story.

MARLENE. Twenty-nine's an excellent age.

NIJO. Well I was only fourteen and I knew he meant something but I didn't know what. He sent me an eight-layered gown and I sent it back. So when the time came I did nothing but cry. My thin gowns were badly ripped. But even that morning when he left / — he'd a green robe with a scarlet lining and

MARLENE. Are you saying he raped you?

NIJO. very heavily embroidered trousers, I already felt different about him. It made me uneasy. No, of course not, Marlene, I belonged to him, it was what I was brought up for from a baby. I soon found I was sad if he stayed away. It was depressing day after day not knowing when he would come. I never enjoyed taking other women to him.

ISABELLA. I certainly never saw my father drunk. He was a clergyman. / And I didn't get married till I was fifty.

The WAITRESS *brings menus.*

NIJO. Oh, my father was a very religious man. Just before he died he said to me, 'Serve His Majesty, be respectful, if you lose his favour enter holy orders.'

MARLENE. But he meant stay in a convent, not go wandering round the country.

NIJO. Priests were often vagrants, so why not a nun? You think I shouldn't? /I still did what my father wanted.

MARLENE. No no, I think you should. / I think it was wonderful.

DULL GRET *arrives.*

ISABELLA. I tried to do what my father wanted.

MARLENE. Gret, good. Nijo. Gret. / I know Griselda's going to be late, but should we wait for Joan? / Let's get you a drink.

ISABELLA. Hello Gret! (*Continues to* NIJO:) I tried to be a clergyman's daughter. Needlework, music, charitable schemes. I had a tumour removed from my spine and spent a great deal of time on the sofa. I studied the metaphysical poets and hymnology. / I thought I enjoyed intellectual pursuits.

NIJO. Ah, you like poetry. I come of a line of eight generations of poets. Father had a poem / in the anthology.

ISABELLA. My father taught me Latin although I was a girl. / But

MARLENE. They didn't have Latin at my school.

ISABELLA. really I was more suited to manual work. Cooking, washing, mending, riding horses. / Better than reading books,

NIJO. Oh but I'm sure you're very clever.

ISABELLA. eh Gret? A rough life in the open air.

NIJO. I can't say I enjoyed my rough life. What I enjoyed most was being the Emperor's favourite / and wearing thin silk.

ISABELLA: Did you have any horses, Gret?

GRET. Pig.

POPE JOAN arrives.

MARLENE. Oh Joan, thank God, we can order. Do you know everyone? We were just talking about learning Latin and being clever girls. Joan was by way of an infant prodigy. Of course you were. What excited you when you were ten?

JOAN. Because angels are without matter they are not individuals. Every angel is a species.

MARLENE. There you are.

They laugh. They look at menus.

ISABELLA. Yes, I forgot all my Latin. But my father was the mainspring of my life and when he died I was so grieved. I'll have the chicken, please, / and the soup.

NIJO. Of course you were grieved. My father was saying his prayers and he dozed off in the sun. So I touched his knee to rouse him. 'I wonder what will happen,' he said, and then he was dead before he finished the sentence. / If he'd died saying

MARLENE. What a shock.

NIJO. his prayers he would have gone straight to heaven. / Waldorf salad.

JOAN. Death is the return of all creatures to God.

NIJO. I shouldn't have woken him.

JOAN. Damnation only means ignorance of the truth. I was always attracted by the teachings of John the Scot, though he was inclined to confuse / God and the world.

ISABELLA. Grief always overwhelmed me at the time.

MARLENE. What I fancy is a rare steak. Gret?

ISABELLA. I am of course a member of the / Church of England.*

GRET. Potatoes.

MARLENE. *I haven't been to church for years. / I like Christmas carols.

ISABELLA. Good works matter more than church attendance.

MARLENE. Make that two steaks and a lot of potatoes. Rare. But I don't do good works either.

JOAN. Canelloni, please, / and a salad.

ISABELLA. Well, I tried, but oh dear. Hennie did good works.

NIJO. The first half of my life was all sin and the second / all repentance.*

MARLENE. Oh what about starters?

GRET. Soup.

JOAN. *And which did you like best?

MARLENE. Were your travels just a penance? Avocado vinaigrette. Didn't you / enjoy yourself?

JOAN. Nothing to start with for me, thank you.

NIJO. Yes, but I was very unhappy. / It hurt to remember

MARLENE. And the wine list.

NIJO. the past. I think that was repentance.

MARLENE. Well I wonder.

NIJO. I might have just been homesick.

MARLENE. Or angry.

NIJO. Not angry, no, / why angry?

GRET. Can we have some more bread?

MARLENE. Don't you get angry? I get angry.

NIJO. But what about?

MARLENE. Yes let's have two more Frascati. And some more bread, please.

The WAITRESS *exits.*

ISABELLA. I tried to understand Buddhism when I was in Japan but all this birth and death succeeding each other through eternities just filled me with the most profound melancholy. I do like something more active.

NIJO. You couldn't say I was inactive. I walked every day for twenty years.

ISABELLA. I don't mean walking. / I mean in the head.

NIJO. I vowed to copy five Mahayana sutras. / Do you know how

MARLENE. I don't think religious beliefs are something we have in common. Activity yes.

NIJO. long they are? My head was active. / My head ached.

JOAN. It's no good being active in heresy.

ISABELLA. What heresy? She's calling the Church of England / a heresy.

JOAN. There are some very attractive / heresies.

NIJO. I had never heard of Christianity. Never / heard of it. Barbarians.

MARLENE. Well I'm not a Christian. / And I'm not a Buddhist.

ISABELLA. You have heard of it?

MARLENE. We don't all have to believe the same.

ISABELLA. I knew coming to dinner with a pope we should keep off religion.

JOAN. I always enjoy a theological argument. But I won't try to convert you, I'm not a missionary. Anyway I'm a heresy myself.

ISABELLA. There are some barbaric practices in the east.

NIJO. Barbaric?

ISABELLA. Among the lower classes.

NIJO. I wouldn't know.

ISABELLA. Well theology always made my head ache.

MARLENE. Oh good, some food.

WAITRESS *is bringing the first course.*

NIJO. How else could I have left the court if I wasn't a nun? When father died I had only His Majesty. So when I fell out of favour I had nothing. Religion is a kind of nothing / and I dedicated what was left of me to nothing.

ISABELLA. That's what I mean about Buddhism. It doesn't brace.

MARLENE. Come on, Nijo, have some wine.

NIJO. Haven't you ever felt like that? Nothing will ever happen again. I am dead already. You've all felt / like that.

ISABELLA. You thought your life was over but it wasn't.

JOAN. You wish it was over.

GRET. Sad.

MARLENE. Yes, when I first came to London I sometimes . . . and when I got back from America I did. But only for a few hours. Not twenty years.

ISABELLA. When I was forty I thought my life was over. / Oh I

NIJO. I didn't say I felt it for twenty years. Not every minute.

ISABELLA. was pitiful. I was sent on a cruise for my health and I felt even worse. Pains in my bones, pins and needles in my hands, swelling behind the ears, and − oh, stupidity. I shook all over, indefinable terror. And Australia seemed to me a hideous country, the acacias stank like drains. / I had a

NIJO. You were homesick.

ISABELLA. photograph for Hennie but I told her I wouldn't send it, my hair had fallen out and my clothes were crooked, I looked completely insane and suicidal.

NIJO. So did I, exactly, dressed as a nun. I was wearing walking shoes for the first time.

ISABELLA. I longed to go home, / but home to what? Houses

NIJO. I longed to go back ten years.

ISABELLA. are so perfectly dismal.

MARLENE. I thought travelling cheered you both up.

ISABELLA. Oh it did / of course. It was on the trip from

NIJO. I'm not a cheerful person, Marlene. I just laugh a lot.

ISABELLA. Australia to the Sandwich Isles, I fell in love with the sea. There were rats in the cabin and ants in the food but suddenly it was like a new world. I woke up every morning happy, knowing there would be nothing to annoy me. No nervousness. No dressing.

NIJO. Don't you like getting dressed? I adored my clothes. / When I was chosen to give sake to His Majesty's brother,

MARLENE. You had prettier colours than Isabella.

NIJO. the Emperor Kameyana, on his formal visit, I wore raw silk pleated trousers and a seven-layered gown in shades of red, and two outer garments, / yellow lined with green and a light

MARLENE. Yes, all that silk must have been very . . .

The WAITRESS *starts to clear the first course.*

JOAN. I dressed as a boy when I left home.*

NIJO. green jacket. Lady Betto had a five-layered gown in shades of green and purple.

ISABELLA. *You dressed as a boy?

MARLENE. Of course, / for safety.

JOAN. It was easy, I was only twelve. Also women weren't / allowed in the library. We wanted to study in Athens.

MARLENE. You ran away alone?

JOAN. No, not alone, I went with my friend. / He was sixteen

NIJO. Ah, an elopement.

JOAN. but I thought I knew more science than he did and almost as much philosophy.

ISABELLA. Well I always travelled as a lady and I repudiated strongly any suggestion in the press that I was other than feminine.

MARLENE. I don't wear trousers in the office. / I could but I don'

ISABELLA. There was no great danger to a woman of my age and appearance.

MARLENE. And you got away with it, Joan?

JOAN. I did then.

The WAITRESS starts to bring the main course.

MARLENE. And nobody noticed anything?

JOAN. They noticed I was a very clever boy. / And when I

MARLENE. I couldn't have kept pretending for so long.

JOAN. shared a bed with my friend, that was ordinary — two poor students in a lodging house. I think I forgot I was pretending.

ISABELLA. Rocky Mountain Jim, Mr Nugent, showed me no disrespect. He found it interesting, I think, that I could make scones and also lasso cattle. Indeed he declared his love for me, which was most distressing.

NIJO. What did he say? / We always sent poems first.

MARLENE. What did you say?

ISABELLA. I urged him to give up whisky, / but he said it was too late.

MARLENE. Oh Isabella.

ISABELLA. He had lived alone in the mountains for many years.

MARLENE. But did you — ?

The WAITRESS goes.

ISABELLA. Mr Nugent was a man that any woman might love but none could marry. I came back to England.

NIJO. Did you write him a poem when you left? / Snow on the

MARLENE. Did you never see him again?

ISABELLA. No, never.

NIJO. mountains. My sleeves are wet with tears. In England no tears, no snow.

ISABELLA. Well, I say never. One morning very early in Switzerland, it was a year later, I had a vision of him as I last saw him / in his trapper's clothes with his hair round his face,

NIJO. A ghost!

ISABELLA. and that was the day, / I learnt later, he died with a

NIJO. Ah!

ISABELLA. bullet in his brain. / He just bowed to me and
vanished.

MARLENE. Oh Isabella.

NIJO. When your lover dies – One of my lovers died. / The priest
Ariake.

JOAN. My friend died. Have we all got dead lovers?

MARLENE. Not me, sorry.

NIJO (to ISABELLA). I wasn't a nun, I was still at court, but he
was a priest, and when he came to me he dedicated his whole
life to hell. / He knew that when he died he would fall into
one of the three lower realms. And he died, he did die.

JOAN (to MARLENE). I'd quarrelled with him over the teachings
of John the Scot, who held that our ignorance of God is the
same as his ignorance of himself. He only knows what he
creates because he creates everything he knows but he himself
is above being – do you follow?

MARLENE. No, but go on.

NIJO. I couldn't bear to think / in what shape would he be reborn. *

JOAN. St. Augustine maintained that the Neo-Platonic Ideas are
indivisible from God, but I agreed with John that the created

ISABELLA. *Buddhism is really most uncomfortable.

JOAN. world is essences derived from Ideas which derived from
God. As Denys the Areopagite said – the pseudo-Denys –
first we give God a name, then deny it / then reconcile the

NIJO. In what shape would he return?

JOAN contradiction by looking beyond / those terms –

MARLENE. Sorry, what? Denys said what?

JOAN. Well we disagreed about it, we quarrelled. And next day he was ill, /I was so annoyed with him, all the time I was

NIJO. Misery in this life and worse in the next, all because of me.

JOAN. nursing him I kept going over the arguments in my mind.
Matter is not a means of knowing the essence. The source of
the species is the Idea. But then I realised he'd never
understand my arguments again, and that night he died. John
the Scot held that the individual disintegrates / and there is no
personal immortality.

ISABELLA. I wouldn't have you think I was in love with Jim
Nugent. It was yearning to save him that I felt.

MARLENE (to JOAN). So what did you do?

JOAN. First I decided to stay a man. I was used to it. And I
wanted to devote my life to learning. Do you know why I
went to Rome? Italian men didn't have beards.

ISABELLA. The loves of my life were Hennie, my own pet, and
my dear husband the doctor, who nursed Hennie in her last
illness. I knew it would be terrible when Hennie died but I
didn't know how terrible. I felt half of myself had gone. How
could I go on my travels without that sweet soul waiting at
home for my letters? It was Doctor Bishop's devotion to her
in her last illness that made me decide to marry him. He and
Hennie had the same sweet character. I had not.

NIJO. I thought his majesty had sweet character because when
he found out about Ariake he was so kind. But really it was
because he no longer cared for me. One night he even sent
me out to a man who had been pursuing me. /He lay awake
on the other side of the screens and listened.

ISABELLA. I did wish marriage had seemed more of a step. I
tried very hard to cope with the ordinary drudgery of life. I
was ill again with carbuncles on the spine and nervous
prostration. I ordered a tricycle, that was my idea of adventure
then. And John himself fell ill, with erysipelas and anaemia. I
began to love him with my whole heart but it was too late. He
was a skeleton with transparent white hands. I wheeled him on
various seafronts in a bathchair. And he faded and left me.
There was nothing in my life. The doctors said I had gout /

and my heart was much affected.

NIJO. There was nothing in my life, nothing, without the
Emperor's favour. The Empress had always been my enemy,
Marlene, she said I had no right to wear three-layered gowns. /
But I was the adopted daughter of my grandfather the Prime
Minister. I had been publicly granted permission to wear thin
silk.

JOAN. There was nothing in my life except my studies. I was
obsessed with pursuit of the truth. I taught at the Greek
School in Rome, which St Augustine had made famous. I was
poor, I worked hard. I spoke apparently brilliantly, I was still
very young, I was a stranger; suddenly I was quite famous,
I was everyone's favourite. Huge crowds came to hear me. The
day after they made me cardinal I fell ill and lay two weeks
without speaking, full of terror and regret. / But then I got up

MARLENE. Yes, success is very . . .

JOAN. determined to go on. I was seized again / with a desperate
longing for the absolute.

ISABELLA. Yes, yes, to go on. I sat in Tobermory among
Hennie's flowers and sewed a complete outfit in Jaeger
flannel. / I was fifty-six years old.

NIJO. Out of favour but I didn't die. I left on foot, nobody saw
me go. For the next twenty years I walked through Japan.

GRET. Walking is good.

The WAITRESS *enters.*

JOAN. Pope Leo died and I was chosen. All right then. I would
be Pope. I would know God. I would know everything.

ISABELLA. I determined to leave my grief behind and set off for
Tibet.

MARLENE. Magnificent all of you. We need some more wine,
please, two bottles I think, Griselda isn't even here yet, and
I want to drink a toast to you all.

ISABELLA. To yourself surely, / we're here to celebrate your
success.

NIJO. Yes, Marlene.

JOAN. Yes, what is it exactly, Marlene?

MARLENE. Well it's not Pope but it is managing director.*

JOAN. And you find work for people.

MARLENE. Yes, an employment agency.

NIJO. *Over all the women you work with. And the men.

ISABELLA. And very well deserved too. I'm sure it's just the beginning of something extraordinary.

MARLENE. Well it's worth a party.

ISABELLA. To Marlene.*

MARLENE. And all of us.

JOAN. *Marlene.

NIJO. Marlene.

GRET. Marlene.

MARLENE. We've all come a long way. To our courage and the way we changed our lives and our extraordinary achievements.

They laugh and drink a toast.

ISABELLA. Such adventures. We were crossing a mountain pass at seven thousand feet, the cook was all to pieces, the muleteers suffered fever and snow blindness. But even though my spine was agony I managed very well.

MARLENE. Wonderful.

NIJO. Once I was ill for four months lying alone at an inn. Nobody to offer a horse to Buddha. I had to live for myself, and I did live.

ISABELLA. Of course you did. It was far worse returning to Tobermory. I always felt dull when I was stationary. / That's why I could never stay anywhere.

NIJO. Yes, that's it exactly. New sights. The shrine by the beach, the moon shining on the sea. The goddess had vowed to save all living things. /She would even save the fishes. I was full of hope.

JOAN. I had thought the Pope would know everything. I thought God would speak to me directly. But of course he knew I was a woman.

MARLENE. But nobody else even suspected?

The WAITRESS *brings more wine.*

JOAN. In the end I did take a lover again.*

ISABELLA. In the Vatican?

GRET. *Keep you warm.

NIJO. *Ah, lover.

MARLENE. *Good for you.

JOAN. He was one of my chamberlains. There are such a lot of servants when you're a Pope. The food's very good. And I realised I did know the truth. Because whatever the Pope says, that's true.

NIJO. What was he like, the chamberlain?*

GRET. Big cock.

ISABELLA. Oh Gret.

MARLENE. *Did he fancy you when he thought you were a fella?

NIJO. What was he like?

JOAN. He could keep a secret.

MARLENE. So you did know everything.

JOAN. Yes, I enjoyed being Pope. I consecrated bishops and let people kiss my feet. I received the King of England when he came to submit to the church. Unfortunately there were earthquakes, and some village reported it had rained blood, and in France there was a plague of giant grasshoppers, but I don't think that can have been my fault, do you?*

Laughter.

The grasshoppers fell on the English Channel and were

washed up on shore and their bodies rotted and poisoned the air and everyone in those parts died.

Laughter.

ISABELLA. *Such superstition! I was nearly murdered in China by a howling mob. They thought the barbarians ate babies and put them under railway sleepers to make the tracks steady, and ground up their eyes to make the lenses of cameras. / So

MARLENE. And you had a camera!

ISABELLA. they were shouting, 'child-eater, child-eater.' Some people tried to sell girl babies to Europeans for cameras or stew!

Laughter.

MARLENE. So apart from the grasshoppers it was a great success.

JOAN. Yes, if it hadn't been for the baby I expect I'd have lived to an old age like Theodora of Alexandria, who lived as a monk. She was accused by a girl / who fell in love with her of being the father of her child and --

NIJO. But tell us what happened to your baby. I had some babies.

MARLENE. Didn't you think of getting rid of it?

JOAN. Wouldn't that be a worse sin than having it? / But a Pope with a child was about as bad as possible.

MARLENE. I don't know, you're the Pope.

JOAN. But I wouldn't have known how to get rid of it.

MARLENE. Other Popes had children, surely.

JOAN. They didn't give birth to them.

NIJO. Well you were a woman.

JOAN. Exactly and I shouldn't have been a woman. Women, children and lunatics can't be Pope.

MARLENE. So the only thing to do / was to get rid of it somehow.

NIJO. You had to have it adopted secretly.

JOAN. But I didn't know what was happening. I thought I was getting fatter, but then I was eating more and sitting about, the life of a Pope is quite luxurious. I don't think I'd spoken to a woman since I was twelve. The chamberlain was the one who realised.

MARLENE. And by then it was too late.

JOAN. Oh I didn't want to pay attention. It was easier to do nothing.

NIJO. But you had to plan for having it. You had to say you were ill and go away.

JOAN. That's what I should have done I suppose.

MARLENE. Did you want them to find out?

NIJO. I too was often in embarrassing situations, there's no need for a scandal. My first child was His Majesty's, which unfortunately died, but my second was Akebono's. I was seventeen. He was in love with me when I was thirteen, he was very upset when I had to go to the Emperor, it was very romantic, a lot of poems. Now His Majesty hadn't been near me for two months so he thought I was four months pregnant when I was really six, so when I reached the ninth month / I

JOAN. I never knew what month it was.

NIJO. announced I was seriously ill, and Akebono announced he had gone on a religious retreat. He held me round the waist and lifted me up as the baby was born. He cut the cord with a short sword, wrapped the baby in white and took it away. It was only a girl but I was sorry to lose it. Then I told the Emperor that the baby had miscarried because of my illness, and there you are. The danger was past.

JOAN. But Nijo, I wasn't used to having a woman's body.

ISABELLA. So what happened?

JOAN. I didn't know of course that it was near the time. It was Rogation Day, there was always a procession. I was on the horse dressed in my robes and a cross was carried in front of me, and all the cardinals were following, and all the clergy of Rome, and a huge crowd of people. / We set off from

MARLENE. Total Pope.

JOAN. St Peter's to go to St John's. I had felt a slight pain earlier,
I thought it was something I'd eaten, and then it came back,
and came back more often. I thought when this is over I'll go
to bed. There were still long gaps when I felt perfectly all right
and I didn't want to attract attention to myself and spoil the
ceremony. Then I suddenly realised what it must be. I had to
last out till I could get home and hide. Then something
changed, my breath started to catch, I couldn't plan things
properly any more. We were in a little street that goes between
St Clement's and the Colosseum, and I just had to get off the
horse and sit down for a minute. Great waves of pressure were
going through my body, I heard sounds like a cow lowing,
they came out of my mouth. Far away I heard people
screaming, 'The Pope is ill, the Pope is dying.' And the baby
just slid out onto the road.*

MARLENE. The cardinals / won't have known where to put
themselves.

NIJO. Oh dear, Joan, what a thing to do! In the street!

ISABELLA. *How embarrassing.

GRET. In a field, yah.

They are laughing.

JOAN. One of the cardinals said, 'The Antichrist!' and fell over
in a faint.

They all laugh.

MARLENE. So what did they do? They weren't best pleased.

JOAN. They took me by the feet and dragged me out of town
and stoned me to death.

They stop laughing.

MARLENE. Joan, how horrible.

JOAN. I don't really remember.

NIJO. And the child died too?

JOAN. Oh yes, I think so, yes.

Pause.

The WAITRESS *enters to clear the plates. They start talking quietly.*

ISABELLA (*to* JOAN). I never had any children. I was very fond of horses.

NIJO (*to* MARLENE). I saw my daughter once. She was three years old. She wore a plum-red / small-sleeved gown. Akebono's

ISABELLA. Birdie was my favourite. A little Indian bay mare I rode in the Rocky Mountains.

NIJO. wife had taken the child because her own died. Everyone thought I was just a visitor. She was being brought up carefully so she could be sent to the palace like I was.

ISABELLA. Legs of iron and always cheerful, and such a pretty face. If a stranger led her she reared up like a bronco.

NIJO. I never saw my third child after he was born, the son of Ariake the priest. Ariake held him on his lap the day he was born and talked to him as if he could understand, and cried. My fourth child was Ariake's too. Ariake died before he was born. I didn't want to see anyone, I stayed alone in the hills. It was a boy again, my third son. But oddly enough I felt nothing for him.

MARLENE. How many children did you have, Gret?

GRET. Ten.

ISABELLA. Whenever I came back to England I felt I had so much to atone for. Hennie and John were so good. I did no good in my life. I spent years in self-gratification. So I hurled myself into committees, I nursed the people of Tobermory in the epidemic of influenza, I lectured the Young Women's Christian Association on Thrift. I talked and talked explaining how the East was corrupt and vicious. My travels must do good to someone beside myself. I wore myself out with good causes.

MARLENE. Oh God, why are we all so miserable?

JOAN. The procession never went down that street again.

MARLENE. They rerouted it specially?

JOAN. Yes they had to go all round to avoid it. And they introduced a pierced chair.

MARLENE. A pierced chair?

JOAN. Yes, a chair made out of solid marble with a hole in the seat / and it was in the Chapel of the Saviour, and after he was

MARLENE. You're not serious.

JOAN. elected the Pope had to sit in it.

MARLENE. And someone looked up his skirts? / Not really?

ISABELLA. What an extraordinary thing.

JOAN. Two of the clergy / made sure he was a man.

NIJO. On their hands and knees!

MARLENE. A pierced chair!

GRET. Balls!

GRISELDA *arrives unnoticed.*

NIJO. Why couldn't he just pull up his robe?

JOAN. He had to sit there and look dignified.

MARLENE. You could have made all your chamberlains sit in it.*

GRET. Big one, small one.

NIJO. Very useful chair at court.

ISABELLA. *Or the laird of Tobermory in his kilt.

They are quite drunk. They get the giggles.

MARLENE *notices* GRISELDA.

MARLENE. Griselda! / There you are. Do you want to eat?

GRISELDA. I'm sorry I'm so late. No, no, don't bother.

MARLENE. Of course it's no bother. / Have you eaten?

GRISELDA. No really, I'm not hungry.

MARLENE. Well have some pudding.

GRISELDA. I never eat pudding.

MARLENE. Griselda, I hope you're not anorexic. We're having pudding, I am, and getting nice and fat.

GRISELDA. Oh if everyone is. I don't mind.

MARLENE. Now who do you know? This is Joan who was Pope in the ninth century, and Isabella Bird, the Victorian traveller, and Lady Nijo from Japan, Emperor's concubine and Buddhist nun, thirteenth century, nearer your own time, and Gret who was painted by Brueghel. Griselda's in Boccaccio and Petrarch and Chaucer because of her extraordinary marriage. I'd like profiteroles because they're disgusting.

JOAN. Zabaglione, please.

ISABELLA. Apple pie / and cream.

NIJO. What's this?

MARLENE. Zabaglione, it's Italian, it's what Joan's having, / it's delicious.

NIJO. A Roman Catholic / dessert? Yes please.

MARLENE. Gret?

GRET. Cake.

GRISELDA. Just cheese and biscuits, thank you.

MARLENE. Yes, Griselda's life is like a fairy-story, except it starts with marrying the prince.

GRISELDA. He's only a marquis, Marlene.

MARLENE. Well everyone for miles around is his liege and he's absolute lord of life and death and you were the poor but beautiful peasant girl and he whisked you off. / Near enough a prince.

NIJO. How old were you?

GRISELDA. Fifteen.

NIJO. I was brought up in court circles and it was still a shock. Had you ever seen him before?

GRISELDA. I'd seen him riding by, we all had. And he'd seen me in the fields with the sheep.*

ISABELLA. I would have been well suited to minding sheep.

NIJO. And Mr Nugent riding by.

ISABELLA. Of course not, Nijo, I mean a healthy life in the open air.

JOAN. *He just rode up while you were minding the sheep and asked you to marry him?

GRISELDA. No, no, it was on the wedding day. I was waiting outside the door to see the procession. Everyone wanted him to get married so there'd be an heir to look after us when he died, / and at last he announced a day for the wedding but

MARLENE. I don't think Walter wanted to get married. It is Walter? Yes.

GRISELDA. nobody knew who the bride was, we thought it must be a foreign princess, we were longing to see her. Then the carriage stopped outside our cottage and we couldn't see the bride anywhere. And he came and spoke to my father.

NIJO. And your father told you to serve the Prince.

GRISELDA. My father could hardly speak. The Marquis said it wasn't an order, I could say no, but if I said yes I must always obey him in everything.

MARLENE. That's when you should have suspected.

GRISELDA. But of course a wife must obey her husband. / And of course I must obey the Marquis.*

ISABELLA. I swore to obey dear John, of course, but it didn't seem to arise. Naturally I wouldn't have wanted to go abroad while I was married.

MARLENE. *Then why bother to mention it at all? He'd got a thing about it, that's why.

GRISELDA. I'd rather obey the Marquis than a boy from the village.

MARLENE. Yes, that's a point.

JOAN. I never obeyed anyone. They all obeyed me.

NIJO. And what did you wear? He didn't make you get married in your own clothes? That would be perverse.*

MARLENE. Oh, you wait.

GRISELDA. *He had ladies with him who undressed me and they had a white silk dress and jewels for my hair.

MARLENE. And at first he seemed perfectly normal?

GRISELDA. Marlene, you're always so critical of him. / Of course he was normal, he was very kind.

MARLENE. But Griselda, come on, he took your baby.

GRISELDA. Walter found it hard to believe I loved him. He couldn't believe I would always obey him. He had to prove it.

MARLENE. I don't think Walter likes women.

GRISELDA. I'm sure he loved me, Marlene, all the time.

MARLENE. He just had a funny way / of showing it.

GRISELDA. It was hard for him too.

JOAN. How do you mean he took away your baby?

NIJO. Was it a boy?

GRISELDA. No, the first one was a girl.

NIJO. Even so it's hard when they take it away. Did you see it at all?

GRISELDA. Oh yes, she was six weeks old.

NIJO. Much better to do it straight away.

ISABELLA. But why did your husband take the child?

GRISELDA. He said all the people hated me because I was just one of them. And now I had a child they were restless. So he had to get rid of the child to keep them quiet. But he said he wouldn't snatch her, I had to agree and obey and give her up. So when I was feeding her a man came in and took her away. I thought he was going to kill her even before he was out of the room.

MARLENE. But you let him take her? You didn't struggle?

GRISELDA. I asked him to give her back so I could kiss her. And I asked him to bury her where no animals could dig her up. / It

ISABELLA. Oh my dear.

GRISELDA. was Walter's child to do what he liked with.*

MARLENE. Walter was bonkers.

GRET. Bastard.

ISABELLA. *But surely, murder.

GRISELDA. I had promised.

MARLENE. I can't stand this. I'm going for a pee.

MARLENE *goes out.*

The WAITRESS *brings dessert.*

[handwritten margin note: nijo empathi zes ↑]

NIJO. No, I understand. Of course you had to, he was your life. And were you in favour after that?

GRISELDA. Oh yes, we were very happy together. We never spoke about what had happened.

ISABELLA. I can see you were doing what you thought was your duty. But didn't it make you ill?

GRISELDA. No, I was very well, thank you.

NIJO. And you had another child?

GRISELDA. Not for four years, but then I did, yes, a boy.

NIJO. Ah a boy. / So it all ended happily.

GRISELDA. Yes he was pleased. I kept my son till he was two years old. A peasant's grandson. It made the people angry. Walter explained.

ISABELLA. But surely he wouldn't kill his children / just because —

GRISELDA. Oh it wasn't true. Walter would never give in to the people. He wanted to see if I loved him enough.

JOAN. He killed his children / to see if you loved him enough?

NIJO. Was it easier the second time or harder?

GRISELDA. It was always easy because I always knew I would do what he said.

Pause. They start to eat.

ISABELLA. I hope you didn't have any more children.

GRISELDA. Oh no, no more. It was twelve years till he tested me again.

ISABELLA. So whatever did he do this time ? / My poor John, I never loved him enough, and he would never have dreamt . . .

GRISELDA. He sent me away. He said the people wanted him to marry someone else who'd give him an heir and he'd got special permission from the Pope. So I said I'd go home to my father. I came with nothing / so I went with nothing. I

NIJO. Better to leave if your master doesn't want you.

GRISELDA. took off my clothes. He let me keep a slip so he wouldn't be shamed. And I walked home barefoot. My father came out in tears. Everyone was crying except me.

NIJO. At least your father wasn't dead. / I had nobody.

ISABELLA. Well it can be a relief to come home. I loved to see Hennie's sweet face again.

GRISELDA. Oh yes, I was perfectly content. And quite soon he sent for me again.

JOAN. I don't think I would have gone.

GRISELDA. But he told me to come. I had to obey him. He wanted me to help prepare his wedding. He was getting married to a young girl from France / and nobody except me knew how to arrange things the way he liked them.

NIJO. It's always hard taking him another woman.

MARLENE *comes back.*

JOAN. I didn't live a woman's life. I don't understand it.

GRISELDA. The girl was sixteen and far more beautiful than me. I could see why he loved her. / She had her younger brother with her as a page.

The WAITRESS *enters.*

MARLENE. Oh God, I can't bear it. I want some coffee. Six coffees. Six brandies. / Double brandies. Straightaway.

GRISELDA. They all went in to the feast I'd prepared. And he stayed behind and put his arms round me and kissed me. / I felt half asleep with the shock.

NIJO. Oh, like a dream.

MARLENE. And he said, 'This is your daughter and your son.'

GRISELDA. Yes.

JOAN. What?

NIJO. Oh. Oh I see. You got them back.

ISABELLA. I did think it was remarkably barbaric to kill them but you learn not to say anything. / So he had them brought up secretly I suppose.

MARLENE. Walter's a monster. Weren't you angry? What did you do?

GRISELDA. Well I fainted. Then I cried and kissed the children. / Everyone was making a fuss of me.

NIJO. But did you feel anything for them?

GRISELDA. What?

NIJO. Did you feel anything for the children?

GRISELDA. Of course, I loved them.

JOAN. So you forgave him and lived with him?

GRISELDA. He suffered so much all those years.

ISABELLA. Hennie had the same sweet nature.

NIJO. So they dressed you again?

GRISELDA. Cloth of gold.

JOAN. I can't forgive anything.

MARLENE. You really are exceptional, Griselda.

NIJO. Nobody gave me back my children.

   NIJO *cries. The* WAITRESS *brings brandies.*

ISABELLA. I can never be like Hennie. I was always so busy in England, a kind of business I detested. The very presence of people exhausted my emotional reserves. I could not be like

Hennie however I tried. I tried and was as ill as could be. The
doctor suggested a steel net to support my head, the weight of
my own head was too much for my diseased spine. / It is
dangerous to put oneself in depressing circumstances. Why
should I do it?

JOAN. Don't cry.

NIJO. My father and the Emperor both died in the autumn. So
much pain.

JOAN. Yes, but don't cry.

NIJO. They wouldn't let me into the palace when he was dying.
I hid in the room with his coffin, then I couldn't find where
I'd left my shoes, I ran after the funeral procession in bare
feet, I couldn't keep up. When I got there it was over, a few
wisps of smoke in the sky, that's all that was left of him. What
I want to know is, if I'd still been at court, would I have been
allowed to wear full mourning?

MARLENE. I'm sure you would.

NIJO. Why do you say that? You don't know anything about it.
Would I have been allowed to wear full mourning?

ISABELLA. How can people live in this dim pale island and wear
our hideous clothes? I cannot and will not live the life of a
lady.

NIJO. I'll tell you something that made me angry. I was eighteen,
at the Full Moon Ceremony. They make a special rice gruel
and stir it with their sticks, and then they beat their women
across the loins so they'll have sons and not daughters. So
the Emperor beat us all / very hard as usual — that's not it,

MARLENE. What a sod.

NIJO. Marlene, that's normal, what made us angry, he told his
attendants they could beat us too. Well they had a wonderful
time. / So Lady Genki and I made a plan, and the ladies all hid

The WAITRESS *has entered with coffees.*

MARLENE. I'd like another brandy please. Better make it six.

NIJO. in his rooms, and Lady Mashimizu stood guard with a stick at the door, and when His Majesty came in Genki seized him and I beat him till he cried out and promised he would never order anyone to hit us again. Afterwards there was a terrible fuss. The nobles were horrified. 'We wouldn't even dream of stepping on your Majesty's shadow.' And I had hit him with a stick. Yes, I hit him with a stick.

JOAN. Suave, mari magno turbantibus aequora ventis,
   e terra magnum alterius spectare laborem;
   non quia vexari quemquamst iucunda voluptas,
   sed quibus ipse malis careas quia cernere suave est.
   Suave etiam belli certamina magna tueri
   per campos instructa tua sine parte pericli.
   Sed nil dulcius est, bene quam munita tenere
   edita doctrina sapientum templa serena, /
   despicere unde queas alios passimque videre
   errare atque viam palantis quaerere vitae,

GRISELDA. I do think — I do wonder — it would have been nicer if Walter hadn't had to.

ISABELLA. Why should I? Why should I?

MARLENE. Of course not.

NIJO. I hit him with a stick.

JOAN. certare ingenio, contendere nobilitate,
   noctes atque dies niti praestante labore
   ad summas emergere opes retumque potiri.
   O miseras / hominum mentis, o pectora caeca!*

ISABELLA. Oh miseras!

NIJO. *Pectora caeca.

JOAN. qualibus in tenebris vitae quantisque periclis
   degitur hoc aevi quodcumquest! / nonne videre
   nil aliud sibi naturam latrare, nisi utqui
   corpore seiunctus dolor absit, mente fruatur

   JOAN subsides.

GRET. We come into hell through a big mouth. Hell's black and red. / It's like the village where I come from. There's a river and

MARLENE (*to* JOAN). Shut up, pet.

ISABELLA. Listen, she's been to hell.

GRET. a bridge and houses. There's places on fire like when the
    soldiers come. There's a big devil sat on a roof with a big hole
    in his arse and he's scooping stuff out of it with a big ladle and
    it's falling down on us, and it's money, so a lot of the women
    stop and get some. But most of us is fighting the devils.
    There's lots of little devils, our size, and we get them down all
    right and give them a beating. There's lots of funny creatures
    round your feet, you don't like to look, like rats and lizards,
    and nasty things, a bum with a face, and fish with legs, and
    faces on things that don't have faces on. But they don't hurt,
    you just keep going. Well we'd had worse, you see, we'd had
    the Spanish. We'd all had family killed. My big son die on a
    wheel. Birds eat him. My baby, a soldier run her through with
    a sword. I'd had enough, I was mad, I hate the bastards. I
    come out my front door that morning and shout till my
    neighbours come out and I said, 'Come on, we're going where
    the evil come from and pay the bastards out.' And they all
    come out just as they was / from baking or washing in their

NIJO. All the ladies come.

GRET. aprons, and we push down the street and the ground
    opens up and we go through a big mouth into a street just like
    ours but in hell. I've got a sword in my hand from somewhere
    and I fill a basket with gold cups they drink out of down
    there. You just keep running on and fighting / you didn't stop
    for nothing. Oh we give them devils such a beating.

NIJO. Take that, take that.

JOAN. Something something something mortisque timores
    tum vacuum pectus — damn.
    Quod si ridicula —
    something something on and on and on and something
        splendorem purpureai.

ISABELLA. I thought I would have a last jaunt up the west river
    in China. Why not? But the doctors were so very grave. I just
    went to Morocco. The sea was so wild I had to be landed by

ship's crane in a coal bucket. / My horse was a terror to me a

GRET. Coal bucket, good.

JOAN. nos in luce timemus
something
terrorem.

ISABELLA. powerful black charger.

NIJO *is laughing and crying.*
JOAN *gets up and is sick in a corner.*
MARLENE *is drinking* ISABELLA's *brandy.*

So off I went to visit the Berber sheikhs in full blue trousers and great brass spurs. I was the only European woman ever to have seen the Emperor of Morocco. I was seventy years old. What lengths to go to for a last chance of joy. I knew my return of vigour was only temporary, but how marvellous while it lasted.

shared pain of motherhood
+ deaths of past
lovers. Is Joan alive?
Are these women
ghost

ACT TWO

Scene One

Employment Agency. MARLENE *and* JEANINE.

MARLENE. Right Jeanine, you are Jeanine aren't you? Let's have a look. Os and As. / No As, all those Os you probably

JEANINE. Six Os.

MARLENE. could have got an A. / Speeds, not brilliant, not too bad.

JEANINE. I wanted to go to work.

MARLENE. Well, Jeanine, what's your present job like?

JEANINE. I'm a secretary.

MARLENE. Secretary or typist?

JEANINE. I did start as a typist but the last six months I've been a secretary.

MARLENE. To?

JEANINE. To three of them, really, they share me. There's

Mr Ashford, he's the office manager, and Mr Philby / is sales, and —

MARLENE. Quite a small place?

JEANINE. A bit small.

MARLENE. Friendly?

JEANINE. Oh it's friendly enough.

MARLENE. Prospects?

JEANINE. I don't think so, that's the trouble. Miss Lewis is secretary to the managing director and she's been there forever, and Mrs Bradford/ is —

MARLENE. So you want a job with better prospects?

JEANINE. I want a change.

MARLENE. So you'll take anything comparable?

JEANINE. No, I do want prospects. I want more money.

MARLENE. You're getting — ?

JEANINE. Hundred.

MARLENE. It's not bad you know. You're what? Twenty?

JEANINE. I'm saving to get married.

MARLENE. Does that mean you don't want a long-term job, Jeanine?

JEANINE. I might do.

MARLENE. Because where do the prospects come in? No kids for a bit?

JEANINE. Oh no, not kids, not yet.

MARLENE. So you won't tell them you're getting married?

JEANINE. Had I better not?

MARLENE. It would probably help.

JEANINE. I'm not wearing a ring. We thought we wouldn't spend on a ring.

MARLENE. Saves taking it off.

JEANINE. I wouldn't take it off.

MARLENE. There's no need to mention it when you go for an interview. / Now Jeanine do you have a feel for any particular

JEANINE. But what if they ask?

MARLENE. kind of company?

JEANINE. I thought advertising.

MARLENE. People often do think advertising. I have got a few vacancies but I think they're looking for something glossier.

JEANINE. You mean how I dress? / I can dress different. I

MARLENE. I mean experience.

JEANINE. dress like this on purpose for where I am now.

MARLENE. I have a marketing department here of a knitwear manufacturer. / Marketing is near enough advertising. Secretary

JEANINE. Knitwear?

MARLENE. to the marketing manager, he's thirty-five, married, I've sent him a girl before and she was happy, left to have a baby, you won't want to mention marriage there. He's very fair I think, good at his job, you won't have to nurse him along. Hundred and ten, so that's better than you're doing now.

JEANINE. I don't know.

MARLENE. I've a fairly small concern here, father and two sons, you'd have more say potentially, secretarial and reception duties, only a hundred but the job's going to grow with the concern and then you'll be in at the top with new girls coming in underneath you.

JEANINE. What is it they do?

MARLENE. Lampshades. / This would be my first choice for you.

JEANINE. Just lampshades?

MARLENE. There's plenty of different kinds of lampshade. So we'll send you there, shall we, and the knitwear second choice. Are you free to go for an interview any day they call you?

JEANINE. I'd like to travel.

MARLENE. We don't have any foreign clients. You'd have to go elsewhere.

JEANINE. Yes I know. I don't really . . . I just mean . . .

MARLENE. Does your fiancé want to travel?

JEANINE. I'd like a job where I was here in London and with him and everything but now and then — I expect it's silly. Are there jobs like that?

MARLENE. There's personal assistant to a top executive in a multinational. If that's the idea you need to be planning ahead. Is that where you want to be in ten years?

JEANINE. I might not be alive in ten years.

MARLENE. Yes but you will be. You'll have children.

JEANINE. I can't think about ten years.

MARLENE. You haven't got the speeds anyway. So I'll send you to these two shall I? You haven't been to any other

agency? Just so we don't get crossed wires. Now Jeanine I
want you to get one of these jobs, all right? If I send you
that means I'm putting myself on the line for you. Your
presentation's OK, you look fine, just be confident and
go in there convinced that this is the best job for you and
you're the best person for the job. If you don't believe it they
won't believe it.

JEANINE. Do you believe it?

MARLENE. I think you could make me believe it if you put
your mind to it.

JEANINE. Yes, all right.

Scene Two

JOYCE's *back yard. The house with back door is upstage.
Downstage a shelter made of junk, made by children. Two girls,
ANGIE and KIT, are in it, squashed together. ANGIE is 16, KIT
is 12. They cannot be seen from the house. JOYCE calls from the
house.*

JOYCE. Angie. Angie are you out there?

*Silence. They keep still and wait. When nothing else happens
they relax.*

ANGIE. Wish she was dead.

KIT. Wanna watch *The Exterminator?*

ANGIE. You're sitting on my leg.

KIT. There's nothing on telly. We can have an ice cream. Angie?

ANGIE. Shall I tell you something?

KIT. Do you wanna watch *The Exterminator?*

ANGIE. It's X, innit.

KIT. I can get into Xs.

ANGIE. Shall I tell you something?

KIT. We'll go to something else. We'll go to Ipswich. What's on
the Odeon?

ANGIE. She won't let me, will she?

KIT. Don't tell her.

ANGIE. I've no money.

KIT. I'll pay.

ANGIE. She'll moan though, won't she?

KIT. I'll ask her for you if you like.

ANGIE. I've no money, I don't want you to pay.

KIT. I'll ask her.

ANGIE. She don't like you.

KIT. I still got three pounds birthday money. Did she say she
    don't like me? I'll go by myself then.

ANGIE. Your mum don't let you. I got to take you.

KIT. She won't know.

ANGIE. You'd be scared who'd sit next to you.

KIT. No I wouldn't.
    She does like me anyway.
    Tell me then.

ANGIE. Tell you what?

KIT. It's you she doesn't like.

ANGIE. Well I don't like her so tough shit.

JOYCE (off). Angie. Angie. Angie. I know you're out there. I'm
    not coming out after you. You come in here.

    Silence. Nothing happens.

ANGIE. Last night when I was in bed. I been thinking yesterday
    could I make things move. You know, make things move
    by thinking about them without touching them. Last night
    I was in bed and suddenly a picture fell down off the wall.

KIT. What picture?

ANGIE. My gran, that picture. Not the poster. The photograph
    in the frame.

KIT. Had you done something to make it fall down?

ANGIE. I must have done.

KIT. But were you thinking about it?

ANGIE. Not about it, but about something.

KIT. I don't think that's very good.

ANGIE. You know the kitten?

KIT. Which one?

ANGIE. There only is one. The dead one.

KIT. What about it?

ANGIE. I heard it last night.

KIT. Where?

ANGIE. Out here. In the dark. What if I left you here in the dark all night?

KIT. You couldn't. I'd go home.

ANGIE. You couldn't.

KIT. I'd / go home.

ANGIE. No you couldn't, not if I said.

KIT. I could.

ANGIE. Then you wouldn't see anything. You'd just be ignorant.

KIT. I can see in the daytime.

ANGIE. No you can't. You can't hear it in the daytime.

KIT. I don't want to hear it.

ANGIE. You're scared that's all.

KIT. I'm not scared of anything.

ANGIE. You're scared of blood.

KIT. It's not the same kitten anyway. You just heard an old cat, / you just heard some old cat.

ANGIE. You don't know what I heard. Or what I saw. You don't know nothing because you're a baby.

KIT. You're sitting on me.

ANGIE. Mind my hair / you silly cunt.

KIT. Stupid fucking cow, I hate you.

ANGIE. I don't care if you do.

KIT. You're horrible.

ANGIE. I'm going to kill my mother and you're going to watch.

KIT. I'm not playing.

ANGIE. You're scared of blood.

> KIT *puts her hand under her dress, brings it out with blood on her finger.*

KIT. There, see, I got my own blood, so.

> ANGIE *takes* KIT's *hand and licks her finger.*

ANGIE. Now I'm a cannibal. I might turn into a vampire now.

KIT. That picture wasn't nailed up right.

ANGIE. You'll have to do that when I get mine.

KIT. I don't have to.

ANGIE. You're scared.

KIT. I'll do it, I might do it. I don't have to just because you say. I'll be sick on you.

ANGIE. I don't care if you are sick on me, I don't mind sick. I don't mind blood. If I don't get away from here I'm going to die.

KIT. I'm going home.

ANGIE. You can't go through the house. She'll see you.

KIT. I won't tell her.

ANGIE. Oh great, fine.

KIT. I'll say I was by myself. I'll tell her you're at my house and I'm going there to get you.

ANGIE. She knows I'm here, stupid.

KIT. Then why can't I go through the house?

ANGIE. Because I said not.

KIT. My mum don't like you anyway.

ANGIE. I don't want her to like me. She's a slag.

KIT. She is not.

ANGIE. She does it with everyone.

KIT. She does not.

ANGIE. You don't even know what it is.

KIT. Yes I do.

ANGIE. Tell me then.

KIT. We get it all at school, cleverclogs. It's on television. You haven't done it.

ANGIE. How do you know?

KIT. Because I know you haven't.

ANGIE. You know wrong then because I have.

KIT. Who with?

ANGIE. I'm not telling you / who with.

KIT. You haven't anyway.

ANGIE. How do you know?

KIT. Who with?

ANGIE. I'm not telling you.

KIT. You said you told me everything.

ANGIE. I was lying wasn't I?

KIT. Who with? You can't tell me who with because / you never —

ANGIE. Sh.

JOYCE has come out of the house. She stops half way across the yard and listens. They listen.

JOYCE. You there Angie? Kit? You there Kitty? Want a cup of tea? I've got some chocolate biscuits. Come on now I'll put the kettle on. Want a choccy biccy, Angie?

They all listen and wait.

Fucking rotten little cunt. You can stay there and die. I'll lock the back door.

They all wait.

JOYCE *goes back to the house.*

ANGIE *and* KIT *sit in silence for a while.*

KIT. When there's a war, where's the safest place?

ANGIE. Nowhere.

KIT. New Zealand is, my mum said. Your skin's burned right off.
    Shall we go to New Zealand?

ANGIE. I'm not staying here.

KIT. Shall we go to New Zealand?

ANGIE. You're not old enough.

KIT. You're not old enough.

ANGIE. I'm old enough to get married.

KIT. You don't want to get married.

ANGIE. No but I'm old enough.

KIT. I'd find out where they were going to drop it and stand right
    in the place.

ANGIE. You couldn't find out.

KIT. Better than walking round with your skin dragging on the
    ground. Eugh. / Would you like walking round with your
    skin dragging on the ground?

ANGIE. You couldn't find out, stupid, it's a secret.

KIT. Where are you going?

ANGIE. I'm not telling you.

KIT. Why?

ANGIE. It's a secret.

KIT. But you tell me all your secrets.

ANGIE. Not the true secrets.

KIT. Yes you do.

ANGIE. No I don't.

KIT. I want to go somewhere away from the war.

ANGIE. Just forget the war.

KIT. I can't.

ANGIE. You have to. It's so boring.

KIT. I'll remember it at night.

ANGIE. I'm going to do something else anyway.

KIT. What? Angie come on. Angie.

ANGIE. It's a true secret.

KIT. It can't be worse than the kitten. And killing your mother. And the war.

ANGIE. Well I'm not telling you so you can die for all I care.

KIT. My mother says there's something wrong with you playing with someone my age. She says why haven't you got friends your own age. People your own age know there's something funny about you. She says you're a bad influence. She says she's going to speak to your mother.

ANGIE *twists* KIT's *arm till she cries out.*

ANGIE. Say you're a liar.

KIT. She said it not me.

ANGIE. Say you eat shit.

KIT. You can't make me.

ANGIE *lets go.*

ANGIE. I don't care anyway. I'm leaving.

KIT. Go on then.

ANGIE. You'll all wake up one morning and find I've gone.

KIT. Good.

ANGIE. I'm not telling you when.

KIT' Go on then.

ANGIE. I'm sorry I hurt you.

KIT. I'm tired.

ANGIE. Do you like me?

KIT. I don't know.

ANGIE. You do like me.

KIT. I'm going home.

> KIT *gets up.*

ANGIE. No you're not.

KIT. I'm tired.

ANGIE. She'll see you.

KIT. She'll give me a chocolate biscuit.

ANGIE. Kitty.

KIT. Tell me where you're going.

ANGIE. Sit down.

> KIT *sits in the hut again.*

KIT. Go on then.

ANGIE. Swear?

KIT. Swear.

ANGIE. I'm going to London. To see my aunt.

KIT. And what?

ANGIE. That's it.

KIT. I see my aunt all the time.

ANGIE. I don't see my aunt.

KIT. What's so special?

ANGIE. It is special. She's special.

KIT. Why?

ANGIE. She is.

KIT. Why?

ANGIE. She is.

KIT. Why?

ANGIE. My mother hates her.

KIT. Why?

ANGIE. Because she does.

KIT. Perhaps she's not very nice.

ANGIE. She is nice.

KIT. How do you know?

ANGIE. Because I know her.

KIT. You said you never see her.

ANGIE. I saw her last year. You saw her.

KIT. Did I?

ANGIE. Never mind.

KIT. I remember her. That aunt. What's so special?

ANGIE. She gets people jobs.

KIT. What's so special?

ANGIE. I think I'm my aunt's child. I think my mother's really my aunt.

KIT. Why?

ANGIE. Because she goes to America, now shut up.

KIT. I've been to London.

ANGIE. Now give us a cuddle and shut up because I'm sick.

KIT. You're sitting on my arm.

   Silence.

   JOYCE *comes out and comes up to them quietly.*

JOYCE. Come on.

KIT. Oh hello.

JOYCE. Time you went home.

KIT. We want to go to the Odeon.

JOYCE. What time?

KIT. Don't know.

JOYCE. What's on?

KIT. Don't know.

JOYCE. Don't know much do you?

KIT. That all right then?

JOYCE. Angie's got to clean her room first.

ANGIE. No I don't.

JOYCE. Yes you do, it's a pigsty.

ANGIE. Well I'm not.

JOYCE. Then you're not going. I don't care.

ANGIE. Well I am going.

JOYCE. You've no money, have you?

ANGIE. Kit's paying anyway.

JOYCE. No she's not.

KIT. I'll help you with your room.

JOYCE. That's nice.

ANGIE. No you won't. You wait here.

KIT. Hurry then.

ANGIE. I'm not hurrying. You just wait.

ANGIE goes into the house. Silence.

JOYCE. I don't know.

Silence.

How's school then?

KIT. All right.

JOYCE. What are you now? Third year?

KIT. Second year.

JOYCE. Your mum says you're good at English.

Silence.

Maybe Angie should've stayed on.

KIT. She didn't like it.

JOYCE. I didn't like it. And look at me. If your face fits at school it's going to fit other places too. It wouldn't make no difference to Angie. She's not going to get a job when jobs are hard to get. I'd be sorry for anyone in charge of her. She'd better get married. I don't know who'd have her, mind. She's one of those girls might never leave home. What do you want to be when you grow up, Kit?

KIT. Physicist.

JOYCE. What?

KIT. Nuclear physicist.

JOYCE. Whatever for?

KIT. I could, I'm clever.

JOYCE. I know you're clever, pet.

Silence.

I'll make a cup of tea.

Silence.

Looks like it's going to rain.

Silence.

Don't you have friends your own age?

KIT. Yes.

JOYCE. Well then.

KIT. I'm old for my age.

JOYCE. And Angie's simple is she? She's not simple.

KIT. I love Angie.

JOYCE. She's clever in her own way.

KIT. You can't stop me.

JOYCE. I don't want to.

KIT. You can't, so.

JOYCE. Don't be cheeky, Kitty. She's always kind to little children.

KIT. She's coming so you better leave me alone.

ANGIE *comes out. She has changed into an old best dress, slightly small for her.*

JOYCE. What you put that on for? Have you done your room? You can't clean your room in that.

ANGIE. I looked in the cupboard and it was there.

JOYCE. Of course it was there, it's meant to be there. Is that why it was a surprise, finding something in the right place? I should think she's surprised, wouldn't you Kit, to find something in her room in the right place.

ANGIE. I decided to wear it.

JOYCE. Not today, why? To clean your room? You're not going to the pictures till you've done your room. You can put your dress on after if you like.

ANGIE *picks up a brick.*

Have you done your room? You're not getting out of it, you know.

KIT. Angie, let's go.

JOYCE. She's not going till she's done her room.

KIT. It's starting to rain.

JOYCE. Come on, come on then. Hurry and do your room, Angie, and then you can go to the cinema with Kit. Oh it's wet, come on. We'll look up the time in the paper. Does your mother know, Kit, it's going to be a late night for you, isn't it? Hurry up, Angie. You'll spoil your dress. You make me sick.

JOYCE *and* KIT *run in.*

ANGIE *stays where she is. Sound of rain.*

KIT *comes out of the house and shouts.*

KIT. Angie. Angie, come on, you'll get wet.

KIT *comes back to* ANGIE.

ANGIE. I put on this dress to kill my mother.

KIT. I suppose you thought you'd do it with a brick.

ANGIE. You can kill people with a brick.

KIT. Well you didn't, so.

Scene Three

Office of 'Top Girls' Employment Agency. Three desks and a small interviewing area. Monday morning. WIN and NELL have just arrived for work.

NELL. Coffee coffee coffee coffee / coffee.

WIN. The roses were smashing. / Mermaid.

NELL. Ohhh.

WIN. Iceberg. He taught me all their names.

   NELL *has some coffee now.*

NELL. Ah. Now then.

WIN. He has one of the finest rose gardens in West Sussex. He exhibits.

NELL. He what?

WIN. His wife was visiting her mother. It was like living together.

NELL. Crafty, you never said.

WIN. He rang on Saturday morning.

NELL. Lucky you were free.

WIN. That's what I told him.

NELL. Did you hell.

WIN. Have you ever seen a really beautiful rose garden?

NELL. I don't like flowers. / I like swimming pools.

WIN. Marilyn. Esther's Baby. They're all called after birds.

NELL. Our friend's late. Celebrating all weekend I bet you.

WIN. I'd call a rose Elvis. Or John Conteh.

NELL. Is Howard in yet?

WIN. If he is he'll be bleeping us with a problem.

NELL. Howard can just hang onto himself.

WIN. Howard's really cut up.

NELL. Howard thinks because he's a fella the job was his as of right. Our Marlene's got far more balls than Howard and that's that.

WIN. Poor little bugger.

NELL. He'll live.

WIN. He'll move on.

NELL. I wouldn't mind a change of air myself.

WIN. Serious?

NELL. I've never been a staying put lady. Pastures new.

WIN. So who's the pirate?

NELL. There's nothing definite.

WIN. Inquiries?

NELL. There's always inquiries. I'd think I'd got bad breath if there stopped being inquiries. Most of them can't afford me. Or you.

WIN. I'm all right for the time being. Unless I go to Australia.

NELL. There's not a lot of room upward.

WIN. Marlene's filled it up.

NELL. Good luck to her. Unless there's some prospects moneywise.

WIN. You can but ask.

NELL. Can always but ask.

WIN. So what have we got? I've got a Mr Holden I saw last week.

NELL. Any use?

WIN. Pushy. Bit of a cowboy.

NELL. Good-looker?

WIN. Good dresser.

NELL. High flyer?

WIN. That's his general idea certainly but I'm not sure he's got it up there.

NELL. Prestel wants six high flyers and I've only seen two and a half.

WIN. He's making a bomb on the road but he thinks it's time for an office. I sent him to IBM but he didn't get it.

NELL. Prestel's on the road.

WIN. He's not overbright.

NELL. Can he handle an office?

WIN. Provided his secretary can punctuate he should go far.

NELL. Bear Prestel in mind then, I might put my head round the door. I've got that poor little nerd I should never have said I could help. Tender heart me.

WIN. Tender like old boots. How old?

NELL. Yes well forty-five.

WIN. Say no more.

NELL. He knows his place, he's not after calling himself a manager, he's just a poor little bod wants a better commission and a bit of sunshine.

WIN. Don't we all.

NELL. He's just got to relocate. He's got a bungalow in Dymchurch.

WIN. And his wife says.

NELL. The lady wife wouldn't care to relocate. She's going through the change.

WIN. It's his funeral, don't waste your time.

NELL. I don't waste a lot.

WIN. Good weekend you?

NELL. You could say.

WIN. Which one?

NELL. One Friday, one Saturday.

WIN. Aye aye.

NELL. Sunday night I watched telly.

WIN. Which of them do you like best really?

NELL. Sunday was best, I liked the Ovaltine.

WIN. Holden, Barker, Gardner, Duke.

NELL. I've a lady here thinks she can sell.

WIN. Taking her on?

NELL. She's had some jobs.

WIN. Services?

NELL. No, quite heavy stuff, electric.

WIN. Tough bird like us.

NELL. We could do with a few more here.

WIN. There's nothing going here.

NELL. No but I always want the tough ones when I see them. Hang onto them.

WIN. I think we're plenty.

NELL. Derek asked me to marry him again.

WIN. He doesn't know when he's beaten.

NELL. I told him I'm not going to play house, not even in Ascot.

WIN. Mind you, you could play house.

NELL. If I chose to play house I would play house ace.

WIN. You could marry him and go on working.

NELL. I could go on working and not marry him.

    MARLENE *arrives*.

MARLENE. Morning ladies.

WIN *and* NELL *cheer and whistle.*

Mind my head.

NELL. Coffee coffee coffee.

WIN. We're tactfully not mentioning you're late.

MARLENE. Fucking tube.

WIN. We've heard that one.

NELL. We've used that one.

WIN. It's the top executive doesn't come in as early as the poor working girl.

MARLENE. Pass the sugar and shut your face, pet.

WIN. Well I'm delighted.

NELL. Howard's looking sick.

WIN. Howard is sick. He's got ulcers and heart. He told me.

NELL. He'll have to stop then won't he?

WIN. Stop what?

NELL. Smoking, drinking, shouting. Working.

WIN. Well, working.

NELL. We're just looking through the day.

MARLENE. I'm doing some of Pam's ladies. They've been piling up while she's away.

NELL. Half a dozen little girls and an arts graduate who can't type.

WIN. I spent the whole weekend at his place in Sussex.

NELL. She fancies his rose garden.

WIN. I had to lie down in the back of the car so the neighbours wouldn't see me go in.

NELL. You're kidding.

WIN. It was funny.

NELL. Fuck that for a joke.

WIN. It was funny.

MARLENE. Anyway they'd see you in the garden.

WIN. The garden has extremely high walls.

NELL. I think I'll tell the wife.

WIN. Like hell.

NELL. She might leave him and you could have the rose garden.

WIN. The minute it's not a secret I'm out on my ear.

NELL. Don't know why you bother.

WIN. Bit of fun.

NELL. I think it's time you went to Australia.

WIN. I think it's pushy Mr Holden time.

NELL. If you've any really pretty bastards, Marlene, I want some for Prestel.

MARLENE. I might have one this afternoon. This morning it's all Pam's secretarial.

NELL. Not long now and you'll be upstairs watching over us all.

MARLENE. Do you feel bad about it?

NELL. I don't like coming second.

MARLENE. Who does?

WIN. We'd rather it was you than Howard. We're glad for you, aren't we Nell.

NELL. Oh yes. Aces.

Interview
WIN *and* LOUISE.

WIN. Now Louise, hello, I have your details here. You've been very loyal to the one job I see.

LOUISE. Yes I have.

WIN. Twenty-one years is a long time in one place.

LOUISE. I feel it is. I feel it's time to move on.

WIN. And you are what age now?

LOUISE. I'm in my early forties.

WIN. Exactly?

LOUISE. Forty-six.

WIN. It's not necessarily a handicap, well it is of course we have to face that, but it's not necessarily a disabling handicap, experience does count for something.

LOUISE. I hope so.

WIN. Now between ourselves is there any trouble, any reason why you're leaving that wouldn't appear on the form?

LOUISE. Nothing like that.

WIN. Like what?

LOUISE. Nothing at all.

WIN. No long term understandings come to a sudden end, making for an insupportable atmosphere?

LOUISE. I've always completely avoided anything like that at all.

WIN. No personality clashes with your immediate superiors or inferiors?

LOUISE. I've always taken care to get on very well with everyone.

WIN. I only ask because it can affect the reference and it also affects your motivation, I want to be quite clear why you're moving on. So I take it the job itself no longer satisfies you. Is it the money?

LOUISE. It's partly the money. It's not so much the money.

WIN. Nine thousand is very respectable. Have you dependants?

LOUISE. No, no dependants. My mother died.

WIN. So why are you making a change?

LOUISE. Other people make changes.

WIN. But why are you, now, after spending most of your life in the one place?

LOUISE. There you are, I've lived for that company, I've given my life really you could say because I haven't had a great deal of social life, I've worked in the evenings. I haven't had office entanglements for the very reason you just mentioned and if you are committed to your work you don't move in many other circles. I had management status from the age of twenty-seven and you'll appreciate what that means. I've built up a department. And there it is, it works extremely well, and I feel I'm stuck there. I've spent twenty years in middle management. I've seen young men who I trained go on, in my own company or elsewhere, to higher things. Nobody notices me, I don't expect it, I don't attract attention by making mistakes, everybody takes it for granted that my work is perfect. They will notice me when I go, they will be sorry I think to lose me, they will offer me more money of course, I will refuse. They will see when I've gone what I was doing for them.

WIN. If they offer you more money you won't stay?

LOUISE. No I won't.

WIN. Are you the only woman?

LOUISE. Apart from the girls of course, yes. There was one, she was my assistant, it was the only time I took on a young woman assistant, I always had my doubts. I don't care greatly for working with women, I think I pass as a man at work. But I did take on this young woman, her qualifications were excellent, and she did well, she got a department of her own, and left the company for a competitor where she's now on the board and good luck to her. She has a different style, she's a new kind of attractive well-dressed — I don't mean I don't dress properly. But there is a kind of woman who is thirty now who grew up in a different climate. They are not so careful. They take themselves for granted. I have had to justify my existence every minute, and I have done so, I have proved — well.

WIN. Let's face it, vacancies are going to be ones where you'll be in competition with younger men. And there are companies that will value your experience enough you'll be in with a chance. There are also fields that are easier for a woman, there is a cosmetic company here where your

experience might be relevant. It's eight and a half, I don't
know if that appeals.

LOUISE. I've proved I can earn money. It's more important to
get away. I feel it's now or never. I sometimes / think —

WIN. You shouldn't talk too much at an interview.

LOUISE. I don't. I don't normally talk about myself. I know very
well how to handle myself in an office situation. I only talk
to you because it seems to me this is different, it's your job
to understand me, surely. You asked the questions.

WIN. I think I understand you sufficiently.

LOUISE. Well good, that's good.

WIN. Do you drink?

LOUISE. Certainly not. I'm not a teetotaller, I think that's very
suspect, it's seen as being an alcoholic if you're teetotal. What
do you mean? I don't drink. Why?

WIN. I drink.

LOUISE. I don't.

WIN. Good for you.

Main office
MARLENE *and* ANGIE.
ANGIE *arrives.*

ANGIE. Hello.

MARLENE. Have you an appointment?

ANGIE. It's me. I've come.

MARLENE. What? It's not Angie?

ANGIE. It was hard to find this place. I got lost.

MARLENE. How did you get past the receptionist? The girl on
the desk, didn't she try to stop you?

ANGIE. What desk?

MARLENE. Never mind.

ANGIE. I just walked in. I was looking for you.

MARLENE. Well you found me.

ANGIE. Yes.

MARLENE. So where's your mum? Are you up in town for the day?

ANGIE. Not really.

MARLENE. Sit down. Do you feel all right?

ANGIE. Yes thank you.

MARLENE. So where's Joyce?

ANGIE. She's at home.

MARLENE. Did you come up on a school trip then?

ANGIE. I've left school.

MARLENE. Did you come up with a friend?

ANGIE. No. There's just me.

MARLENE. You came up by yourself, that's fun. What have you been doing? Shopping? Tower of London?

ANGIE. No, I just come here. I come to you.

MARLENE. That's very nice of you to think of paying your aunty a visit. There's not many nieces make that the first port of call. Would you like a cup of coffee?

ANGIE. No thank you.

MARLENE. Tea, orange?

ANGIE. No thank you.

MARLENE. Do you feel all right?

ANGIE. Yes thank you.

MARLENE. Are you tired from the journey?

ANGIE. Yes, I'm tired from the journey.

MARLENE. You sit there for a bit then. How's Joyce?

ANGIE. She's all right.

MARLENE. Same as ever.

ANGIE. Oh yes.

MARLENE. Unfortunately you've picked a day when I'm rather busy, if there's ever a day when I'm not, or I'd take you out to lunch and we'd go to Madame Tussaud's. We could go shopping. What time do you have to be back? Have you got a day return?

ANGIE. No.

MARLENE. So what train are you going back on?

ANGIE. I came on the bus.

MARLENE. So what bus are you going back on? Are you staying the night?

ANGIE. Yes.

MARLENE. Who are you staying with? Do you want me to put you up for the night, is that it?

ANGIE. Yes please.

MARLENE. I haven't got a spare bed.

ANGIE. I can sleep on the floor.

MARLENE. You can sleep on the sofa.

ANGIE. Yes please.

MARLENE. I do think Joyce might have phoned me. It's like her.

ANGIE. This is where you work is it?

MARLENE. It's where I have been working the last two years but I'm going to move into another office.

ANGIE. It's lovely.

MARLENE. My new office is nicer than this. There's just the one big desk in it for me.

ANGIE. Can I see it?

MARLENE. Not now, no, there's someone else in it now. But he's leaving at the end of next week and I'm going to do his job.

ANGIE. Is that good?

MARLENE. Yes, it's very good.

ANGIE. Are you going to be in charge?

MARLENE. Yes I am.

ANGIE. I knew you would be.

MARLENE. How did you know?

ANGIE. I knew you'd be in charge of everything.

MARLENE. Not quite everything.

ANGIE. You will be.

MARLENE. Well we'll see.

ANGIE. Can I see it next week then?

MARLENE. Will you still be here next week?

ANGIE. Yes.

MARLENE. Don't you have to go home?

ANGIE. No.

MARLENE. Why not?

ANGIE. It's all right.

MARLENE. Is it all right?

ANGIE. Yes, don't worry about it.

MARLENE. Does Joyce know where you are?

ANGIE. Yes of course she does.

MARLENE. Well does she?

ANGIE. Don't worry about it.

MARLENE. How long are you planning to stay with me then?

ANGIE. You know when you came to see us last year?

MARLENE. Yes, that was nice wasn't it?

ANGIE. That was the best day of my whole life.

MARLENE. So how long are you planning to stay?

ANGIE. Don't you want me?

MARLENE. Yes yes, I just wondered.

ANGIE. I won't stay if you don't want me.

MARLENE. No, of course you can stay.

ANGIE. I'll sleep on the floor. I won't be any bother.

MARLENE. Don't get upset.

ANGIE. I'm not, I'm not. Don't worry about it.

MRS KIDD *comes in*.

MRS KIDD. Excuse me.

MARLENE. Yes.

MRS KIDD. Excuse me.

MARLENE. Can I help you?

MRS KIDD. Excuse me bursting in on you like this but I have to talk to you.

MARLENE. I am engaged at the moment. / If you could go to reception —

MRS KIDD. I'm Rosemary Kidd, Howard's wife, you don't recognise me but we did meet, I remember you of course / but you wouldn't —

MARLENE. Yes of course, Mrs Kidd, I'm sorry, we did meet. Howard's about somewhere I expect, have you looked in his office?

MRS KIDD. Howard's not about, no. I'm afraid it's you I've come to see if I could have a minute or two.

MARLENE. I do have an appointment in five minutes.

MRS KIDD. This won't take five minutes. I'm very sorry. It is a matter of some urgency.

MARLENE. Well of course. What can I do for you?

MRS KIDD. I just wanted a chat, an informal chat. It's not something I can simply — I'm sorry if I'm interrupting your work. I know office work isn't like housework / which is all interruptions.

MARLENE. No no, this is my niece. Angie. Mrs Kidd.

MRS KIDD. Very pleased to meet you.

ANGIE. Very well thank you.

MRS KIDD. Howard's not in today.

MARLENE. Isn't he?

MRS KIDD. He's feeling poorly.

MARLENE. I didn't know. I'm sorry to hear that.

MRS KIDD. The fact is he's in a state of shock. About what's happened.

MARLENE. What has happened?

MRS KIDD. You should know if anyone. I'm referring to you being appointed managing director instead of Howard. He hasn't been at all well all weekend. He hasn't slept for three nights. I haven't slept.

MARLENE. I'm sorry to hear that, Mrs Kidd. Has he thought of taking sleeping pills?

MRS KIDD. It's very hard when someone has worked all these years.

MARLENE. Business life is full of little setbacks. I'm sure Howard knows that. He'll bounce back in a day or two. We all bounce back.

MRS KIDD. If you could see him you'd know what I'm talking about. What's it going to do to him working for a woman? I think if it was a man he'd get over it as something normal.

MARLENE. I think he's going to have to get over it.

MRS KIDD. It's me that bears the brunt. I'm not the one that's been promoted. I put him first every inch of the way. And now what do I get? You women this, you women that. It's not my fault. You're going to have to be very careful how you handle him. He's very hurt.

MARLENE. Naturally I'll be tactful and pleasant to him, you don't start pushing someone round. I'll consult him over any decisions affecting his department. But that's no different, Mrs Kidd, from any of my other colleagues.

MRS KIDD. I think it is different, because he's a man.

MARLENE. I'm not quite sure why you came to see me.

MRS KIDD. I had to do something.

MARLENE. Well you've done it, you've seen me. I think that's probably all we've time for. I'm sorry he's been taking it out on you. He really is a shit, Howard.

MRS KIDD. But he's got a family to support. He's got three children. It's only fair.

MARLENE. Are you suggesting I give up the job to him then?

MRS KIDD. It had crossed my mind if you were unavailable after all for some reason, he would be the natural second choice I think, don't you? I'm not asking.

MARLENE. Good.

MRS KIDD. You mustn't tell him I came. He's very proud.

MARLENE. If he doesn't like what's happening here he can go and work somewhere else.

MRS KIDD. Is that a threat?

MARLENE. I'm sorry but I do have some work to do.

MRS KIDD. It's not that easy, a man of Howard's age. You don't care. I thought he was going too far but he's right. You're one of these ballbreakers / that's what you are. You'll end up

MARLENE. I'm sorry but I do have some work to do.

MRS KIDD. miserable and lonely. You're not natural.

MARLENE. Could you please piss off?

MRS KIDD. I thought if I saw you at least I'd be doing something.

   MRS KIDD goes.

MARLENE. I've got to go and do some work now. Will you come back later?

ANGIE. I think you were wonderful.

MARLENE. I've got to go and do some work now.

ANGIE. You told her to piss off.

MARLENE. Will you come back later?

ANGIE. Can't I stay here?

MARLENE. Don't you want to go sightseeing?

ANGIE. I'd rather stay here.

MARLENE. You can stay here I suppose, if it's not boring.

ANGIE. It's where I most want to be in the world.

MARLENE. I'll see you later then.

> MARLENE *goes.*

> ANGIE *sits at* WIN's *desk.*

Interview
NELL *and* SHONA.

NELL. Is this right? You are Shona?

SHONA. Yeh.

NELL. It says here you're twenty-nine.

SHONA. Yeh.

NELL. Too many late nights, me. So you've been where you are for four years, Shona, you're earning six basic and three commission. So what's the problem?

SHONA. No problem.

NELL. Why do you want a change?

SHONA. Just a change.

NELL. Change of product, change of area?

SHONA. Both.

NELL. But you're happy on the road?

SHONA. I like driving.

NELL. You're not after management status?

SHONA. I would like management status.

NELL. You'd be interested in titular management status but not come off the road?

SHONA. I want to be on the road, yeh.

NELL. So how many calls have you been making a day?

SHONA. Six.

NELL. And what proportion of those are successful?

SHONA. Six.

NELL. That's hard to believe.

SHONA. Four.

NELL. You find it easy to get the initial interest do you?

SHONA. Oh yeh, I get plenty of initial interest.

NELL. And what about closing?

SHONA. I close, don't I?

NELL. Because that's what an employer is going to have doubts
about with a lady as I needn't tell you, whether she's got
the guts to push through to a closing situation. They think
we're too nice. They think we listen to the buyer's doubts.
They think we consider his needs and his feelings.

SHONA. I never consider people's feelings.

NELL. I was selling for six years, I can sell anything, I've sold in
three continents, and I'm jolly as they come but I'm not
very nice.

SHONA. I'm not very nice.

NELL. What sort of time do you have on the road with the other
reps? Get on all right? Handle the chat?

SHONA. I get on. Keep myself to myself.

NELL. Fairly much of a loner are you?

SHONA. Sometimes.

NELL. So what field are you interested in?

SHONA. Computers.

NELL. That's a top field as you know and you'll be up against
some very slick fellas there, there's some very pretty boys in
computers, it's an American-style field.

SHONA. That's why I want to do it.

NELL. Video systems appeal? That's a high-flying situation.

SHONA. Video systems appeal OK.

NELL. Because Prestel have half a dozen vacancies I'm looking to fill at the moment. We're talking in the area of ten to fifteen thousand here and upwards.

SHONA. Sounds OK.

NELL. I've half a mind to go for it myself. But it's good money here if you've got the top clients. Could you fancy it do you think?

SHONA. Work here?

NELL. I'm not in a position to offer, there's nothing officially going just now, but we're always on the lookout. There's not that many of us. We could keep in touch.

SHONA. I like driving.

NELL. So the Prestel appeals?

SHONA. Yeh.

NELL. What about ties?

SHONA. No ties.

NELL. So relocation wouldn't be a problem.

SHONA. No problem.

NELL. So just fill me in a bit more could you about what you've been doing.

SHONA. What I've been doing. It's all down there.

NELL. The bare facts are down here but I've got to present you to an employer.

SHONA. I'm twenty-nine years old.

NELL. So it says here.

SHONA. We look young. Youngness runs in the family in our family.

NELL. So just describe your present job for me.

SHONA. My present job at present. I have a car. I have a Porsche.
I go up the M1 a lot. Burn up the M1 a lot. Straight up the
M1 in the fast lane to where the clients are, Staffordshire,
Yorkshire, I do a lot in Yorkshire. I'm selling electric things.
Like dishwashers, washing machines, stainless steel tubs are
a feature and the reliability of the programme. After sales
service, we offer a very good after sales service, spare parts,
plenty of spare parts. And fridges, I sell a lot of fridges
specially in the summer. People want to buy fridges in the
summer because of the heat melting the butter and you get fed
up standing the milk in a basin of cold water with a cloth
over, stands to reason people don't want to do that in this
day and age. So I sell a lot of them. Big ones with big freezers.
Big freezers. And I stay in hotels at night when I'm away from
home. On my expense account. I stay in various hotels. They
know me, the ones I go to. I check in, have a bath, have a
shower. Then I go down to the bar, have a gin and tonic, have
a chat. Then I go into the dining room and have dinner. I
usually have fillet steak and mushrooms, I like mushrooms.
I like smoked salmon very much. I like having a salad on the
side. Green salad. I don't like tomatoes.

NELL. Christ what a waste of time.

SHONA. Beg your pardon?

NELL. Not a word of this is true is it?

SHONA. How do you mean?

NELL. You just filled in the form with a pack of lies.

SHONA. Not exactly.

NELL. How old are you?

SHONA. Twenty-nine.

NELL. Nineteen?

SHONA. Twenty-one.

NELL. And what jobs have you done? Have you done any?

SHONA. I could though, I bet you.

Main office
ANGIE *sitting as before.*
WIN *comes in.*

WIN. Who's sitting in my chair?

ANGIE. What? Sorry.

WIN. Who's been eating my porridge?

ANGIE. What?

WIN. It's all right, I saw Marlene. Angie isn't it? I'm Win. And I'm not going out for lunch because I'm knackered. I'm going to set me down here and have a yoghurt. Do you like yoghurt?

ANGIE. No.

WIN. That's good because I've only got one. Are you hungry?

ANGIE. No.

WIN. There's a cafe on the corner.

ANGIE. No thank you. Do you work here?

WIN. How did you guess?

ANGIE. Because you look as if you might work here and you're sitting at the desk. Have you always worked here?

WIN. No I was headhunted. That means I was working for another outfit like this and this lot came and offered me more money. I broke my contract, there was a hell of a stink. There's not many top ladies about. Your aunty's a smashing bird.

ANGIE. Yes I know.

MARLENE. Fan are you? Fan of your aunty's?

ANGIE. Do you think I could work here?

WIN. Not at the moment.

ANGIE. How do I start?

WIN. What can you do?

ANGIE. I don't know. Nothing.

WIN. Type?

ANGIE. Not very well. The letters jump up when I do capitals. I was going to do a CSE in commerce but I didn't.

WIN. What have you got?

ANGIE. What?

WIN. CSE's, O's.

ANGIE. Nothing, none of that. Did you do all that?

WIN. Oh yes, all that, and a science degree funnily enough. I started out doing medical research but there's no money in it. I thought I'd go abroad. Did you know they sell Coca-Cola in Russia and Pepsi-cola in China? You don't have to be qualified as much as you might think. Men are awful bullshitters, they like to make out jobs are harder than they are. Any job I ever did I started doing it better than the rest of the crowd and they didn't like it. So I'd get unpopular and I'd have a drink to cheer myself up. I lived with a fella and supported him for four years, he couldn't get work. After that I went to California. I like the sunshine. Americans know how to live. This country's too slow. Then I went to Mexico, still in sales, but it's no country for a single lady. I came home, went bonkers for a bit, thought I was five different people, got over that all right, the psychiatrist said I was perfectly sane and highly intelligent. Got married in a moment of weakness and he's inside now, he's been inside four years, and I've not been to see him too much this last year. I like this better than sales, I'm not really that aggressive. I started thinking sales was a good job if you want to meet people, but you're meeting people that don't want to meet you. It's no good if you like being liked. Here your clients want to meet you because you're the one doing them some good. They hope.

ANGIE *has fallen asleep*. NELL *comes in*.

NELL. You're talking to yourself, sunshine.

WIN. So what's new?

NELL. Who is this?

WIN. Marlene's little niece.

NELL. What's she got, brother, sister? She never talks about her family.

WIN. I was telling her my life story.

NELL. Violins?

WIN. No, success story.

NELL. You've heard Howard's had a heart attack?

WIN. No, when?

NELL. I heard just now. He hadn't come in, he was at home, he's gone to hospital. He's not dead. His wife was here, she rushed off in a cab.

WIN. Too much butter, too much smoke. We must send him some flowers.

MARLENE *comes in.*

You've heard about Howard?

MARLENE. Poor sod.

NELL. Lucky he didn't get the job if that's what his health's like.

MARLENE. Is she asleep?

WIN. She wants to work here.

MARLENE. Packer in Tesco more like.

WIN. She's a nice kid. Isn't she?

MARLENE. She's a bit thick. She's a bit funny.

WIN. She thinks you're wonderful.

MARLENE. She's not going to make it.

ACT THREE

A year earlier. Sunday evening. JOYCE's kitchen. JOYCE, ANGIE, MARLENE. MARLENE is taking presents out of a bright carrier bag. ANGIE has already opened a box of chocolates.

MARLENE. Just a few little things. / I've no memory for

JOYCE. There's no need.

MARLENE. birthdays have I, and Christmas seems to slip by. So I think I owe Angie a few presents.

JOYCE. What do you say?

ANGIE. Thank you very much. Thank you very much, Aunty Marlene.

She opens a present. It is the dress from Act One, new.

ANGIE. Oh look, Mum, isn't it lovely?

MARLENE. I don't know if it's the right size. She's grown up since I saw her. / I knew she was always tall for her age.

ANGIE. Isn't it lovely?

JOYCE. She's a big lump.

MARLENE. Hold it up, Angie, let's see.

ANGIE. I'll put it on, shall I?

MARLENE. Yes, try it on.

JOYCE. Go on to your room then, we don't want / a strip show thank you.

ANGIE. Of course I'm going to my room, what do you think? Look Mum, here's something for you. Open it, go on. What is it? Can I open it for you?

JOYCE. Yes, you open it, pet.

ANGIE. Don't you want to open it yourself? / Go on.

JOYCE. I don't mind, you can do it.

ANGIE. It's something hard. It's — what is it? A bottle. Drink is it? No, it's what? Perfume, look. What a lot. Open it, look, let's smell it. Oh it's strong. It's lovely. Put it on me. How do you do it? Put it on me.

JOYCE. You're too young.

ANGIE. I can play wearing it like dressing up.

JOYCE. And you're too old for that. Here, give it here, I'll do it, you'll tip the whole bottle over yourself / and we'll have you smelling all summer.

ANGIE. Put it on you. Do I smell? Put it on Aunty too. Put it on Aunty too. Let's all smell.

MARLENE. I didn't know what you'd like.

JOYCE. There's no danger I'd have it already, / that's one thing.

ANGIE. Now we all smell the same.

MARLENE. It's a bit of nonsense.

JOYCE. It's very kind of you Marlene, you shouldn't.

ANGIE. Now. I'll put on the dress and then we'll see.

ANGIE *goes.*

JOYCE. You've caught me on the hop with the place in a mess. / If you'd let me know you was coming I'd have got

MARLENE. That doesn't matter.

JOYCE. something in to eat. We had our dinner dinnertime. We're just going to have a cup of tea. You could have an egg.

MARLENE. No, I'm not hungry. Tea's fine.

JOYCE. I don't expect you take sugar.

MARLENE. Why not?

JOYCE. You take care of yourself.

MARLENE. How do you mean you didn't know I was coming?

JOYCE. You could have written. I know we're not on the phone but we're not completely in the dark ages, / we do have a postman.

MARLENE. But you asked me to come.

JOYCE. How did I ask you to come?

MARLENE. Angie said when she phoned up.

JOYCE. Angie phoned up, did she?

MARLENE. Was it just Angie's idea?

JOYCE. What did she say?

MARLENE. She said you wanted me to come and see you. /
It was a couple of weeks ago. How was I to know that's a

JOYCE. Ha.

MARLENE. ridiculous idea? My diary's always full a couple of
weeks ahead so we fixed it for this weekend. I was meant to
get here earlier but I was held up. She gave me messages from
you.

JOYCE. Didn't you wonder why I didn't phone you myself?

MARLENE. She said you didn't like using the phone. You're shy
on the phone and can't use it. I don't know what you're like,
do I.

JOYCE. Are there people who can't use the phone?

MARLENE. I expect so.

JOYCE. I haven't met any.

MARLENE. Why should I think she was lying?

JOYCE. Because she's like what she's like.

MARLENE. How do I know / what she's like?

JOYCE. It's not my fault you don't know what she's like. You
never come and see her.

MARLENE. Well I have now / and you don't seem over the moon.*

JOYCE. Good.
*Well I'd have got a cake if she'd told me.

   Pause.

MARLENE. I did wonder why you wanted to see me.

JOYCE. I didn't want to see you.

MARLENE. Yes, I know. Shall I go?

JOYCE. I don't mind seeing you.

MARLENE. Great, I feel really welcome.

JOYCE. You can come and see Angie any time you like, I'm not stopping you. / You know where we are. You're the

MARLENE. Ta ever so.

JOYCE. one went away, not me. I'm right here where I was. And will be a few years yet I shouldn't wonder.

MARLENE. All right. All right.

JOYCE *gives* MARLENE *a cup of tea.*

JOYCE. Tea.

MARLENE. Sugar?

JOYCE *passes* MARLENE *the sugar.*

It's very quiet down here.

JOYCE. I expect you'd notice it.

MARLENE. The air smells different too.

JOYCE. That's the scent.

MARLENE. No, I mean walking down the lane.

JOYCE. What sort of air you get in London then?

ANGIE *comes in, wearing the dress. It fits.*

MARLENE. Oh, very pretty. / You do look pretty, Angie.

JOYCE. That fits all right.

MARLENE. Do you like the colour?

ANGIE. Beautiful. Beautiful.

JOYCE. You better take it off, / you'll get it dirty.

ANGIE. I want to wear it. I want to wear it.

MARLENE. It is for wearing after all. You can't just hang it up and look at it.

ANGIE. I love it.

JOYCE. Well if you must you must.

ANGIE. If someone asks me what's my favourite colour I'll tell them it's this. Thank you very much, Aunty Marlene.

MARLENE. You didn't tell your mum you asked me down.

ANGIE. I wanted it to be a surprise.

JOYCE. I'll give you a surprise / one of these days.

ANGIE. I thought you'd like to see her. She hasn't been here since I was nine. People do see their aunts.

MARLENE. Is it that long? Doesn't time fly?

ANGIE. I wanted to.

JOYCE. I'm not cross.

ANGIE. Are you glad?

JOYCE. I smell nicer anyhow, don't I?

KIT *comes in without saying anything, as if she lived there.*

MARLENE. I think it was a good idea, Angie, about time. We are sisters after all. It's a pity to let that go.

JOYCE. This is Kitty, / who lives up the road. This is Angie's Aunty Marlene.

KIT. What's that?

ANGIE. It's a present. Do you like it?

KIT. It's all right. / Are you coming out?*

MARLENE. Hello, Kitty.

ANGIE. *No.

KIT. What's that smell?

ANGIE. It's a present.

KIT. It's horrible. Come on.*

MARLENE. Have a chocolate.

ANGIE. *No, I'm busy.

KIT. Coming out later?

ANGIE. No.

KIT (*to* MARLENE). Hello.

KIT *goes without a chocolate.*

JOYCE. She's a little girl Angie sometimes plays with because she's the only child lives really close. She's like a little sister to her really. Angie's good with little children.

MARLENE. Do you want to work with children, Angie? / Be a teacher or a nursery nurse?

JOYCE. I don't think she's ever thought of it.

MARLENE. What do you want to do?

JOYCE. She hasn't an idea in her head what she wants to do. / Lucky to get anything.

MARLENE. Angie?

JOYCE. She's not clever like you.

Pause.

MARLENE. I'm not clever, just pushy.

JOYCE. True enough.

MARLENE *takes a bottle of whisky out of the bag.*

I don't drink spirits.

ANGIE. You do at Christmas.

JOYCE. It's not Christmas, is it?

ANGIE. It's better than Christmas.

MARLENE. Glasses?

JOYCE. Just a small one then.

MARLENE. Do you want some, Angie?

ANGIE. I can't, can I?

JOYCE. Taste it if you want. You won't like it.

MARLENE. We got drunk together the night your grandfather died.

JOYCE. We did not get drunk.

MARLENE. I got drunk. You were just overcome with grief.

JOYCE. I still keep up the grave with flowers.

MARLENE. Do you really?

JOYCE. Why wouldn't I?

MARLENE. Have you seen Mother?

JOYCE. Of course I've seen Mother.

MARLENE. I mean lately.

JOYCE. Of course I've seen her lately, I go every Thursday.

MARLENE (*to* ANGIE). Do you remember your grandfather?

ANGIE. He got me out of the bath one night in a towel.

MARLENE. Did he? I don't think he ever gave me a bath. Did he
    give you a bath, Joyce? He probably got soft in his old age.
    Did you like him?

ANGIE. Yes of course.

MARLENE. Why?

ANGIE. What?

MARLENE. So what's the news? How's Mrs Paisley? Still going
    crazily? / And Dorothy. What happened to Dorothy?*

ANGIE. Who's Mrs Paisley?

JOYCE. *She went to Canada.

MARLENE. Did she? What to do?

JOYCE. I don't know. She just went to Canada.

MARLENE. Well / good for her.

ANGIE. Mr Connolly killed his wife.

MARLENE. What, Connolly at Whitegates?

ANGIE. They found her body in the garden. / Under the cabbages.

MARLENE. He was always so proper.

JOYCE. Stuck up git. Connolly. Best lawyer money could buy
    but he couldn't get out of it. She was carrying on with
    Matthew.

MARLENE. How old's Matthew then?

JOYCE. Twenty-one. / He's got a motorbike.

MARLENE. I think he's about six.

ANGIE. How can he be six? He's six years older than me. / If he was six I'd be nothing, I'd be just born this minute.

JOYCE. Your aunty knows that, she's just being silly. She means it's so long since she's been here she's forgotten about Matthew.

ANGIE. You were here for my birthday when I was nine. I had a pink cake. Kit was only five then, she was four, she hadn't started school yet. She could read already when she went to school. You remember my birthday? / You remember me?

MARLENE. Yes, I remember the cake.

ANGIE. You remember me?

MARLENE. Yes, I remember you.

ANGIE. And Mum and Dad was there, and Kit was.

MARLENE. Yes, how is your dad? Where is he tonight? Up the pub?

JOYCE. No, he's not here.

MARLENE. I can see he's not here.

JOYCE. He moved out.

MARLENE. What? When did he? / Just recently?*

ANGIE. Didn't you know that? You don't know much.

JOYCE. *No, it must be three years ago. Don't be rude, Angie.

ANGIE. I'm not, am I Aunty? What else don't you know?

JOYCE. You was in America or somewhere. You sent a postcard.

ANGIE. I've got that in my room. It's the Grand Canyon. Do you want to see it? Shall I get it? I can get it for you.

MARLENE. Yes, all right.

ANGIE goes.

JOYCE. You could be married with twins for all I know. You must have affairs and break up and I don't need to know about any of that so I don't see what the fuss is about.

MARLENE. What fuss?

ANGIE comes back with the postcard.

ANGIE. 'Driving across the states for a new job in L.A. It's a long way but the car goes very fast. It's very hot. Wish you were here. Love from Aunty Marlene.'

JOYCE. Did you make a lot of money?

MARLENE. I spent a lot.

ANGIE. I want to go to America. Will you take me?

JOYCE. She's not going to America, she's been to America, stupid.

ANGIE. She might go again, stupid. It's not something you do once. People who go keep going all the time, back and forth on jets. They go on Concorde and Laker and get jet lag. Will you take me?

MARLENE. I'm not planning a trip.

ANGIE. Will you let me know?

JOYCE. Angie, / you're getting silly.

ANGIE. I want to be American.

JOYCE. It's time you were in bed.

ANGIE. No it's not. / I don't have to go to bed at all tonight.

JOYCE. School in the morning.

ANGIE. I'll wake up.

JOYCE. Come on now, you know how you get.

ANGIE. How do I get? / I don't get anyhow.

JOYCE. Angie.
   Are you staying the night?

MARLENE. Yes, if that's all right. / I'll see you in the morning.

ANGIE. You can have my bed. I'll sleep on the sofa.

JOYCE. You will not, you'll sleep in your bed. / Think I can't

ANGIE. Mum.

JOYCE. see through that? I can just see you going to sleep / with us talking.

ANGIE. I would, I would go to sleep, I'd love that.

JOYCE. I'm going to get cross, Angie.

ANGIE. I want to show her something.

JOYCE. Then bed.

ANGIE. It's a secret.

JOYCE. Then I expect it's in your room so off you go. Give us a shout when you're ready for bed and your aunty'll be up and see you.

ANGIE. Will you?

MARLENE. Yes of course.

> ANGIE *goes.*
> *Silence.*

It's cold tonight.

JOYCE. Will you be all right on the sofa? You can / have my bed.

MARLENE. The sofa's fine.

JOYCE. Yes the forecast said rain tonight but it's held off.

MARLENE. I was going to walk down to the estuary but I've left it a bit late. Is it just the same?

JOYCE. They cut down the hedges a few years back. Is that since you were here?

MARLENE. But it's not changed down the end, all the mud? And the reeds? We used to pick them when they were bigger than us. Are there still lapwings?

JOYCE. You get strangers walking there on a Sunday. I expect they're looking at the mud and the lapwings, yes.

MARLENE. You could have left.

JOYCE. Who says I wanted to leave?

MARLENE. Stop getting at me then, you're really boring.

JOYCE. How could I have left?

MARLENE. Did you want to?

JOYCE. I said how, / how could I?

MARLENE. If you'd wanted to you'd have done it.

JOYCE. Christ.

MARLENE. Are we getting drunk?

JOYCE. Do you want something to eat?

MARLENE. No, I'm getting drunk.

JOYCE. Funny time to visit, Sunday evening.

MARLENE. I came this morning. I spent the day.

ANGIE (*off*). Aunty! Aunty Marlene!

MARLENE. I'd better go.

JOYCE. Go on then.

MARLENE. All right.

ANGIE (*off*). Aunty! Can you hear me? I'm ready.

MARLENE *goes.*

JOYCE *goes on sitting.*

MARLENE *comes back.*

JOYCE. So what's the secret?

MARLENE. It's a secret.

JOYCE. I know what it is anyway.

MARLENE. I bet you don't. You always said that.

JOYCE. It's her exercise book.

MARLENE. Yes, but you don't know what's in it.

JOYCE. It's some game, some secret society she has with Kit.

MARLENE. You don't know the password. You don't know the code.

JOYCE. You're really in it, aren't you. Can you do the handshake?

MARLENE. She didn't mention a handshake.

JOYCE. I thought they'd have a special handshake. She spends hours writing that but she's useless at school. She copies things out of books about black magic, and politicians out of the paper. It's a bit childish.

MARLENE. I think it's a plot to take over the world.

JOYCE. She's been in the remedial class the last two years.

MARLENE. I came up this morning and spent the day in Ipswich.
  I went to see mother.

JOYCE. Did she recognise you?

MARLENE. Are you trying to be funny?

JOYCE. No, she does wander.

MARLENE. She wasn't wandering at all, she was very lucid thank
  you.

JOYCE. You were very lucky then.

MARLENE. Fucking awful life she's had.

JOYCE. Don't tell me.

MARLENE. Fucking waste.

JOYCE. Don't talk to me.

MARLENE. Why shouldn't I talk? Why shouldn't I talk to you? /
  Isn't she my mother too?

JOYCE. Look, you've left, you've gone away, / we can do
  without you.

MARLENE. I left home, so what, I left home. People do leave
  home / it is normal.

JOYCE. We understand that, we can do without you.

MARLENE. We weren't happy. Were you happy?

JOYCE. Don't come back.

MARLENE. So it's just your mother is it, your child, you never
  wanted me round, / you were jealous of me because I was the

JOYCE. Here we go.

MARLENE. little one and I was clever.

JOYCE. I'm not clever enough for all this psychology / if that's
  what it is.

MARLENE. Why can't I visit my own family / without all this?*

JOYCE. Aah.
  *Just don't go on about Mum's life when you haven't been to
  see her for how many years. / I go and see her every week.*

MARLENE. It's up to me.
  *Then don't go and see her every week.

JOYCE. Somebody has to.

MARLENE. No they don't. / Why do they?

JOYCE. How would I feel if I didn't go?

MARLENE. A lot better.

JOYCE. I hope you feel better.

MARLENE. It's up to me.

JOYCE. You couldn't get out of here fast enough.

MARLENE. Of course I couldn't get out of here fast enough. What was I going to do? Marry a dairyman who'd come home pissed? / Don't you fucking this fucking that fucking bitch

JOYCE. Christ.

MARLENE. fucking tell me what to fucking do fucking.

JOYCE. I don't know how you could leave your own child.

MARLENE. You were quick enough to take her.

JOYCE. What does that mean?

MARLENE. You were quick enough to take her.

JOYCE. Or what? Have her put in a home? Have some stranger / take her would you rather?

MARLENE. You couldn't have one so you took mine.

JOYCE. I didn't know that then.

MARLENE. Like hell, / married three years.

JOYCE. I didn't know that. Plenty of people / take that long.

MARLENE. Well it turned out lucky for you, didn't it?

JOYCE. Turned out all right for you by the look of you. You'd be getting a few less thousand a year.

MARLENE. Not necessarily.

JOYCE. You'd be stuck here / like you said.

MARLENE. I could have taken her with me.

JOYCE. You didn't want to take her with you. It's no good coming back now, Marlene, / and saying —

MARLENE. I know a managing director who's got two children, she breast feeds in the board room, she pays a hundred pounds a week on domestic help alone and she can afford that because she's an extremely high-powered lady earning a great deal of money.

JOYCE. So what's that got to do with you at the age of seventeen?

MARLENE. Just because you were married and had somewhere to live —

JOYCE. You could have lived at home. / Or live with me

MARLENE. Don't be stupid.

JOYCE. and Frank. / You said you weren't keeping it. You

MARLENE. You never suggested.

JOYCE. shouldn't have had it / if you wasn't going to keep it.

MARLENE. Here we go.

JOYCE. You was the most stupid, / for someone so clever you was the most stupid, get yourself pregnant, not go to the doctor, not tell.

MARLENE. You wanted it, you said you were glad, I remember the day, you said I'm glad you never got rid of it, I'll look after it, you said that down by the river. So what are you saying, sunshine, you don't want her?

JOYCE. Course I'm not saying that.

MARLENE. Because I'll take her, / wake her up and pack now.

JOYCE. You wouldn't know how to begin to look after her.

MARLENE. Don't you want her?

JOYCE. Course I do, she's my child.

MARLENE. Then what are you going on about / why did I have her?

JOYCE. You said I got her off you / when you didn't —

MARLENE. I said you were lucky / the way it —

JOYCE. Have a child now if you want one. You're not old.

MARLENE. I might do.

JOYCE. Good.

Pause.

MARLENE. I've been on the pill so long / I'm probably sterile.

JOYCE. Listen when Angie was six months I did get pregnant
and I lost it because I was so tired looking after your fucking
baby / because she cried so much — yes I did tell

MARLENE. You never told me.

JOYCE. you — / and the doctor said if I'd sat down all day with

MARLENE. Well I forgot.

JOYCE. my feet up I'd've kept it / and that's the only chance
I ever had because after that —

MARLENE. I've had two abortions, are you interested? Shall I
tell you about them? Well I won't, it's boring, it wasn't a
problem. I don't like messy talk about blood / and what a bad

JOYCE. If I hadn't had your baby. The doctor said.

MARLENE. time we all had. I don't want a baby. I don't want to
talk about gynaecology.

JOYCE. Then stop trying to get Angie off of me.

MARLENE. I come down here after six years. All night you've
been saying I don't come often enough. If I don't come for
another six years she'll be twenty-one, will that be OK?

JOYCE. That'll be fine, yes, six years would suit me fine.

Pause.

MARLENE. I was afraid of this.
I only came because I thought you wanted . . .
I just want . . .

MARLENE *cries.*

JOYCE. Don't grizzle, Marlene, for God's sake.
Marly? Come on, pet. Love you really.
Fucking stop it, will you?

MARLENE. No, let me cry. I like it.

They laugh, MARLENE *begins to stop crying.*

I knew I'd cry if I wasn't careful.

JOYCE. Everyone's always crying in this house. Nobody takes any notice.

MARLENE. You've been wonderful looking after Angie.

JOYCE. Don't get carried away.

MARLENE. I can't write letters but I do think of you.

JOYCE. You're getting drunk. I'm going to make some tea.

MARLENE. Love you.

JOYCE *gets up to make tea.*

JOYCE. I can see why you'd want to leave. It's a dump here.

MARLENE. So what's this about you and Frank?

JOYCE. He was always carrying on, wasn't he? And if I wanted to go out in the evening he'd go mad, even if it was nothing, a class, I was going to go to an evening class. So he had this girlfriend, only twenty-two poor cow, and I said go on, off you go, hoppit. I don't think he even likes her.

MARLENE. So what about money?

JOYCE. I've always said I don't want your money.

MARLENE. No, does he send you money?

JOYCE. I've got four different cleaning jobs. Adds up. There's not a lot round here.

MARLENE. Does Angie miss him?

JOYCE. She doesn't say.

MARLENE. Does she see him?

JOYCE. He was never that fond of her to be honest.

MARLENE. He tried to kiss me once. When you were engaged.

JOYCE. Did you fancy him?

MARLENE. No, he looked like a fish.

JOYCE. He was lovely then.

MARLENE. Ugh.

JOYCE. Well I fancied him. For about three years.

MARLENE. Have you got someone else?

JOYCE. There's not a lot round here. Mind you, the minute you're on your own, you'd be amazed how your friends' husbands drop by. I'd sooner do without.

MARLENE. I don't see why you couldn't take my money.

JOYCE. I do, so don't bother about it.

MARLENE. Only got to ask.

JOYCE. So what about you? Good job?

MARLENE. Good for a laugh. / Got back from the US of A a bit

JOYCE. Good for more than a laugh I should think.

MARLENE. wiped out and slotted into this speedy employment agency and still there.

JOYCE. You can always find yourself work then.

MARLENE. That's right.

JOYCE. And men?

MARLENE. Oh there's always men.

JOYCE. No one special?

MARLENE. There's fellas who like to be seen with a high-flying lady. Shows they've got something really good in their pants. But they can't take the day to day. They're waiting for me to turn into the little woman. Or maybe I'm just horrible of course.

JOYCE. Who needs them?

MARLENE. Who needs them? Well I do. But I need adventures more. So on on into the sunset. I think the eighties are going to be stupendous.

JOYCE. Who for?

MARLENE. For me. / I think I'm going up up up.

JOYCE. Oh for you. Yes, I'm sure they will.

MARLENE. And for the country, come to that. Get the economy

back on its feet and whoosh. She's a tough lady, Maggie. I'd
give her a job. / She just needs to hang in there. This country

JOYCE. You voted for them, did you?

MARLENE. needs to stop whining. / Monetarism is not stupid.

JOYCE. Drink your tea and shut up, pet.

MARLENE. It takes time, determination. No more slop. / And

JOYCE. Well I think they're filthy bastards.

MARLENE. who's got to drive it on? First woman prime
minister. Terrifico. Aces. Right on. / You must admit.
Certainly gets my vote.

JOYCE. What good's first woman if it's her? I suppose you'd have
liked Hitler if he was a woman. Ms Hitler. Got a lot done,
Hitlerina. / Great adventures.

MARLENE. Bosses still walking on the workers' faces? Still
Dadda's little parrot? Haven't you learned to think for yourself?
I believe in the individual. Look at me.

JOYCE. I am looking at you.

MARLENE. Come on, Joyce, we're not going to quarrel over
politics.

JOYCE. We are though.

MARLENE. Forget I mentioned it. Not a word about the slimy
unions will cross my lips.

Pause.

JOYCE. You say Mother had a wasted life.

MARLENE. Yes I do. Married to that bastard.

JOYCE. What sort of life did he have? / Working in the fields like

MARLENE. Violent life?

JOYCE. an animal. / Why wouldn't he want a drink?

MARLENE. Come off it.

JOYCE. You want a drink. He couldn't afford whisky.

MARLENE. I don't want to talk about him.

JOYCE. You started, I was talking about her. She had a rotten life because she had nothing. She went hungry.

MARLENE. She was hungry because he drank the money. / He used to hit her.

JOYCE. It's not all down to him. / Their lives were rubbish. They

MARLENE. She didn't hit him.

JOYCE. were treated like rubbish. He's dead and she'll die soon and what sort of life / did they have?

MARLENE. I saw him one night. I came down.

JOYCE. Do you think I didn't? / They didn't get to America and

MARLENE. I still have dreams.

JOYCE. drive across it in a fast car. / Bad nights, they had bad days.

MARLENE. America, America, you're jealous. / I had to get out,

JOYCE. Jealous?

MARLENE. I knew when I was thirteen, out of their house, out of them, never let that happen to me, / never let him, make my own way, out.

JOYCE. Jealous of what you've done, you're ashamed of me if I came to your office, your smart friends, wouldn't you, I'm ashamed of you, think of nothing but yourself, you've got on, nothing's changed for most people / has it?

MARLENE. I hate the working class / which is what you're going

JOYCE. Yes you do.

MARLENE. to go on about now, it doesn't exist any more, it means lazy and stupid. / I don't like the way they talk. I don't

JOYCE. Come on, now we're getting it.

MARLENE. like beer guts and football vomit and saucy tits / and brothers and sisters —

JOYCE. I spit when I see a Rolls Royce, scratch it with my ring / Mercedes it was.

MARLENE. Oh very mature —

JOYCE. I hate the cows I work for / and their dirty dishes with blanquette of fucking veau.

MARLENE. and I will not be pulled down to their level by a flying picket and I won't be sent to Siberia / or a loony bin

JOYCE. No, you'll be on a yacht, you'll be head of Coca-Cola and you wait, the eighties is going to be stupendous all right because we'll get you lot off our backs —

MARLENE. just because I'm original. And I support Reagan even if he is a lousy movie star because the reds are swarming up his map and I want to be free in a free world —

JOYCE. What? / What?

MARLENE. I know what I mean / by that — not shut up here.

JOYCE. So don't be round here when it happens because if someone's kicking you I'll just laugh.

Silence.

MARLENE. I don't mean anything personal. I don't believe in class. Anyone can do anything if they've got what it takes.

JOYCE. And if they haven't?

MARLENE. If they're stupid or lazy or frightened, I'm not going to help them get a job, why should I?

JOYCE. What about Angie?

MARLENE. What about Angie?

JOYCE. She's stupid, lazy and frightened, so what about her?

MARLENE. You run her down too much. She'll be all right.

JOYCE. I don't expect so, no. I expect her children will say what a wasted life she had. If she has children. Because nothing's changed and it won't with them in.

MARLENE. Them, them. / Us and them?

JOYCE. And you're one of them.

MARLENE. And you're us, wonderful us, and Angie's us / and Mum and Dad's us.

JOYCE. Yes, that's right, and you're them.

MARLENE. Come on, Joyce, what a night. You've got what it takes.

JOYCE. I know I have.

MARLENE. I didn't really mean all that.

JOYCE. I did.

MARLENE. But we're friends anyway.

JOYCE. I don't think so, no.

MARLENE. Well it's lovely to be out in the country. I really must make the effort to come more often.
I want to go to sleep.
I want to go to sleep.

JOYCE *gets blankets for the sofa.*

JOYCE. Goodnight then. I hope you'll be warm enough.

MARLENE. Goodnight. Joyce —

JOYCE. No, pet. Sorry.

JOYCE *goes.*

MARLENE *sits wrapped in a blanket and has another drink.*

ANGIE *comes in.*

ANGIE. Mum?

MARLENE. Angie? What's the matter?

ANGIE. Mum?

MARLENE. No, she's gone to bed. It's Aunty Marlene.

ANGIE. Frightening.

MARLENE. Did you have a bad dream? What happened in it?
Well you're awake now, aren't you pet?

ANGIE. Frightening.

FEN

'It was work, work, work, it was all their lives.'
Retired School Teacher

'What's the point of working till you drop?'
Union Branch Secretary

'I'm the only Marxist in the Fens.'
Smallholder

'They must think I'm off the road.'
Smallholder

'If you don't believe, you don't see anything.'
Retired Landworker

2   a character sometimes continues speaking right through
     another's speech.

eg.   GEOFFREY: We had terrible times. If I had cracked tomatoes
     for my tea / I
     SHIRLEY: It's easy living here like I do now.
     GEOFFREY: thought I was lucky. etc

Production Note

From the workshop and from talking to Les Waters and Annie
Smart before I wrote the play, I had some idea of what the play
was like physically while I was writing it, and certain things are an
essential part of its structure: no interval, almost continuous
action (the scenes following with hardly a break), all furniture
and props on stage throughout and one set which doesn't change.
In the original production this was achieved by Annie Smart's
design of a field in a room, which was brilliant but which I can't
claim as part of the play as I wrote it.

In the earlier edition there was a musical setting of lines from
Rilke's *Duino Elegies*, which was cut very early in the production.
Though I miss having two songs, the Girls' Song about particular
and limited wants and the Rilke about a vaster yearning, I do on
the whole prefer this version.

I have kept the line near the end where the Boy from the
beginning of the play reappears and says 'Jarvis . . .' In practice
we cut it, as we wanted to keep Angela on stage and the parts
were doubled. But I like the idea that that boy was that old man,
so I've kept it, for reading anyway.

May sings, ie she stands as if singing and we hear what she
would have liked to sing. So something amazing and beautiful —
she wouldn't sing unless she could sing like that. In the original
production it was a short piece of opera on tape.

Fen was first performed by the Joint Stock Theatre Group at the University of Essex Theatre on 20 January 1983 and opened at the Almeida Theatre, London on 16 February 1983, with the following cast:

SHIRLEY SHONA MISS CADE MARGARET	Linda Bassett
BOY ANGELA DEB MRS FINCH	Amelda Brown
JAPANESE BUSINESSMAN NELL MAY MAVIS	Cecily Hobbs
MRS HASSETT BECKY ALICE IVY	Tricia Kelly
VAL GHOST	Jennie Stoller
WILSON FRANK MR TEWSON GEOFFREY	Bernard Strother

Directed by Les Waters
Designed by Annie Smart
Lighting by Tom Donnellan
Original music by Ilona Sekacz

This play was written after a workshop in a village in the Fens.

Note on layout
A speech usually follows the one immediately before it BUT:
1. when one character starts speaking before the other has finished, the point of interruption is marked / .
eg. DEB: You shut up, / none of your business.
    MAY: Don't speak to your mum like that. etc

As the audience comes in, a BOY *from the last century, barefoot and in rags, is alone in a field, in a fog, scaring crows. He shouts and waves a rattle. As the day goes on his voice gets weaker till he is hoarse and shouting in a whisper. It gets dark.*

Scene One

It gets lighter, but still some mist. It is the present. JAPANESE BUSINESSMAN, *in suit, with camera.*

JAPANESE BUSINESSMAN. Mr Takai, Tokyo Company, welcomes you to the fen. Most expensive earth in England. Two thousand pounds acre. Long time ago, under water. Fishes and eels swimming here. Not true people had webbed feet but did walk on stilts. Wild people, fen tigers. In 1630 rich lords planned to drain fen, change swamp into grazing land, far thinking men, brave investors. Fen people wanted to keep fishes and eels to live on, no vision. Refuse work on drainage, smash dykes, broke sluices. Many problems. But in the end we have this beautiful earth. Very efficient, flat land, plough right up to edge, no waste. This farm, one of our twenty-five farms, very good investment. Belongs to Baxter Nolesford Ltd, which belongs to Reindorp Smith Farm Land trust, which belongs 65% to our company. We now among many illustrious landowners, Esso, Gallagher, Imperial Tobacco, Equitable Life, all love this excellent earth. How beautiful English countryside. I think it is too foggy to take pictures. Now I find teashop, warm fire, old countryman to tell tales.

Scene Two

WOMEN *and a* BOY *working in a row, potato picking down a field. When their buckets are full they tip the potatoes into a potato grave at the top of the field.*

    VAL *thirty,* ANGELA *twenty-eight,* SHIRLEY *fifty,* NELL *forty,* WILSON *sixteen.*

    MRS HASSETT *forty-five, gangmaster, stands at the bottom of the field watching them. They pick down and back once, and start down again.*

    SHIRLEY *sings the fireman's song from children's TV programme* Trumpton.

SHIRLEY (*sings*). Pugh, Pugh, Barney McGrew,
    Cuthbert, Dibble, Grub.
    Da da diddidi da
    Diddidi diddidi diddidi da
    Da da diddidi da
    Diddidi diddidi da, pom.

    ANGELA *joins in and sings with her.*

    NELL *joins in.*

    VAL *stops and stands staring.*

NELL. You all right, girl?

    NELL *doesn't stop working.*

    VAL *goes down the field to the end where* MRS HASSETT *is.*

MRS HASSETT. What's the matter, Val? Took short?

VAL. I've got to leave now.

MRS HASSETT. What do you mean, got to leave? It ent three o'clock.

VAL. I know, but I'm going.

MRS HASSETT. Who's going to do your work then? Mr Coleman wants this done today. How does it make me look?

VAL. Sorry, I can't help it.

MRS HASSETT. You think twice before you ask me for work again because I'll think twice an' all. So where you off to so fast?

VAL. Just back home.

MRS HASSETT. What's waiting there then?

VAL. I've got to. I've gone. Never mind.

MRS HASSETT. Wait then, I'll give you a lift halfway. I've another lot at Mason's I've got to look in on.

VAL. I've got to go now.

MRS. HASSETT. You'll be quicker waiting. I don't owe you nothing for today.

VAL. You do.

MRS HASSETT. Not with you messing me about like this, not if you want another chance.

VAL. I'll start walking and you pick me up.

VAL *goes.*

The others arrive at the end of the field. WILSON *is first.*

MRS HASSETT. What's your name? Wilson? The idea's to get the work done properly not win the Derby. Want to come again?

WILSON. Yes, Mrs Hassett.

MRS HASSETT. Because if you work regular with me it's done proper with stamps. I don't want you signing on at the same time because that makes trouble for me, never mind you. And if I catch you with them moonlighting gangs out of town you don't work for me again. Work for peanuts them buggers, spoil it for the rest of you, so keep well clear.

NELL. Spoil it for you, Mrs Hassett.

MRS HASSETT. Spoil it for all of us, Nell.

ANGELA. What's up with Val?

NELL. You've got two colour tellies to spoil.

MRS HASSETT. Think you'd get a better deal by yourself? Think you'd get a job at all?

ANGELA. Where's she gone? Ent she well?

MRS HASSETT. She don't say she's ill. She don't say what.

NELL. You paying her what she's done?

MRS HASSETT. Will you mind your own business or she won't be the only one don't get picked up tomorrow morning.

NELL. It is my business. You'd treat me the same.

ANGELA. Nell, do give over.

SHIRLEY. Come on, Nell, let's get on with it.

NELL. She treat you the same.

WILSON. If I do hers, do I get her money?

MRS HASSETT. You'll have enough to do to finish your own.

WILSON. Can I try?

MRS HASSETT. If you do it careful.

NELL. Am I crazy? Am I crazy? Am I crazy?

MRS HASSETT. I'm off now, ladies and gent. Can't stand about in this wind. I should get a move on, you've plenty to do.

ANGELA. Nell, you're just embarrassing.

> MRS HASSETT *goes.* SHIRLEY *and* WILSON *have already started work.*
>
> ANGELA *starts.*
>
> NELL *starts.*

Scene Three

FRANK, *thirty, driving a tractor.*
> *Earphones. We can hear the music he's listening to.*
> *The music fades down, we hear him talking to himself.*

FRANK. Mr Tewson, Can I have a word with you?
> Yes, Frank, what can I do for you lad?
> I'm finding things a bit difficult.
> So am I, Frank. Hard times.
> Fellow come round from the union last week.
> Little fellow with a squint?
> I don't hold with strikes myself.

I'm not against the union, Frank. I can see the sense of it for
your big newfangle farms. Not when people are friends.

Fact is, Mr Tewson, living separate from the wife and kids I
can't seem to manage.

It's lucky I'm able to let them stay on in the cottage. The
council housing's not up to much eh?

I'm very grateful. But Mr Tewson I can't live on the money.
You'd get half as much again in a factory, Frank. I wouldn't
blame you. But I remember when your dad worked for my
dad and you and your brother played about the yard. Your
poor old brother, eh Frank? It was great we got him into that
home when your mum died. We're like family. We'd both put
up with a lot to go on living this good old life here.

I hate you, you old bugger.

FRANK *hits* MR TEWSON, *that is he hits himself across the*
face.

VAL *arrives with* DEB *nine and* SHONA *six. They have a*
suitcase. She leaves them at the side of the field with the
suitcase and goes to speak to FRANK. *She has to attract his*
attention, shouting 'Frank! Frank!' He stops the tractor, takes
off the earphones.

FRANK. What happened?

VAL. Suddenly came to me.

FRANK. What's wrong?

VAL. I'm leaving him. I'm going to London on the train, I'm
taking the girls, I've left him a note and that's it. You follow
us soon as you can. It's the only thing. New life.

FRANK. Where are you going to live?

VAL. We'll find somewhere together.

FRANK. How much money you got?

VAL. Fifty-six pounds. I'll get a job. I just want to be with you.

FRANK. I want to be with you, Val.

VAL. All right then.

FRANK. What am I supposed to do in London?

VAL. Where do you want to go? You say. I don't mind. You
    don't like it here. You're always grumbling about Mr Tewson.

FRANK. He's not a bad old boy.

VAL. He don't pay what he should.

FRANK. He was good to my brother.

VAL. I'm in a panic.

FRANK. Shall I see you tonight?

VAL. In London?

FRANK. Here.

VAL. How can I get out? I'm going crazy all this dodging about.

FRANK. Come and live with me. If you're ready to leave.

VAL. With the girls?

FRANK. With or without.

VAL. He'll never let me. He'll have them off me.

FRANK. Please do.

    They kiss.

VAL. I suppose I go home now. Unpack.

    She gets the CHILDREN *and they go.*

Scene Four

VAL *and* DEB.

VAL. You're to be a good girl Deb, and look after Shona.
    Mummy will come and see you all the time. You can come and
    see Mummy and Frank. Mummy loves you very much. Daddy
    loves you very much. I'll only be down the road.

DEB. I want to go on the train.

VAL. We will go on the train sometime. We can't go now.
    Mummy's got to go and live with Frank because I love him.
    You be a good girl and look after Shona. Daddy's going to look
    after you. And Nan's going to look after you. Daddy loves you

very much. I'll come and see you all the time.

DEB. I want new colours.

VAL. You've still got your old ones, haven't you. Lucky we
didn't go away, you've still got all your things.

DEB. I want new colours.

VAL. I'll get you some new colours. Mummy's sorry. Love you
very much. Look after Shona.

Scene Five

VAL *and* FRANK *dance together. Old-fashioned, formal,*
romantic, happy.

Scene Six

ANGELA *and* BECKY, *her stepdaughter, fifteen.*
   BECKY *is standing still.* ANGELA *has a cup of very hot water.*

ANGELA. You shouldn't let me treat you like this.

BECKY. Can I sit down now, Angela?

ANGELA. No, because you asked. Drink it standing up. And you
didn't call me mum.

BECKY. You're not, that's why.

ANGELA. Wouldn't want to be the mother of a filthy little cow
like you. Pity you didn't die with her. Your dad wishes you'd
died with her. Now drink it quick.

   BECKY *takes the cup and drops it. She goes to pick it up.*

   Now look. Don't you dare pick it up. That's your trick is it, so
   I'll let you move? I'll have to punish you for breaking a cup.
   Why do you push me?

BECKY. Too hot.

   ANGELA *fills another cup from a kettle.*

ANGELA. It's meant to be hot. What you made of, girl? Ice cream? Going to melt in a bit of hot? I'll tell your dad what a bad girl you are if he phones up tonight and then he won't love you. He'll go off in his lorry one day and not come back and he'll send for me and he won't send for you. Say sorry and you needn't drink it.

BECKY *starts to drink it.*

Faster than that. Crybaby. Hurts, does it? Say sorry now. Sorry mummy.

BECKY *stands in silence.*

I'm not bothered. No one's going to come you know. No chance of anyone dropping in. We've got all afternoon and all evening and all night. We can do what we like so long as we get your dad's tea tomorrow.

BECKY. I'm going to tell him.

ANGELA. You tell him what you like and what won't I tell him about you.

BECKY. I'll tell someone. You'll be put in prison, you'll be burnt.

ANGELA. You can't tell because I'd kill you. You know that. Do you know that?

BECKY. Yes.

ANGELA. Do you?

BECKY. Yes.

ANGELA. Now why not say sorry and we'll have a biscuit and see what's on telly. You needn't say mummy, you can say, 'Sorry, Angela, I'm bad all through.' I don't want you driving me into a mood.

BECKY. Sorry, Angela, bad all through.

ANGELA *strokes* BECKY's *hair then yanks it.*

ANGELA. No stamina, have you? 'Sorry Angela.' What you made of, girl?

Scene Seven

NELL *is hoeing her garden.*
     BECKY, DEB, SHONA *spying on her.*

DEB. Is she a man?

BECKY. No, she's a morphrodite.

DEB. What's that?

BECKY. A man and a woman both at once.

DEB. Can it have babies by itself?

BECKY. It has them with another morphrodite. Like snails. But
     she's never met one yet.

SHONA. Is she a witch?

BECKY. She eats little children, so watch out.

DEB. She talks to herself. That's spells.

BECKY. Angela says she makes trouble.

DEB. She goes in the gang with my mum.

BECKY. She makes trouble.

DEB. Let's get her wild.

BECKY. I hate her, don't you?

DEB. She makes me feel sick.

BECKY. Let's make her shout.

SHONA. Poo bum! Poo bum!

DEB. Shut up, Shona.

NELL. What you doing there?

BECKY. Watching you, so what?

NELL. Come out and watch me close up then.

DEB. Can I ask you something?

NELL. What?

DEB. Have you got — have you got — ?

NELL. What?

They giggle.

NELL. Well I don't know what you want. Want to help me with my garden? You can do some weeding.

BECKY. That's a funny hat.

NELL. That's a good old hat. It's a funny old hat.

SHONA. Poo bum.

NELL. You watch out, Shona, or you'll have a smack.

DEB. You hit my sister and I'll kill you.

BECKY. I'll kill you. Kill you with the hoe. You're horrible.

BECKY *takes the garden hoe and pokes it at* NELL.

NELL. Watch what you're doing. Put it down.

DEB. Make her run. Give her a poke.

BECKY. Jump. Jump.

SHONA. Poo poo poo poo.

NELL. You stop that.

NELL *grabs* SHONA, *holds her in front of her, between herself and the hoe.*

Now you mind who you poke.

SHONA *screams and struggles.*

Give me my hoe and get on home.

DEB. You let her go.

BECKY. I'll have your foot. I'll have your eyes.

NELL. Right then, you stop in there like a little rabbit.

NELL *pushes* SHONA *into a rabbit hutch.*

SHONA. Let me out.

DEB. Kill her.

BECKY. Let her out.

NELL. Give me that hoe first. Now shut up, Shona, or I'll have you for tea.

DEB. Kill her.

BECKY *screams and stabs at* NELL, *who ducks and gets her hat knocked off.*

NELL. Now give me my hoe.

BECKY *gives her the hoe.*

Give me my hat.

BECKY *gives her the hat.*

And get out of my garden.

DEB. Shona.

NELL. What if I keep Shona an hour or two? Teach you a lesson.

DEB. Please let her go.

SHONA. Deb, get me out, I can't move, get me out.

NELL. Nasty, nasty children. What will you grow up like? Nasty. You should be entirely different. Everything. Everything.

NELL *lets* SHONA *out.*

You're the poo bum now, all rabbit business.

SHONA. Are you a witch?

NELL. No, I'm a princess. Now get out.

Girls' Song (BECKY, DEB, SHONA)

I want to be a nurse when I grow up
And I want to have children and get married.
But I don't think I'll leave the village when I grow up.

I'm never going to leave the village when I grow up even when
I get married.
I think I'll stay in the village and be a nurse.

I want to be a hairdresser when I grow up or perhaps a teacher.
I don't really care if I get married or be a hairdresser.

I want to be a cook when I grow up.
If I couldn't be a cook I'd be a hairdresser.
But I don't really want to leave the village when I grow up.

I don't think much about what I want to be.
I don't mind housework.

I think I want to be a housewife until I think of another job.

When I grow up I'm going to be a nurse and if not a hairdresser.

I'm going to be a hairdresser when I grow up and if not a nurse.

Scene Eight

MAY, VAL's *mother, sixty, filling in a pools coupon.* DEB *and* SHONA *colouring.*

MAY. When the light comes down from behind the clouds it comes down like a ladder into the graveyards. And the dead people go up the light into heaven.

SHONA. Can you see them going up?

MAY. I never have. You look for them, my sugar.

A long silence.

DEB. Sing something, nan.

MAY. I can't sing, my sugar.

Silence.

SHONA. Go on, sing something.

MAY. I can't, I can't sing.

Silence.

SHONA. Mum can sing.

MAY. Yes, she's got a nice voice, Val.

DEB. Sing something.

Pause. MAY *seems about to sing.*

MAY. I can't sing, my sugar.

DEB. You're no good then, are you.

MAY. There's other things besides singing.

DEB. Like what?

Silence.

VAL *comes. They all go on with what they're doing.*

VAL. Hello, mum. Hello, Deb. Oh Deb, hello. Shona, Shona. What are you drawing? Can't I look?

MAY. They're telling me off because I can't sing. You can sing them something since you're here.

VAL. You want me to sing you something, Deb?

DEB. No.

VAL. Shona?

Pause.

VAL *starts to sing. She stops.*

MAY. How long is this nonsense going to last?

VAL. Don't.

MAY. I'm ashamed of you.

VAL. Not in front.

MAY. What you after? Happiness? Got it have you? Bluebird of happiness? Got it have you? Bluebird?

Silence.

What you after?

DEB. Shut up.

VAL. Don't speak to your nan like that.

DEB. You shut up, / none of your business.

MAY. Don't speak to your mum like that. She's getting dreadful, Val. / You've only yourself to blame.

DEB. I'm not. You are. You're getting dreadful.

MAY. You see what I mean.

VAL. You're winding her up.

MAY. I'm winding her up? She was good as gold till you come in. / You better think what you're doing.

VAL. Don't start on me. Just because you had nothing.

MAY. Don't speak to me like that, / my girl, or it's out you go.

DEB. Don't speak to my mum.

VAL. I've not been here / five minutes.

DEB. Don't speak to my nan.

VAL. Shut up, Deb.

MAY. Don't speak to the child like that.

>SHONA *screams and runs off. Silence.*

>Don't go after her.

VAL. Don't you go after her.

MAY. Deb, you go and look after your sister.

DEB. No.

>*Pause.*

VAL. I'd better go after her.

DEB. Leave her alone.

MAY. Leave her alone a bit, best thing.

>*Silence.*

VAL. Never mind, Deb.

MAY. Get one thing straight. It's no trouble having them. They've always a place here.

VAL. I know that.

MAY. I'll stand by you. I stand by my children.

>*Silence.*

>I'd never have left you, Val.

VAL. Just don't.

MAY. I'd go through fire. What's stronger than that?

VAL. Just don't.

MAY. What's stronger?

>*Silence.*

DEB. I'll get Shona.

Scene Nine

MR TEWSON *fifty-five, farmer, and* MISS CADE, *thirty-five from the City.*

TEWSON. Suppose I was to die. I can claim fifty percent working farmer relief on my land value.

CADE. And thirty percent on the value of your working capital.

TEWSON. My son would still have a bill of —

CADE. Three hundred thousand pounds.

TEWSON. Which I don't have.

CADE. That's the position exactly.

TEWSON. It would mean selling a hundred and fifty acres.

CADE. That's what it would mean.

TEWSON. He could do that.

CADE. It's certainly an option.

TEWSON. Take a good few generations before the whole farm disappears. Eh?

CADE. Alternatively you can give land direct to the Inland Revenue.

Pause.

Alternatively.

TEWSON. I need to be bloody immortal. Then I'd never pay tax. You're bloody immortal, eh? City institutions are immortal.

CADE. The farmers who have sold to us are happy, Mr Tewson.

TEWSON. Bloody driven to it. Don't have to like you as well. I've read about you, Miss Cade. Moguls.

CADE. The popular farming press unfortunately —

TEWSON. And tycoons. And barons.

CADE. The specialist journals take a longer view.

TEWSON. Who pushed the price of land up?

CADE. Not in fact the City.

TEWSON. I don't want these fields to be worth hundreds of thousands. More tax I have to pay.

CADE. We follow the market. The rise in prices is caused by government policies. Ever since the Heath administration introduced rollover relief —

TEWSON. Same old fields. My great great grandfather, Miss Cade.

Pause.

I am a member of the Country Landowners Association. We have ears in the corridors of power. My family are landowners. If I sell to you I become a tenant on my grandfather's land. Our president appealed to us to keep our nerve.

CADE. With us, your grandson will farm his grandfather's acres. The same number of acres. More. You'll have the capital to reinvest. Land and machinery.

Pause.

TEWSON. My family hold this land in trust for the nation.

CADE. We too have a sense of heritage.

Pause.

TEWSON. Grandson, eh?

CADE. No reason why not.

TEWSON. When I say nation. You don't want to go too far in the public responsibility direction. You raise the spectre of nationalisation.

CADE. No danger of that. Think of us as yourself.

TEWSON. No problem getting a new tractor then.

CADE. I can leave the papers with you.

TEWSON. Cup of tea? Daresay Mrs Tewson's made a cake. You want to watch the Transport and General Workers. The old agricultural union was no trouble. We'll have these buggers stopping the trains.

MISS CADE *goes.* TEWSON *is following her. He is stopped by the sight of a* WOMAN *working in the fields. She is as real as the other women workers but barefoot and wearing nineteenth century rags. She is a* GHOST.

TEWSON. Good afternoon. Who's that? You're not one of Mrs Hassett's girls.

GHOST. We are starving, we will not stand this no longer. Rather than starve we are torment to set you on fire. You bloody farmers could not live if it was not for the poor, tis them that keep you bloody rascals alive, but there will be a slaughter made amongst you very soon. I should very well like to hang you the same as I hanged your beasts. You bloody rogue, I will light up a little fire for you the first opportunity I can make.

TEWSON. My father saw you. I didn't believe him.

GHOST. I been working in this field a hundred and fifty years. There ain't twenty in this parish but what hates you, bullhead.

TEWSON. Are you angry because I'm selling the farm?

GHOST. What difference will it make?

TEWSON. None, none, everything will go on the same.

GHOST. That's why I'm angry.

TEWSON. I'm going.

GHOST. Get home then. I live in your house. I watch television with you. I stand beside your chair and watch the killings. I watch the food and I watch what makes people laugh. My baby died starving.

Scene Ten

WOMEN *onion packing.* SHIRLEY, NELL, ANGELA, ALICE, *a Baptist, 35. They have a large box of onions which they pack a few at a time in small bags for the supermarket, discarding those that don't make the grade. They keep working hard throughout the scene, including* NELL.

SHIRLEY. No Val today?

ANGELA. No time for onions.

NELL. Need the money though, won't she?

ALICE. Not surprised she don't come. You shouldn't be surprised.

SHIRLEY. What's that mean?

ALICE. Way you treat her.

SHIRLEY. What's that mean?

ALICE. Everyone's acting funny with her.

ANGELA. She's the one acting funny. Leave her own kiddies. If I had my own kiddies I wouldn't leave them.

ALICE. I know she's wicked but she's still my friend.

SHIRLEY. What you talking about wicked?

ALICE. It was sinners Jesus Christ come for so don't you judge.

SHIRLEY. Who said anything?

ALICE. Outside school yesterday, collecting time, no one said hello except me.

SHIRLEY. I wasn't there, was I. Expect me to shout from the other end of the street. Hello Val! Say hello now, shall I? Hello, Val! That'll cheer her up wherever she is. Altogether now, Hello —

ALICE. Never mind. You're all so — never mind.

NELL. Did I ever tell you about my grandfather?

SHIRLEY. When he was a boy and run away, that one?

NELL. I know you know, you'll have to hear it again.

ALICE. People are all miserable sinners. Miserable.

SHIRLEY. You want to tell Val not us. Give her a fright.

ANGELA. This one of your dirty stories, Nell? Or one of your frightening ones?

SHIRLEY. It's funny.

NELL. He used to swear this really happened. When he was ten his mother died in childbirth, and his father soon got a woman in he said was a housekeeper, but she slept with him from the first night. My grandfather hated her and she hated him, and she'd send him to bed without any tea, and his father always

took her side. So after a few months of this, early one morning
when his father had gone to work but she wasn't up yet, he
took some bread and some cold tea and he run off. He walked
all day and it got real dark and he was frit as hell. There was
no houses on the road, just an old green drove sometimes
going off towards the coast, so he thought he'd have to sleep
by the road. Then he sees a little light shining so he set off
down the drove that led to it and he comes to an old stone
house. So he knocks on the door and the woman comes, and
she'd a candlestick in one hand and a big old copper stick in the
other. But when she sees it's only a boy she says come in and
she makes him sit by the fire and gives him a bowl of hot milk
with some fat bacon in it and a hunk of brown bread. Then
she says, 'Me and my husband are going out but you can sleep
by the fire. But you must stay here in the kitchen,' she says,
'whatever you do, you mustn't go through that door,' and she
points to the door at the back of the kitchen. Then her
husband came and said the pony trap was ready and he didn't
look too pleased to see the boy but he didn't say nothing and
off they went for their night out. So he sat by the fire and sat
by the fire, and he thought I'll just take a look through that
door. So he turned the handle but it was locked. And he saw a
key lay on the dresser and he tried it and slowly opened the
door, and then he wished he hadn't. There was a candle in the
window which was the light he'd seen, and a long table, and on
the table was a coffin with the lid off, and inside the coffin
there was a body. And he was just going to shut the door and
hurry back by the fire when the body in the coffin sat up and
opened its eyes, and said, 'Who are you boy?' Oh he were
petrified. But the body said, 'Don't be afraid, I'm not dead,'
he said, 'Where have they gone?' meaning the woman and the
husband. When he heard they were out he got out of the
coffin and come in the kitchen and made some cocoa. Then he
told my grandfather his missus had been having an affair with
the chap from the next smallholding, and she was trying to get
rid of him by putting rat poison in his food, and he'd fed it to
some pigeons and they'd died. So what he'd done, he'd
pretended to die, and she'd told the doctor he'd had a heart
attack, and he'd been put in the coffin. And before that he'd

sold the farm without telling the wife and had the money safe in the bank under another name. So he give my grandfather a screwdriver and said when the couple came home and screwed down the coffin, after they was in bed he was to unscrew it again. So he went back by the fire and pretended to be asleep, and he heard them screw up the coffin and laughing about how they'd got the old man's farm and kissing, and later he got the old fellow out and he were real glad because he said he wanted a pee so bad he could almost taste it. Then he got a large two tined pitchfork and a pickaxe handle and he said 'Come on it's time to go.' My grandfather thought they were going to leave, but the old fellow crept upstairs, and gave the boy the candle and the pickaxe handle to carry, and he crept up and opened the door of the bedroom. There was the couple lying close together, completely naked and fast asleep. Then suddenly he raised the pitchfork and brung it down as hard as he could directly over their bare stomachs, so they were sort of stitched together. They screamed and screamed and he grabbed the pickaxe handle off of my grandfather and clubbed them on their heads till they lay still. Then he gets the man and takes him downstairs and puts him in the coffin and screws it up. He says, 'They'll bury him tomorrow and think it's me, and when they find her dead they'll know she was out drinking with her fellow and they'll think he killed her and done a bunk, so the police won't be looking for me,' he said, 'they'll be looking for him. And I'm going to start a new life in London or Australia, and if you talk about it I'll find you and slit your throat from ear to ear.' And he never did till he was so old he knew the old man must be dead, and even then he waited a good few years more, and I was the first person he ever told. The old fellow gave my grandfather a gold sovereign and told him to walk west and look for a job on a farm over that way, so he walked five days and slept five nights in barns, and got a job on a farm near Doncaster.

ANGELA. He never heard no more about it?

NELL. If it was in the paper he wouldn't know because he couldn't read. He never heard nothing about it, and his father never found him neither.

ALICE. You said it was funny, Shirley.

ANGELA. I don't reckon it's true.

SHIRLEY. Funny if it is true, eh Nell?

NELL. I believe it all right. Why not? There's harder things to believe than that. Makes me laugh.

Scene Eleven

SHIRLEY *working in the house. She goes from one job to another, ironing, mending, preparing dinner, minding a baby. VAL is there, not doing anything. SHIRLEY never stops throughout the scene.*

VAL. I made a cake Deb always likes and I had to throw half of it away. Frank and I don't like cake.

SHIRLEY. You're bound to miss them.

VAL. I do see them.

Silence.

It's right he should keep them. I see that. It's not his fault. He's a good father. It's better for them to stay in their own home. Frank's only got the one room. It makes sense. It's all for the best.

SHIRLEY. At harvest dad'd say, 'Come on, Shirley, you're marker.' Then if the shock fell over, 'Who's the marker?' I'd say, 'I'll go outside, let someone else be marker,' but he wouldn't let me. And leading the horse. 'What if he treads on my feet?' I never could work in front of a horse. Many's the time they'd bolt up the field. My mother wouldn't let me off. 'Just get on with it, Shirley.'

VAL. Can I help with something?

SHIRLEY. Thank you but I know how I like it.

Silence.

VAL. Is that Mary's baby?

SHIRLEY. No, it's Susan's.

VAL. You've so many grandchildren I lose track.

SHIRLEY. I'll be a great-grandmother next.

VAL. What, Sukey's never?

SHIRLEY. No, but she's sixteen now and I was a grandmother at thirty-two.

Silence.

Same thing when I went into service. I was fifteen and I hated it. They had me for a week's trial and I could have gone home at the end of it but I didn't want my mother to think she'd bred a gibber. Stayed my full year.

Silence.

I don't think she will somehow, Sukey. She's got green hair. Shocks her mother.

Silence.

Woken up, have we?

SHIRLEY *picks up the baby.*

VAL. I can't remember what they look like.

SHIRLEY. You see them every other day.

VAL. I don't think I can have looked at them when I had them. I was busy with them all the time so I didn't look. Now when I meet them I really stare. But they're not the same.

SHIRLEY. You've too much time on your hands. You start thinking. Can't think when you're working in the field can you? It's work work work, then you think, 'I wonder what the time is,' and it's dinnertime. Then you work again and you think, 'I wonder if it's time to go home,' and it is. Mind you, if I didn't need the money I wouldn't do any bugger out of a job.

VAL. Sukey's a freak round here but if she went to a city she wouldn't be, not so much. And I wouldn't.

SHIRLEY. You can take the baby off me if you want to do something.

VAL *takes the baby.*

SHIRLEY. We have to have something to talk about, Val, you mustn't mind if it's you. We'll soon stop. Same things people do in cities get done here, we're terrible here, you're the latest that's all. If it's what you want, get on with it. Frank left his wife two years ago and everyone's got used to that. What I can't be doing with is all this fuss you're making.

VAL. I can't hold the baby, it makes me cry. I'll do the ironing.

SHIRLEY. Give her here then. You don't want to be so soft. If you can't stop away from them, go back to them.

VAL. I can't leave Frank.

SHIRLEY (*to the baby*). Nothing's perfect is it, my poppet? There's a good girl.

SHIRLEY's husband GEOFFREY, sixty, comes in. By the end of the scene he has had the soup she prepared.

GEOFFREY. Dinner ready?

SHIRLEY. Just about.

VAL. Hello, Geoffrey.

GEOFFREY. Could do with some dinner.

SHIRLEY. Ent you got a civil tongue?

GEOFFREY. I don't hold you personally responsible, Val. You're a symptom of the times. Everything's changing, everything's going down. Strikes, militants, I see the Russians behind it. / All the boys want to do today

SHIRLEY. You expect too much Val. Till Susan was fifteen I never went out. Geoffrey wouldn't either, he wouldn't go to the pub without me. 'She's mine as much as yours', he says,

GEOFFREY. is drive their bikes and waste petrol. When we went to school we got beaten and when we got home we got beaten again. They don't want to work today.

SHIRLEY. 'I've as much right to stop in as what you have.'

Pause.

Lived right out on the fen till ten years ago. You could stand at the door with your baby in your arms and not see a soul from one week's end to the next. / Delivery van come once a week. My sister come at Christmas.

GEOFFREY. Don't talk to me about unemployment. They've got four jobs. Doing other people out of jobs. Being a horseman was proper work, but all your Frank does is sit on a tractor. Sitting down's not work. Common market takes all the work.

Pause.

Only twenty in church on Sunday. Declining morals all round. Not like in the war. Those French sending rockets to the Argies, forgotten what we did for them I should think. / Common market's a good thing for stopping wars.

SHIRLEY. I remember dad said to mum one Bank Holiday, 'Do you want to go out?' 'Yes please,' she said. 'Right,' he said, 'We'll go and pick groundsel.'

GEOFFREY. We had terrible times. If I had cracked tomatoes for my tea / I thought I was lucky. So why shouldn't you have

SHIRLEY. It's easy living here like I do now.

GEOFFREY. terrible times? Who are all these people / who come and live

SHIRLEY. Your bike'd be mud right up to the middle of the wheel.

GEOFFREY. here to have fun? I don't know anybody. Nobody does. Makes me wild. / My mother was glad she could

SHIRLEY. I'd think, 'If anything's after me it'll have to pedal.'

GEOFFREY. keep us alive, that's all. I'm growing Chinese radishes. I've never eaten Chinese food and I never will. Friend of mine grows Japanese radishes and takes them to Bradford, tries to sell them to the Pakis. Pakis don't want them. You want to pull yourself together, girl, that's what you want to do.

Scene Twelve

WOMEN *working down the field, stone picking. Bad weather.*
SHIRLEY, VAL, ANGELA, BECKY, NELL.

SHIRLEY (*sings*). Who would true valour see
  Let him come hither.
  One here will constant be
  Come wind come weather.
  There's no discouragement
  Shall make him once relent
  His first avowed intent
  To be a pilgrim.

It's hard singing in the wind. She's out of breath. No one joins in. They go on working silently. A military jet flies over, very loud. Only NELL looks up, angry.

They go on working.

MR TEWSON *comes out to watch.*

NELL. Sod this.

ANGELA. Keep up, Beck.

They reach the end of the field one by one and stop.

TEWSON. You're good workers, I'll say that for you.

NELL. Thank you very much.

TEWSON. Better workers than men. I've seen women working in my fields with icicles on their faces. I admire that.

SHIRLEY. Better than men all right.

NELL. Bloody fools, that's all.

ANGELA. What you crying for, Beck?

BECKY. I'm not.

SHIRLEY. Cold are you?

BECKY. No.

NELL. I am and so are you. What's going to make us feel better? Sun going to come out? You going to top yourself, Tewson, like that farmer over Chatteris?

TEWSON. She's funny in the head, isn't she.

ANGELA. She likes a joke.

TEWSON. Better watch her tongue.

SHIRLEY. She's a good worker, Mr Tewson, she don't do no harm.

NELL. Don't I though. Don't I do harm. I'll do you some harm one of these days, you old bugger.

ANGELA. What you made of, Becky?

SHIRLEY. You'll get used to it.

BECKY. I want to be a hairdresser.

TEWSON. That was a friend of mine you were speaking of. He found out he had six months to live. So he sold his orchards without telling anyone. Then before he started to suffer he took his life. Never said a word to his family. Carried it out alone, very bravely. I think that's a tragedy.

SHIRLEY. Well it is, yes.

TEWSON. Might clear up tonight.

TEWSON *goes*.

NELL. Best hope if they all top themselves. Start with the queen and work down and I'll tell them when to stop.

VAL *has only now finished her piece and joins them*.

SHIRLEY. All right, Val?

NELL. What's wrong with you?

VAL. Nothing.

NELL. Slows you up a lot for nothing.

VAL. It's like thick nothing. I can't get on. Makes my arms and legs heavy.

SHIRLEY. Still you're back with the kids, best thing. Just get on with it.

VAL *starts working again*.

NELL. You think I'm the loony. Is she eating? Sleeping?

ANGELA. She wants to go to the doctor, get some valium. (*She calls after* VAL:) A man's not worth it, mate. Kids neither.

NELL. I'm not working in this.

SHIRLEY. Don't be soft.

NELL. It's more than rain, it's splinters. Come on, Becky, you've had enough.

BECKY. Can I stop, Angela? Please, mum, can I?

ANGELA. I've had enough myself. Can't work in this.

SHIRLEY. I can.

NELL, ALICE, BECKY *move off.* SHIRLEY *starts working again.* VAL *works too, slower.*

Scene Thirteen

FRANK *and* VAL.

FRANK. What?

VAL. I wanted to see you.

FRANK. Why?

Silence.

Coming back to me?

VAL. No.

FRANK. Then what? What?

Silence.

I don't want to see you, Val.

VAL. No.

FRANK. Stay with me tonight.

Silence.

VAL. No.

FRANK. Please go away.

Scene Fourteen

Baptist women's meeting. MRS FINCH, *40, the minister's wife, is taking the meeting.* MAVIS *and* MARGARET, *thirties, are two of the congregation. Happy, loving. They are singing when* VAL *and* ALICE *arrive. Song: 'He's Our Lord'*

MRS FINCH. God is doing wonderful things among us.

MAVIS. I hope you'll stay with us because we all love each other.

ALICE. She's a friend of mine. I brought her.

MAVIS. Alice is a beautiful friend to have.

They sing: 'Thank you Jesus'.

ALICE *puts her arm round* VAL. MRS FINCH *comforts* VAL *too.* VAL *likes this.*

MRS FINCH. How lovely to be here again with all my sisters. And specially lovely to welcome new faces. We hope you will commit yourself to the Lord because with him you will have everything. And without him, nothing. This is not a perfect world and we can't be perfect in it. You know how we work cleaning our houses or weeding our gardens, but they're never perfect, there's always another job to start again. But our Lord Jesus is perfect, and in him we are made perfect. That doesn't mean I'm perfect. You know I'm not. I know you're not. But we've plunged ourselves body and soul in the water of God. Next Sunday Margaret will be baptised and she'll testify before the whole congregation. Tonight she's going to share with her loving sisters how she accepted the Lord into her life.

MARGARET. I thought I would be nervous but I'm not. Because Jesus is giving me strength to speak. I don't know where to begin because I've been unhappy as long as I can remember. My mother and father were unhappy too. I think my grandparents were unhappy. My father was a violent man. You'd hear my mother, you'd say, 'Are you all right, mum?' But that's a long time ago. I wasn't very lucky in my marriage. So after that I was on my own except I had my little girl. Some of you knew her. But for those of you who didn't, she couldn't see. I thought at first that was why she couldn't learn things but it turned out to be in her head as well. But I taught her to walk, they said she wouldn't but she did. She slept in my bed, she wouldn't let me turn away from her, she'd put her hand on my face. It was after she died I started drinking, which has been my great sin and brought misery to myself and those who love me. I betrayed them again and again by saying I would give it up, but the drink would have me hiding a little away. But my loving sisters in Christ stood by me. I thought if God wants me he'll give me a sign, because I couldn't believe he really would want someone as terrible as me. I thought if I hear two words today, one beginning with M for Margaret, my name, and one with J for Jesus, close together, then I'll know how close I am to him. And that very afternoon I was at Mavis's house and her little boy was having his tea, and he said, 'More jam, mum.' So that was how close Jesus was to me, right inside my heart. That was when I decided to be baptised. But I slid back and had a drink again and next day I was in despair. I thought God can't want me, nobody can want me. And a thrush got into my kitchen. I thought if that bird can fly out, I can fly out of my pain. I stood there and watched, I didn't open another window, there was just the one window open. The poor bird beat and beat round the room, the tears were running down my face. And at last as it found the window and went straight through into the air. I cried tears of joy because I knew Jesus would save me. / So I went to Malcolm and said 'Baptise me now because I'm ready'. I want to give myself over completely to God so there's nothing else of me left, and then the pain will be gone and I'll be saved. Without the love of my sisters I would never have got through.

VAL. I want to go.

ALICE. What? Val?

VAL. I'm going. You needn't.

ALICE. Aren't you well?

VAL. I feel sick.

ALICE. I'm coming, I'm coming.

VAL and ALICE leave.

They are outside alone. Night.

ALICE. It's a powerful effect.

VAL. Yes.

ALICE. I'm glad I brought you, Val.

VAL. I hated it.

ALICE. What do you mean?

VAL. That poor woman.

ALICE. She's all right now, thank the Lord.

VAL. She just liked a drink. No wonder. Can't you understand her wanting a drink?

ALICE. Of course I can. So can Jesus. That's why he forgives her.

VAL. She thinks she's rubbish.

ALICE. We're all rubbish but Jesus still loves us so it's all right.

VAL. It was kind of you to bring me. I loved the singing. And everyone was so loving.

ALICE. Well then? That's it, isn't it? Better than we get every day, isn't it? How cold everyone is to each other? All the women there look after each other. I was dreadful after the miscarriage and they saved my life. Let Jesus help you, Val, because I know you're desperate. You need to plunge in. What else are you going to do? Poor Val.

ALICE *hugs* VAL.

VAL. Can't you give me a hug without Jesus?

ALICE. Of course not, we love better in Jesus.

VAL. I'd rather take valium.

Scene Fifteen

VAL *and* FRANK.

VAL. I was frightened.

FRANK. When?

VAL. When I left you.

FRANK. I was frightened when you came back.

VAL. Are you now?

FRANK. Thought of killing myself after you'd gone. Lucky I didn't.

VAL. What are you frightened of?

FRANK. Going mad. Heights. Beauty.

VAL. Lucky we live in a flat country.

Scene Sixteen

IVY's *birthday.* IVY, *ninety,* MAY's *mother.* MAY, DEB, SHONA.
   They sing 'Happy Birthday' — 'dear mum' 'dear greatnan.'

IVY. Sometimes I think I was never there. You can remember a thing because someone told you. When they were dredging the mud out of the leat. I can picture the gantry clear as a bell. But whether I was there or someone told me, I don't know. Am I ninety? Ninety is it? 'Are you the bloody union man?' he'd say to Jack. 'Are you the bloody union man?' And Jack'd say, 'Are you going to pay him, because if not I'll splash it all over.'

MAY. Kiss your greatnan, Shona.

IVY. Ever kill a mouse, Shona? Tuppence a score. How old are you?

SHONA. Six.

IVY. I come home late from school on purpose so I wouldn't have to help mum with the beet. So I had to go without my tea and straight out to the field. 'You can have tea in the dark,' mum said, 'but you can't pick beet in the dark.' I were six then. Jack didn't wear shoes till he were fourteen. You could stick a pin in. Walked through the night to the union meeting. Fellow come round on his bike and made his speech in the empty street and everybody'd be in the house listening because they daren't go out because what old Tewson might say. 'Vote for the blues, boys,' he'd say and he'd give them money to drink. They'd pull off the blue ribbons behind the hedge. Still have the drink though. You'd close your eyes at night, it was time to open them in the morning. Jack'd be out in the yard at midnight. 'It's my tilley lamp and my wick,' I said, 'you owe me for that, Mr Tewson.' Chased him with a besom. 'You join that union, Jack,' I said. Nothing I couldn't do then. Now my balance takes me and I go over backwards.

There was five of us if you count my brother John that had his face bit off by the horse. 'Are you the bloody union man?' That quack who said he could cure cancer. Took the insides of sheep and said it was the cancer he got out. I didn't believe it but most of them did. Stoned the doctor's house when he drove him out. Welcomed him back with a brass band. Laudanum pills were a great thing for pain. Walk from Littleport to Wisbech in no time.

Ninety is it? Old fellow lived next to us, he was a hundred. He'd come out on the bank and shout out to the undertaker lived on the other side, 'Jarvis, Jarvis, come and make my coffin.' 'Are you the bloody union man?' he'd say. 'Yes I am,' he'd say, 'and what about it?' They don't marry today with the same love. 'Jarvis, come and make my coffin.'

Scene Seventeen

VAL *and* FRANK. *Outdoors. Night.*

FRANK. What you doing?

VAL. Can't sleep.

FRANK. Come back to bed. I can't sleep with you up.

VAL. I'm not too bad in the day, am I?

FRANK. Go back to them then.

VAL. Tried that.

FRANK. He'd have you back still.

VAL. Tried it already.

FRANK. If I went away it might be easier. We'd know it was for definite.

VAL. You could always come back. I'd come after you.

FRANK. I'd better kill myself hadn't I. Be out of your way then.

VAL. Don't be stupid.

FRANK. The girls are all right, you know.

VAL. I just want them. I can't help it. I just want them.

FRANK. I left my family.

VAL. Not for me.

FRANK. I didn't say it was for you. I said I manage.

VAL. I'm the one who should kill themself. I'm the one can't get used to how things are. I can't bear it either way, without them or without you.

FRANK. Try and get them off him again.

VAL. We've been over that. They're his just as much. Why should he lose everything? He's got the place. We've been over that.

FRANK. Let's go to bed. I'm cold.

VAL. One of us better die I think.

Scene Eighteen

WOMEN *playing darts in the pub.* SHIRLEY, ALICE, ANGELA, NELL.

    FRANK *alone. He is joined by* NELL.

NELL. How's Mr Tewson then?

    FRANK *doesn't answer.*

    You're his right-hand man.

FRANK. I do my job.

NELL. I'm nobody's right hand. And proud of it. I'm their left foot more like. Two left feet.

FRANK. Bloody trouble-maker.

NELL. I just can't think like they do. I don't know why. I was
brought up here like everyone else. My family thinks like
everyone else. Why can't I? I've tried to. I've given up now. I
see it all as rotten. What finished me off was my case. Acton's
that closed down.

FRANK. Made trouble there.

NELL. I wanted what they owed me — ten years I'd topped their
effing carrots. You all thought I was off the road. You'll never
think I'm normal now. Thank God, eh?

NELL *goes to play darts.*

ANGELA *joins* FRANK.

ANGELA. All alone?

FRANK. Just having a pint.

ANGELA. How's Val?

FRANK. Fine.

ANGELA. Never thought you were the type.

FRANK. What type?

ANGELA. After the married women.

FRANK. I'm not.

ANGELA. I got married too soon you know. I think forty-five's a
good age to get married. Before that you want a bit of fun.
You having fun?

FRANK. No.

ANGELA. Maybe it's gone on too long.

FRANK. Should never have started.

ANGELA. You can always try again.

FRANK. Too late for that.

ANGELA. You've got no spirit, Frank. Nobody has round here.
Flat and dull like the landscape. I am too. I want to live in the
country.

FRANK. What's this then?

ANGELA. I like more scenery. The Lake District's got scenery. We went there on our honeymoon. He said we were going to live in the country. I wouldn't have come. Real country is romantic. Away from it all. Makes you feel better.

FRANK. This is real country. People work in it. You want a holiday.

ANGELA. I want more than two weeks. You wouldn't consider running away with me?

FRANK. I'm thinking of killing myself.

ANGELA. God, so am I, all the time. We'll never do it. We'll be two old dears of ninety in this pub and never even kissed each other.

ANGELA *goes back to the darts.*

NELL *talks to* FRANK *again.*

NELL. Tell you something about Tewson. He's got a sticker in the back of his car, Buy British Beef. And what sort of car is it?

FRANK. Opel.

NELL. There, see?

FRANK. He's sold the farm, hasn't he? He's just a tenant himself. He had to, to get money for new equipment.

NELL. So who's boss? Who do you have a go at? Acton's was Ross, Ross is Imperial Foods, Imperial Foods is Imperial Tobacco, so where does that stop? He's your friend, I know that. Good to your brother, all that. Nice old fellow.

FRANK. That's right.

NELL. You don't think I'm crackers, do you?

FRANK. No.

NELL. I don't think you are neither. You cheer up anyway. Don't give them the satisfaction.

FRANK. I'm fine, thank you.

NELL. You never see a farmer on a bike.

Scene Nineteen

ANGELA *and* BECKY. ANGELA *has an exercise book of* BECKY's.

BECKY. It's private.

ANGELA. Nothing's private from me.

BECKY. Give it back.

ANGELA. Ashamed of it? I should think so. It's rubbish. And it's dirty. And it doesn't rhyme properly. Listen to this.

BECKY. No.

ANGELA. You're going to listen to this, Becky. You wrote it, you hear it. (*She reads:*)

When I'm dead and buried in the earth
Everyone will cry and be sorry then.
Nightingales will sing and wolves will howl.
I'll come back and frighten you to death.

Who? Me, I suppose. Me?

BECKY. No.

ANGELA. Who?

BECKY. Anyone.

ANGELA. Me, but you won't. You've got a horrible mind. (*She reads:*)

The saint was burnt alive
The crackling fat ran down.
Everyone ran to hear her scream
They thought it was a bad dream.

Eugh.
Oh this is very touching. (*She reads:*)

Mother where are you sweet and dear?
Your lonely child is waiting here.

BECKY. No, no, shut up.

ANGELA. If you could see what's done to me
You'd come and get me out of here. /

My love for you is always true —

BECKY. Mother where are you sweet and dear?
  Your lonely child is waiting here.
  If you could see what's done to me /
  You'd come and get me out of here.
  My love for you is always true
  Mother mother sweet and dear.

ANGELA. You shut up, Becky. I never said you could. Becky I'm
  warning you. Just for that you've got to hear another one. Not
  a word. Now this is dirty. Wrote this in bed I expect. (*She
  reads:*)

He pressed her with a passionate embrace
Tears ran down all over her face.
He put his hand upon her breast
Which gave her a sweet rest.
He put his hand upon her cunt
And put his cock up her.

That doesn't even rhyme, you filthy child.

He made love to her all night long.
They listened to the birdsong.

What puts filth like that into your head? What if I showed
your dad?

BECKY. No.

ANGELA. Lucky I'm your friend.

BECKY. I'll never do another one.

ANGELA. I don't care. Hope you don't. You should do one for
  Frank.

BECKY. I don't love Frank.

ANGELA. You love Frank, do you? I hadn't guessed that.

BECKY. I don't. I said I don't. You do.

ANGELA. What? Watch out, Becky, don't get me started. Make a
  poem about him dying.

BECKY. He's not dead?

ANGELA. He tried to. He took some pills, but Val got the ambulance.

BECKY. When? When?

ANGELA. I'll make one.

Frank was miserable and wished he was dead.
He had horrible thoughts in his head.
He took some pills to end his life.
Too bad he got saved by his silly wife. Not his wife.
Now he's got to go on being alive
Like all the rest of us here who survive.
I stay alive so Frank may as well.
He won't go to heaven and he's already in hell.
Poor Frank was never very cheerful —

She stops, stuck for a rhyme.

BECKY. Except when he goes to the pub and then he's beerful.

They laugh.

ANGELA. Those pills must have made him feel sick
And wish he'd never followed his prick.

They laugh.

BECKY. That's quite good.

Silence.

ANGELA. Becky, why do you like me? I don't want you to like me.

Silence.

BECKY. Poor Frank. Imagine.

Scene Twenty

VAL *and* SHONA.

VAL. Shona. I hoped I'd see you.

SHONA. I've been to the shop for nan.

VAL. What did you get?

SHONA. Sliced loaf, pound of sausages, butterscotch Instant Whip, and a Marathon for me and Deb, I'm going to cut it in half. The warts have gone off my hands because nan said get some meat and she got some meat yesterday and it was liver and it wasn't cooked yet but she cooked it for tea but I didn't like it but I liked the bacon. She cut off a bit and rubbed it on my warts, Deb said Eugh. Then me and Deb buried it in the garden near where nan's dog's buried. There was one here and one here and another one and some more. I watched 'Top of the Pops' last night and I saw Madness. Deb likes them best but I don't.

VAL. What do you like?

SHONA. I don't like Bucks Fizz because Mandy does. She's not my friend because I took the blue felt tip for doing eskimos and Miss said use the wax ones but I have to have felt tips so I got it and Mandy says she won't choose me when it's sides.

VAL. She'll probably have forgotten by tomorrow.

SHONA. Nan says you mustn't cut your toenails on Sunday or the devil gets you.

VAL. It's just a joke.

SHONA. My toenails don't need cutting because nan cut them already. What hangs on a tree and it's brown?

VAL. What?

SHONA. Des O'Conker. What's yellow and got red spots?

VAL. The sun with measles.

SHONA. Knock knock.

VAL. Who's there?

SHONA. A man without a hat on.

VAL. What?

SHONA. Why did the mouse run up the clock?

VAL. Why?

SHONA. To see what time it is.

VAL. Shona, when you grow up I hope you're happy.

SHONA. I'm going to be an eskimo. Mandy can't because she can't make an igloo. She can come on my sledge. Nan said to be quick.

VAL. Why does an elephant paint its toenails red?

SHONA. Footprints in the butter.

VAL. No, that's how you know it's been in the fridge.

SHONA. Why then?

VAL. So it can hide in a cherry tree.

SHONA. Deb knows that one. Nan doesn't.

SHONA *goes*.

Scene Twenty-One

VAL *and* FRANK.

VAL. I've got it all worked out.

VAL *pulls up her shirt*.

VAL. Look. I marked the place with a biro. That's where the knife has to go in. I can't do it to myself.

FRANK. I can't even kill a dog.

VAL. I've been feeling happy all day because I decided.

FRANK. You marked the place with a biro.

VAL. I know it's funny but I want it to work.

FRANK. It's ridiculous.

VAL. Just say you love me and put the knife in and hold me till it's over.

VAL *gives* FRANK *the knife*.

FRANK. We don't have to do this.

Silence.

VAL. Say you love me.

FRANK. You know that.

VAL. But say it.

FRANK. I nearly did it. I nearly killed you.

He puts the knife down.

VAL. Do it. Do it.

FRANK. How can I?

VAL. Just do it.

Silence.

FRANK. Aren't you cold? I'm shivering. Let's have a fire and some tea. Eh, Val?

FRANK *picks up an axe and is about to go out.*

Remember —

VAL. What?

FRANK. Early on. It wasn't going to be like this.

Silence.

Why do you — ?

VAL. What?

FRANK. All right then. All right.

He kills her with the axe.

He puts her body in the wardrobe.

He sits on the floor with his back against the wardrobe door.

She comes in through the door on the other side of the stage.

VAL. It's dark. I can see through you. No, you're better now.

FRANK. Does it go on?

VAL. There's so much happening. There's all those people and I know about them. There's a girl who died. I saw you put me in the wardrobe, I was up by the ceiling, I watched. I could have gone but I wanted to stay with you and I found myself coming back in.

There's so many of them all at once. He drowned in the river carrying his torch and they saw the light shining up through the water.

There's the girl again, a long time ago when they believed in boggarts.

The boy died of measles in the first war.

The girl, I'll try and tell you about her and keep the others out. A lot of children died that winter and she's still white and weak though it's nearly time to wake the spring — stand at the door at dawn and when you see a green mist rise from the fields you throw out bread and salt, and that gets the boggarts to make everything grow again. She's getting whiter and sillier and she wants the spring. She says maybe the green mist will make her strong. So every day they're waiting for the green mist.

I can't keep them out. Her baby died starving. She died starving. Who?

She says if the green mist don't come tomorrow she can't wait. 'If I could see spring again I wouldn't ask to live longer than one of the cowslips at the gate.' The mother says, 'Hush, the boggarts'll hear you.'

Next day, the green mist. It's sweet, can you smell it? Her mother carries her to the door. She throws out bread and salt. The earth is awake.

Every day she's stronger, the cowslips are budding, she's running everywhere. She's so strange and beautiful they can hardly look. Is that all? A boy talks to her at the gate. He picks a cowslip without much noticing. 'Did you pick that?'

She's a wrinkled white dead thing like the cowslip.

There's so many, I can't keep them out. They're not all dead. There's someone crying in her sleep. It's Becky.

FRANK. I can hear her.

VAL. She's having a nightmare. She's running downstairs away from Angela. She's out on the road but she can't run fast enough. She's running on her hands and feet to go faster, she's swimming up the road, she's trying to fly but she can't get up because Angela's after her, and she gets to school and sits down at her desk. But the teacher's Angela. She comes nearer. But she knows how to wake herself up, she's done it before, she doesn't run away, she must hurl herself at Angela — jump! jump! and she's falling — but it's wrong, instead of waking up in bed she's falling into another dream and she's here.

BECKY *is there.*

BECKY. I want to wake up.

VAL. It's my fault.

BECKY. I want to wake up. Angela beats me. She shuts me in the dark. She put a cigarette on my arm. She's here.

ANGELA *is there.*

ANGELA. Becky, do you feel it? I don't, not yet. There's a pain somewhere. I can see so far and nothing's coming. I stand in a field and I'm not there. I have to make something happen. I can hurt you, can't I? You feel it, don't you? Let me burn you. I have to hurt you worse. I think I can feel something. It's my own pain. I must be here if it hurts.

BECKY. You can't, I won't, I'm not playing. You're not here.

ANGELA *goes.*

NELL *crosses on stilts.*

NELL. I was walking out on the fen. The sun spoke to me. It said, 'Turn back, turn back.' I said, 'I won't turn back for you or anyone.'

NELL *goes.*

SHIRLEY *is ironing the field.*

SHIRLEY. My grandmother told me her grandmother said when times were bad they'd mutilate the cattle. Go out in the night and cut a sheep's throat or hamstring a horse or stab a cow with a fork. They didn't take the sheep, they didn't want the meat. She stabbed a lamb. She slashed a foal. 'What for?' I said. They felt quieter after that. I cried for the hurt animals. I'd forgotten that. I'd forgotten what it was like to be unhappy. I don't want to.

FRANK. I've killed the only person I love.

VAL. It's what I wanted.

FRANK. You should have wanted something different.

The BOY *who scares crows is there.*

BOY. Jarvis, Jarvis, come and make my coffin.

VAL. My mother wanted to be a singer. That's why she'd never sing.

MAY *is there. She sings.*

Girls' Song

SERIOUS MONEY

Serious Money was first performed at the Royal Court Theatre, London, on 21 March 1987, with the following cast:

SCILLA TODD *a LIFFE dealer*	Lesley Manville
JAKE TODD *Scilla's brother, a commercial paper dealer*	Julian Wadham
GRIMES *a gilts dealer*	Gary Oldman
ZACKERMAN *a banker with Klein Merrick*	Alfred Molina
MERRISON *a banker, co-chief executive of Klein Merrick*	Burt Caesar
DURKFELD *a trader, co-chief executive of Klein Merrick*	Allan Corduner
GREVILLE TODD *Jake and Scilla's father, a stockbroker*	Allan Corduner
FROSBY *a jobber*	Julian Wadham
T.K. *personal assistant*	Burt Caesar
MARYLOU BAINES *an American arbitrageur*	Linda Bassett
JACINTA CONDOR *a Peruvian businesswoman*	Meera Syal
NIGEL ABJIBALA *an importer from Ghana*	Burt Caesar
BILLY CORMAN *a corporate reader*	Gary Oldman
MRS ETHERINGTON *a stockbroker*	Linda Bassett
DUCKETT *chairman of Albion*	Allan Corduner
MS BIDDULPH *a white knight*	Lesley Manville
DOLCIE STARR *a PR consultant*	Linda Bassett
GREVETT *a DTI inspector*	Julian Wadham
SOAT *president of Missouri Gumballs*	Allan Corduner
GLEASON *a Cabinet Minister*	Allan Corduner

Other parts played by the Company and members of the Royal Court Young Peoples' Theatre.

KEYBOARDS	Colin Sell

Director	Max Stafford-Clark
Designer	Peter Hartwell
Lighting Designer	Rick Fisher
Sound Designer	Christopher Shutt
Musical Director and Arranger	Colin Sell
Assistant Director	Bo Barton
Stage Manager	Bo Barton

Futures song: words by Ian Dury, music by Micky Gallagher
Freedom song: words by Ian Dury, music by Chaz Jankel

The play includes a scene from *The Volunteers, or The Stockjobbers* by Thomas Shadwell, 1692.

Note on layout

A speech usually follows the one immediately before it BUT:

1: When one character starts speaking before the other has finished, the point of interruption is marked / .

eg. SCILLA: Leave the country. / Are you serious?
    JAKE.   They've taken my passport.

2: A character sometimes continues speaking right through another's speech:

eg. JAKE: No, it's just . . . I'm in a spot of bother with the authorities/but it's no problem, I'm sorting it
    SCILLA: What have you done?
    JAKE: out, it's more what the sorting might lead to

3: Sometimes a speech follows on from a speech earlier than the one immediately before it, and continuity is marked*.

eg. BRIAN: How much would it cost to shoot her through the head?*
    TERRY: You can't get rid of your money in Crete.
                       Hire every speedboat, drink till you pass out, eat
                       Till you puke and you're still loaded with drachs.
    MARTIN: ⎱
    DAVE: ⎰   Drach attack! drach attack!
    VINCE: Why's a clitoris like a filofax?
    DAVE and OTHERS: Every cunt's got one.
    BRIAN: *And he says five grand.

where 'shoot her through the head?' is the cue to 'You can't get rid and 'And he says five grand.'

4: Superior numerals appear where several conversations overlap at the same time.

eg. DAVE: I've got a certain winner for the 3.30 if anyone's interested.[4]
    BRIAN: You haven't paid us yesterday's winnings yet.
    DAVE: Leave it out, Brian, I always pay you.
    KATHY: [4]Come on gilts. 2 at 4 the gilts.

where Kathy starts speaking as Dave finishes his first speech, but Brian and Dave continue their dialogue at the same time.

ACT ONE

A scene from The Volunteers or The Stockjobbers by Thomas Shadwell.

HACKWELL, MRS HACKWELL, *and two jobbers.*

HACKWELL.
Well, have ye been enquiring? What Patents are they soliciting for, and what Stocks to dispose of?

FIRST JOBBER.
Why in truth there is one thing liketh me well, it will go all over England.

MRS HACKWELL.
What's that, I am resolved to be in it Husband.

FIRST JOBBER.
Why it is a Mouse-Trap, that will invite all mice in, nay rats too, whether they will or no: a whole share before the Patent is fifteen pound; after the Patent they will not take sixty: there is no family in England will be without 'em.

SECOND JOBBER.
I take it to be great Undertaking: but there is a Patent likewise on foot for one walking under Water, a share twenty pound.

MRS HACKWELL.
That would have been of great use to carry messages under the ice this last frost, before it would bear.

HACKWELL.
Look thee Lamb, between us, it's no matter whether it turns to use or not; the main end verily is to turn the penny in the way of stock jobbing, that's all.

FIRST JOBBER.
There is likewise one who will undertake to kill all fleas in all the families in England –

SECOND JOBBER.
There is likewise a Patent moved for, of bringing some Chinese Rope-Dancers over, the most exquisite in the world; considerable men have shares in it.

FIRST JOBBER.
But verily I question whether this be lawful or not?

HACKWELL.
Look thee, brother, if it be to a good end and that we ourselves
have no share in the vanity or wicked diversion thereof by
beholding of it but only use it whereby we may turn the penny,
always considered that it is like to take and the said Shares will sell
well; and then we shall not care whether the aforesaid dancers
come over or no.

SECOND JOBBER.
There is another Patent in agitation for flying; a great virtuoso
undertakes to outfly any post horse five mile an hour, very good for
expresses and intelligence.

MRS HACKWELL.
May one have a share in him too?

SECOND JOBBER.
Thou mayst.

HACKWELL.
Look ye Brethren, hye ye into the city and learn what ye can; we
are to have a Consultation at my house at four, to settle matters as
to lowing and heightening of Shares: Lamb, let's away, we shall be
too late.

*Three different dealing rooms simultaneously. All have screens and
phones.*

Shares – GREVILLE
Gilts – GRIMES *and* OTHERS
Paper – JAKE *and* OTHERS

Shares

GREVILLE (*on phone*)
It's quite a large placement and what we've done is taken them
onto our own books, one of the first deals of this kind we've done
since Big Bang, yes . . . It's Unicorn Hotels, whom of course you
know, they've acquired a chain of hotels in Belgium, and the main
thing is they're a perfect mirror of their hotels here, 70 per cent
business, 3 and 4 star. They acquired them for sixteen million, the
assets are in fact valued at eleven million but that's historic and
they're quite happy about that. The key to the deal is there's
considerable earnings enhancement. It was a private owner who got
into trouble, not bankrupt but a considerable squeeze on his assets,
and they were able to get them cheap. I can offer you a million

shares, they're 63 to 4 in the market, I can let you have them for 62½ net. At the moment the profits are fourteen million pretax which is eleven million, the shares pay 4.14 with a multiple of 13.3. With the new hotels we expect to see a profit of twenty million next year paying 5.03 with the multiple falling to 12, so it's very attractive. This is only the beginning of a major push into Europe. Essentially the frontiers have been pushed back quite considerably.

The following is heard after the overlapping scenes finish:

I would show them to Joe in New York but it's only five in the morning. He's usually quite yielding when he's in bed but I don't think he'd want to start a whole new story.

Gilts

GRIMES *and his* MATE *in gilts dealing room of Klein Merrick.* SCILLA *on Liffe floor. Each has two phones.*

GRIMES (*to* MATE).
  I'm long on these bastards.
MATE (*to* GRIMES).
  3's a nice sell. They'd be above the mark.

GRIMES (*on phone*).
  Scilla? Sell at 3.
SCILLA (*on two phones. To floor*).
  10 at 3. 10 at 3.
  (*On phone 2.*)
  That's March is it?

MATE (*phone*).
  6 Bid.

GRIMES (*phone*).
  What you doing tonight?

SCILLA (*to floor*).
  4 for 10. 4 for 10. Are you looking at me?
  4 for 10.

GRIMES (*phone*).
  Scilla?

SCILLA (*phone 1*).
  Yes, we sold them.

GREVILLE (*phone*).
  What you doing tonight?

SCILLA (*phone 1*).
  Going out later – hang on.

(*Phone 2.*) 4 for 10 nothing doing. Will he go to 5?
(*To floor.*) 5 for 10! 5 for 10!

GRIMES (*phone 2*).
Bid 28 at the figure.

MATE (*to* GRIMES).
I'm only making a tick.

GRIMES (*to* MATE).
Leg out of it.

SCILLA (*phone*).
Grimes?

GRIMES (*to* MATE).
Futures are up.
(*Phone.*) Champagne bar / at six?

MATE (*phone*).
Selling one at the figure.
(*To* GRIMES.) I'm lifting a leg.

SCILLA (*phone 2*).
We got you 10 for 5 bid, OK?
(*Phone 1.*) Yes, champagne bar at 6.
(*Puts down phone 1, answers phone 2 again.*) Yes?

GRIMES (*phone 2*).
Get off the fucking line, will you please?

MATE (*to* GRIMES).
01 bid, 01 offered.

SCILLA (*phone 2*).
No, it's 5 bid at 6. I can't help you, I'm afraid.

GRIMES (*phone 1*).
Is it a seller or a buyer?
(*To* MATE.) He don't want to take us because he don't want to
pay commission.

MATE (*phone 2*).
Offered at 4. Thanks very much but nothing done.

GRIMES (*phone 2 to* SCILLA).
5 March at 28.
(*To* MATE.) What are we long of?

SCILLA (*phone 1*).
No, it's gone to 29.

GRIMES (*to* MATE).
29 bid.
(*Phone 2.*) All right, 9 for 5.

SCILLA (*to floor*).
  9 for 5! 9 for 5! / Terry!
MATE (*phone 1*).
  You'd better keep up, I'll be off in a minute.
GRIMES (*phone 1*).
  I'll make you a price, what do you want to do?
MATE (*to* GRIMES).
  Bid 4.
  (*Phone 1*.) I'm off, I'm off.
GRIMES (*to* MATE).
  They was offered at 4.
  (*Phone 1*.) Bid 3.
SCILLA (*phone 2*).
  Three month sterling opened at 89.27 for March delivery and
  they've been trading in a 4 tick range.
MATE (*phone 2*).
  Can't help you.
  (*To* GRIMES.) There's a fucking seller trying to make us pay up.
GRIMES (*phone 2*).
  Bid 3.
MATE (*to* GRIMES).
  I think we should buy them.
GRIMES (*phone 1*).
  Bid 4, bid 4 at 6.
SCILLA (*phone 2*).
  No, it's quite quiet.
  (*Phone 1*.) 9 for 5 a deal.
GRIMES.
  You're getting good at this. Extra poo tonight.
MATE (*phone 1*).
  2 bid at 5.
  (*To* GRIMES.) Am I still cheap?
GRIMES (*to* MATE).
  Sold 5 for 9 bid.
SCILLA (*phone 2*).
  Looks as if they may finish at 25.
MATE (*to* GRIMES).
  What shall we do overnight?
GRIMES (*to* MATE).
  I'll be long.

MATE (*to* GRIMES).
  You don't want to be too long.
GRIMES (*phone 2*).
  Closing out now at 4.
  GRIMES *starts going down a list on a piece of paper marking prices.*
MATE (*to* GRIMES).
  Doing the long end?
GRIMES (*to* MATE).
  How shall I mark these, 2 or 3?
MATE (*to* GRIMES).
  3.
GRIMES (*to* MATE).
  Does it make a lot of difference to you?
MATE (*to* GRIMES).
  Hundred thousand.
GRIMES (*to* MATE).
  You must have made that trading in the last half hour.
SCILLA (*to floor*).
  If you've lost any cards, Dave, I'm not helping you.

Paper.
JAKE *and another dealer sitting side by side. Two salespeople who shout from behind. Loud. American sound though they're not.*
SALES 1.
  I tell you what else here. Sweden / just called.
SALES 2.
  If you want to jump on the Hambro / bandwagon you better hurry.
JAKE (*phone*).
  We also have two Japanese. I'll make those 88 6.
SALES 1.
  Sweden first 10 has been called. How do we go these days?
DEALER (*phone*).
  There's also an issue coming out again.
SALES 2.
  The new BFC for World Bank.
DEALER (*to* JAKE).
  I've just sold some paper / like that.
SALES 1 (*phone*).
  They're not taking. I'll give you a level.

DEALER (*to* JAKE).
  Shall we go ahead?

JAKE (*to* DEALER).
  Let's wait a few / minutes before we have the whole world crashing
  down on us.

SALES 2.
  Chase Corporation 68 88.
  He can bash you in with one arm. He's got a black belt in karate.

SALES 1.
  He's a very nice guy.

JAKE (*phone*).
  What I suggested was swapping into something longer, threes or
  whatever.

DEALER (*phone*).
  I've been talking to Hong Kong.

JAKE (*phone*).
  Because / it's up to 14.

SALES 1.
  We're waiting on the Bundesbank here.

JAKE (*phone*).
  He doesn't care at the moment, / David.

SALES 2.
  Paris intervention rate / still at 8%. Buy 10.

DEALER (*phone*).
  It's done.

JAKE (*phone*).
  Band two are at thirteen-sixteenths. It's a softer tone today.

DEALER (*to* JAKE).
  He just said to me 590, I said it's done. He would have said 610
  wouldn't he?

JAKE (*to* DEALER).
  Get back on.

SALES 1.
  We have Frankfurt here, Frankfurt, guys.
  Discount rate remains 3%. Lombard 5. Buy twos / twos, twos,
  twos.

DEALER (*phone*).
  He said to me 595 . . . OK that would be great.

SALES 2.
  Tokyo one month 4.28125.

DEALER (*phone*).
  Discretion is my middle name. Tell me tell me tell me tell me . . .
  you said you were going to tell me after lunch . . . / What, you
  bought some? It's

SALES 1.
  He broke an arm wrestling with a treasury bond dealer.

DEALER.
  going down . . . How fast do you want it to go down? . . . You're
  in profit, it's 7–8 right.

JAKE (*phone*).
  Listen, guy. Listen listen listen listen listen.
  Lombard Intervention steady at 5.

DEALER.
  If it takes at 6 . . . no it's not going to take at 5 . . . if it goes to 7
  . . . You're such a sleaze, you're not really a man of honour, you
  said you'd tell me after lunch . . . / I didn't know

SALES 2.
  The guy dealt with Citibank but got back to them too late.

DEALER.
  that's what your best was . . . tell me tell me . . . Futures are
  crashing off.

JAKE (*phone*).
  The Mori poll put the Tories four up.

SALES 1.
  We're going to lose power any minute, that's official.

DEALER.
  What the fuck?

JAKE (*phone*).
  So the three month interbank sterling rate – no it's a tick under –

SALES 1.
  We have Milan three months 11½.

JAKE (*phone*).
  There's a discrepancy between band 2 and band 3 . . . I thought it
    might give us some arbitrage possibilities.

DEALER (*phone*).
  Come on come on come on guy.

SALES 1.
  What's with the ECU linked deposits for Nomura?

SALES 2.
  Now hurry hurry hurry guys hurry.

Power goes – no screens, no phones.

Outcry.

JAKE.

Marvellous.

DEALER.

If the market moves in a big way we'll get cremated.

JAKE.

They left us a whole lot of orders we're meant to be filling.

DEALER.

I have to speak to Zurich.

SALES 2.

So what happens now?

SALES 1.

They go elsewhere, bozo.

Liffe Champagne Bar

SCILLA (*trader with Liffe*), *her brother* JAKE (*commercial paper dealer*), GRIMES (*gilts dealer*) *drinking together in the champagne bar.*

GRIMES.

Offered me sixty right? So next day
The other lot seventy-five. OK,
So I go to the boss and go 'I don't want to trouble
You', and he goes 'All right you cunt,
Don't mess about, how much do you want?'
So I go – I mean why not – I go 'Double
What I'm getting now', and he goes 'fuck off'. Meanwhile
Zackerman rings and – this'll make you smile –
He goes, he goes, I'll give you a hundred grand,
Plus the car and that, and fifty in your hand,
But no thinking about it, no calling back,
This is my first and last. I say, Zac,
A good dealer don't need time to think.
So there you go. Have another drink.

JAKE.

So there's twenty-seven firms dealing gilts.

SCILLA.

Where there used to be two.

GRIMES.

Half the bastards don't know what to do.

JAKE.
Those of you that do have got it made.
SCILLA.
And all twenty-seven want ten per cent of the trade.
GRIMES.
So naturally there's going to be blood spilt.
JAKE.
Ten per cent? Go in there and get fifty.
SCILLA.
Everyone thinks it's Christmas and it's great to know they love you,
But you mustn't forget there's plenty still above you.
(There's at least two dozen people in the City now getting a million
   a year.)
Think of the ones at the top who can afford
To pay us to make them money, and they're on the board.
GRIMES.
They're for the chop.
JAKE (*simultaneously*).
I'm on the board.
SCILLA.
                    True, you're on the board,
But how many of us will make it to the top?
If we've a Porsche in the garage and champagne in the glass
We don't notice there's a lot of power still held by men of
   daddy's class.
GRIMES.
No but most of them got no feel
For the market. Jake's the only public schoolboy what can really
   deal.
JAKE.
That's because I didn't go to university and learn to think twice.
SCILLA.
Yes, but they regard us as the SAS.
They send us in to smash the place up and get them out of a
   mess.
GRIMES.
Listen, do you want my advice?
SCILLA.
They'll have us on the scrap heap at thirty-five,
JAKE.
I've no intention of working after I'm thirty.

SCILLA.
    Unless we're really determined to survive
        (which I am).

JAKE.
    It probably means you have to fight dirty.

GRIMES.
    Listen, Nomura's recruiting a whole lot of Sloanes.
    Customers like to hear them on the phones
    Because it don't sound Japanese.
    If you want to get in somewhere big –

SCILLA.
                                    Grimes, don't be such a sleaze.
    Daddy could have got me in at the back door
    But you know I'd rather be working on the floor.
    I love it down with the oiks, it's more exciting.

JAKE.
    When Scilla was little she always enjoyed fighting
        (better at it than me).

SCILLA.
    But it's time to go it alone and be a local.
    I'm tired of making money for other people.

GRIMES.
        (Going to make a million a year?

SCILLA.
        I might do.)

GRIMES.
    I tell you what though, Zackerman can recruit
    The very best because he's got the loot.

JAKE. I told him for what he's getting from my team, why be a
        meanie?
    He got rid of the BMW's and got us each a Lamborghini.
    He's quite a useful guy to have as a friend.
    So I thought I'd ask him home for the weekend.
    He's talking to dad about amalgamation.
    Klein needs a brokers.

SCILLA.
                        And daddy needs a banker.

GRIMES.
    Won't survive without one, poor old wanker.

JAKE.
    I told dad / his best bet's a conglomeration.

GRIMES.
Some of them old brokers is real cunts.

JAKE.
But I've got to go to Frankfurt Friday night,
So Scilla, you can drive him down, all right?

SCILLA.
Yes, that's fine. I wonder if he hunts.

JAKE *leaves.*

SCILLA.
I'm beginning to find Zackerman quite impressive.
    (I wonder how he got to where he is now?)

GRIMES.
My school reports used to say I was too aggressive
    (but it's come in quite useful).
My old headmaster wouldn't call me a fool again.
I got a transfer fee like a footballer. He thought I was a hooligan.
He goes, you fool boy, you're never going to get to work,
What use is a CSE in metalwork?
I could kiss his boots the day he kicked me out of school.

GRIMES *and* SCILLA *leave.*
ZAC *enters.*

ZAC.
So cut the nostalgia. I'm the guy they're talking about, Zac.
I'm here for my bank, Klein Merrick, to buy up jobbers and
    brokers.
And turn the best of them into new market makers.
The first time I realised how fast things were changing was
    something that happened at Klein's in New York a few years back.

MERRISON, *a banker, co-chief executive officer of Klein Merrick.*
DURKFELD, *a trader, co-chief executive officer of Klein Merrick.*

MERRISON.
So I told them 83 was a great year,
Profits up ten million on 82.
But we can do better than that by far.
Leveraged buyouts are the way to go
    (I told them).
Take Krafft, put up three million to acquire Hoffman Clocks,
Borrowed the rest of the fifty million, a year later makes a public
    offering, and pockets a whole fifty million plus he retains thirty

million of stock.
That's eighty million dollars on his initial three.
And that's from taking a risk instead of a fee.
We advise other people on acquisitions.
They make the serious money. Fuck it all.
The company should take its own positions.
Partners should be willing to risk their own capital.
I told them, man is a gambling animal.
Risk is one of our company traditions.
Old Benny Klein took risks, the latest news
Meant profit, they'd say on Wall Street 'Let the Jews
Have that one,' and he would. Imagine the scene,
Guy comes and says 'I can make flying machines.'
Benny puts up the money, doesn't bat an eye,
He says, 'OK, so make the machines fly.'
When I was working with Henry under Nixon

DURKFELD.

Jack, I heard this speech before.

MERRISON.

There were quite a few things needed fixing –

DURKFELD.

Jack, I heard it already.

MERRISON.

So, I'm a bore.
Tell me, do you have a problem, Eddie?
I trust you've no more trouble with your wife?
It's a while since you took a good vacation.
None of us gets enough relaxation
        (I never even make it upstairs to the gym get a massage).
Tell me what you want out of life.

DURKFELD.

I'm a simple guy, Jack. I walk in the woods
And shoot things. I don't talk so good
As you, I'm good on my own, I shoot straight,
I don't say, 'Shall I, shan't I?' You guys deliberate
One hell of a lot. I walk on my own
And I know I could run this show on my own.

MERRISON.

I'm not sure I understand what you're saying.

DURKFELD.

I don't have the same alternatives
A guy like you does. You say Henry

Where I say Kissinger. You want to move?
You've talked about some possibility.
For me, this is enough.
I don't look beyond this company.
You ready to go do that stuff?

MERRISON.

Let me understand what you're saying here.

DURKFELD.

I want to go solo running Klein.
I'm saying I'm suggesting you resign.

MERRISON.

I just promoted you.

DURKFELD.

Should I be grateful?

MERRISON.

I made you my equal.

DURKFELD.

Jack. I hate you.
Didn't you know that? You're not so smart.
You're too important to smell your own fart.

MERRISON.

Eddie. I need to understand your problem.

DURKFELD.

There's guys don't want me in their club.
I don't give a rat's ass.
Those guys would have looked the other way
And let the cattle trucks pass.
        (I don't want to play golf with those bastards. I don't even
        play golf. I can walk without hitting a ball.)
I'm good at my job.
I stay on the floor with the guys.
Screw the panelling, screw the Picassos, I am not interested in office
    size.
        (You like lunch, you have lunch.)
I run the best trading floor in New York City,
And traders make two dollars profit for this company
    for every dollar made by you bankers.
And you treat us like a load of shit.
You make me your equal, I'm meant to say thanks
For that? Thanks, Jack. Come off it.
I make this company eighty million dollars and bankers pocket
    most of that profit.
Bankers get on the cover of Time.

MERRISON.

Brother, can you spare a dime?

DURKFELD.

I do OK, sure, I'm not talking greed.

I'm talking how I mean to succeed.

(My father came to this country – forget it.)

Which of us does this company need?

I'm talking indispensable.

MERRISON.

And my father? You think I'm some kind of patrician?

I was sweeping floors in my uncle's delicatessen

So don't –

The company needs us both. Be sensible.

There's two aspects to the institution.

Nobody means to imply they underestimate your invaluable
contribution.

I need to understand what you're saying here so let's set a time
we can have a further talk.

DURKFELD.

You don't seem to get it. You're sitting in my chair. Walk.

ZAC. And the guy walked.

(He walked with twenty million dollars but he walked.)

The financial world won't be the same again

Because the traders are coming down the fast lane.

They don't even know it themselves, they're into fucking or
getting a Porsche, getting a Porsche *and* a Mercedes Benz.

But you can't drive two cars at once.

If you're making the firm ten million you want a piece of the
action.

You know you're got it made the day you're offered stock
options.

There are guys that blow out, sure, stick too much whitener up
their nose.

Guy over forty's got any sense he takes his golden handshake and
goes.

Because the new guys are hungrier and hornier,

They're Jews from the Bronx and spicks from Southern
California.

It's like Darwin says, survival of the fit,

Now, here in England, it's just beginning to hit.

The British Empire was a cartel.

England could buy whatever it wanted cheap

And make a profit on what it made to sell.
The empire's gone but the City of London keeps
On running like a cartoon cat off a cliff – bang.
That's your Big Bang.
End of the City cartel.
Swell.
England's been fucking the world with interest but now it's a
   different scene.
I don't mind bending over and greasing my ass but I sure ain't
   using my own vaseline.

Now as a place to live, England's swell.
Tokyo treats me like a slave, New York tries to kill me, Hong
   Kong
I have to turn a blind eye to the suffering and I feel wrong.
London, I go to the theatre, I don't get mugged, I have classy
   friends,
And I go see them in the country at the weekends.

The meet of a hunt. On horses are ZAC, GREVILLE, *stockbroker,
his daughter* SCILLA, *and other hunt members, e.g.,* MRS
CARRUTHERS, LADY VERE, MAJOR *and* FARMER. FROSBY,
jobber, comes in late, on foot to watch.

MRS CARRUTHERS.
The hound that I walked goes up front with the best.

FARMER.
The best of the pack is that cunning old bitch.

LADY VERE.
His fetlocks swell up so I'll give him a rest.

MAJOR.
Went over his neck and headfirst in the ditch.

GREVILLE.
Stand still will you dammit, whatever's the matter?

MAJOR.
Bottle of sherry he won in a raffle.

LADY VERE.
Hunt saboteurs made a terrible clatter.

MRS CARRUTHERS.
You can't hold her, Greville, in only a snaffle.

FARMER.
It's colder today but the going's much quicker

SCILLA.
Jumped onto the lawn and straight over the vicar.

GREVILLE.
  Good morning
MAJOR.
              Good morning
GREVILLE.
                      Good morning
MRS CARRUTHERS.
                              Hello
GREVILLE.
  Good morning
LADY VERE.
              Good morning
GREVILLE.
                          I don't think you know
  Mr Zackerman here, my colleague and guest.
MRS CARRUTHERS.
  The hound that I walked goes up front with the best.
GREVILLE.
  Mr Zackerman wanted to join us of course
  And Mrs Carruthers provided a horse.
MRS CARRUTHERS.
  He's terribly clever, won't put a foot wrong,
  When he hears the horn blow he'll be off like a rocket.
  His mouth's rather hard and he is very strong,
  Don't fight him, he'll pull out your arms by the socket.
  There's not a horse safer and not a horse faster,
  So don't step on hounds and don't override master.
LADY VERE.
  Making the most of the beautiful weather.
GREVILLE.
  American fellow, a friend of my daughter,
  Colleague of mine, we'll be working together.
SCILLA.
  Left behind at the gate and came off in the water.
FARMER.
  The best of the pack is that cunning old bitch.
MAJOR.
  Went over his neck and headfirst in the ditch.
LADY VERE.
  Hunt saboteurs made a terrible clatter.

GREVILLE.
  Stand still will you dammit, whatever's the matter?
  Priscilla insists upon working for Liffe.
  I was terribly doubtful and so was my wife.
      (The London International Financial Futures Exchange, terrible
      place, full of the most frightful yobs.)
  Hardly the spot for a daughter of mine
  But she buys her own horses and takes her own line.

LADY VERE.
  We've lost our head gardener, bit of a chore.

MAJOR.
  I'm sure Mr Zimmerman's hunted before.

ZAC.
  Not a great deal but I have been out a few times in Ireland with the
    Galway Blazers.

LADY VERE.
  In that case I'm sure you can give us a lead.

MRS CARRUTHERS.
  The girl's putting far too much oat in his feed.

SCILLA.
  Is it true?

ZAC.
      Well I saw both the start and the finish.
  I was on foot drinking plenty of Guinness.

SCILLA.
  There aren't any gates and I'm not waiting for you.

ZAC.
  You're so tenderhearted, that's why I adore you.

FARMER.
  It's colder today but the going's much quicker

SCILLA.
  Jumped onto the lawn and straight over the vicar.
      (So Klein have taken over Daddy. How long will he last? Five
      years?)

ZAC.
  (He could be lucky.)

GREVILLE.
  Not joining us Frosby? Find horses a bore?

MRS CARRUTHERS.
  He's terribly clever, won't put a foot wrong.

LADY VERE.
  We've lost our head gardener, bit of a chore.
CARRUTHERS.
  His mouth's rather hard and he is very strong.
FROSBY.
  I like a stroll to see the meet.
  I'm happier on my own two feet.
  Is that chap there the American?
GREVILLE.
  Yes, it's Klein's Zac Zackerman.
FROSBY (to himself).
  Yanks go home. Yanks are robbers.
GREVILLE.
  Zac, I want you to meet a colleague I've done a great deal of
  business with over the years, one of the jobbers.
  Mr Frosby, Mr Zackerman.
ZAC.
  Hi Mr Frosby, I can't really talk.
  This horse won't stand still and he won't even walk.
MRS CARRUTHERS.
  When he hears the horn blow he'll be off like a rocket.
  Don't fight him, he'll pull out your arms by the socket.
GREVILLE.
  No more long lunches for me, Frosby, no more lying in bed.
  It's up at six now in the godforsaken
  Dark cold mornings. On the bright side
  The company does an excellent egg and bacon.
FROSBY.
  Some things change, some things don't end.
  After all, a friend's a friend.
MRS CARRUTHERS.
  So don't step on hounds and don't override master.
ZAC.
  Is this horse going to do what I tell it Priscilla?
MRS CARRUTHERS.
  There's not a horse safer and not a horse faster.
SCILLA.
  It's generally known around here as a killer.
ZAC.
  (When I end up in bed with a broken leg I only hope you're going
  to look after me.)

SCILLA.

(Drop dead, bozo.)

The horn blows.

They all go in a rush, leaving FROSBY *alone.*

FROSBY.

The stock exchange was a village street.
You strolled about and met your friends.
Now we never seem to meet.
I don't get asked much at weekends.

Everyone had a special name.
We really had a sense of humour.
And everybody played the game.
You learned a thing or two from rumour.

Since Big Bang the floor is bare,
They deal in offices on screens.
But if the chap's not really there
You can't be certain what he means.

I've been asked to retire early.
The firm's not doing awfully well.
I quite enjoy the hurly burly.
Sitting alone at home is hell.

I can't forgive Greville. He's gone with that Yankee bank buying its way in, that Yak, Whack, whatsisname, Zac, trying to keep up with his children. His son Jake's one of these so-called marketmakers. Some of us have been making markets for thirty years. And his daughter Scilla works with those barrow boys in Liffe you'd expect to see on a street corner selling Christmas paper and cheap watches, they earn more than I do, they won't last.

I have a constant funny ache.
I can't see straight because of grief.
I really think my heart will break.
Revenge would give me some relief.

So now I'll phone the DTI,
Who want a clean and honest City.
Jake's no better than a thief
And why should I have any pity?
I've cried and now my friends can cry.

I've had the odd tip from Greville, I know he gets it from Jake and there's far more than I ever see. Let the DTI investigate. The City's not mine any more so let it fall.

I love the masters in their pink
I'm glad traditions still exist.

I think I'll go and have a drink.
I love the valley in the mist.
 (I'm very frightened.)

ZAC *phones* TK *and* MARYLOU BAINES *in New York.*

TK.
This is Marylou Baines' personal assistant.

ZAC.
It's Zac, I've got to speak to her this instant.
I know it's 3 a.m. your time, but I know she's awake.
Tell her it's about Jake.

TK.
Hi, Zac, this is TK here. Can I help you? What's the problem? Is it urgent?

ZAC.
Stop talking like a tubful of detergent /.
I got to speak to her now and not now but five minutes ago.

MARYLOU.
Zac, is there something I should know?

ZAC.
Jake's dead. They think it's suicide.

MARYLOU.
         Thank you, Zac.
Jake was a nice guy but I haven't heard from him since some time back.

She hangs up and speaks to TK.

MARYLOU.
Put anything from Jake Todd in the shredder.

ZAC *phones* JACINTA CONDOR *in London.*

ZAC.
Jacinta, it's me. / Bad news. Jake's been found shot. /
It looks like suicide because he was in some kind of trouble with
 the DTI / though so far nobody seems to know exactly what.

JACINTA. Zac! What? My God.
He was the English colleague I like the most (except for you).
I hope I never meet his unhappy ghost.
I look forward to meeting. /

  JACINTA *phones* NIGEL AJIBALA.

JACINTA.
Nigel, have you read the newspapers today?

NIGEL.
  No, what's the matter?

JACINTA.
                    Don't panic, OK?

This overlaps with CORMAN *phoning* ZAC.

CORMAN.
  Zac, have you seen the fucking *Times* this morning?
  Why didn't Todd give us any warning?
  Why didn't he tell us about the DTI?
  Do you think he's talked?

ZAC.
                    Deny. Deny. Deny.
  (Let them see what they can prove.)

This overlaps with JACINTA *phoning* MARYLOU.

JACINTA.
  Marylou, the delivery. You think we should wait a week?

MARYLOU.
  Hold off for twenty-four hours, OK? We'll speak.

NIGEL *phones* CORMAN.

NIGEL.
  Mr Corman, I'm deeply shocked that anyone associated with your
    company should be touched by the slightest breath / of scandal.

CORMAN.
  The deal's in no way affected by his death.
    (The deal is the priority.)

This overlaps with MARYLOU *phoning* ZAC.

MARYLOU.
  Zac, your news is causing a certain amount of tension.

ZAC.
  Can we still rely / on you?

MARYLOU.
                    Sure, but never mention.

CORMAN *phones* MARYLOU *and gets* TK *on answering machine.*

CORMAN.
  TK? Marylou?

TK (*on machine*).
  Hello, this is the office of Marylou Baines. I'm afraid Ms Baines is
    not available right now to come to the phone,
  But if you wish to leave a message for her or for TK, her

personal assistant, please speak for as long as you wish after the tone.

CORMAN.
Fuck.

ZAC.
I went with Scilla to identify her brother Jake's body which was kind of a mess.
Then we stopped for coffee, which was making me late for work, but it was a special occasion, I guess.
It'd be good if we could handle this
So you don't get associated with anything too scandalous.
   (Just stick to No comment, and let them make things up.)

SCILLA.
Zac, I told the police I had breakfast with Jake at Klein Merrick yesterday morning.
Just to say hello. But in fact he gave me a warning.

ZAC.
They know the DTI paid him a visit.

SCILLA.
But it wasn't just that. He was frightened of . . .

ZAC.
                                  Well, what is it?

SCILLA.
What was Jake like? charming, clever, idle.
He won, he lost, he cheated a bit, he treated it all as a game.
Can you really imagine him killing himself for shame?
   (He didn't know what honour meant.)
He wasn't telling me he was suicidal,
He was telling me . . . You may think it's absurd, but
I'm certain he must have been murdered.

   JAKE *and* SCILLA *at breakfast*.

JAKE.
Don't let me worry you, I'm probably imagining it.

SCILLA.
Have you shared a needle?

JAKE.
Not Aids, I'm perfectly / healthy.

SCILLA.
At work they ask for tea in an Aids cup, they mean / a disposable because the dishwasher –

JAKE.
  Listen, I've a problem. Listen.
SCILLA.
  What?
JAKE.
  No, never mind, you know I left my diary at your place last week? /
  You haven't got it on you?
SCILLA.
  Yes, do you want – ?
  No, but I could – .
JAKE.
  Hold onto it. No, maybe you'd better – No, hold onto it. You can
  always burn it later. Fine.
SCILLA.
  What is this?
JAKE.
  No, it's just . . . I'm in a spot of bother with the authorities / but
  it's no problem. I'm sorting it
SCILLA.
  What have you done?
JAKE.
  out, it's more what the sorting out might lead to / because once I
  start –
SCILLA.
  Are you going to prison?
JAKE.
  No, I'm not going to be in trouble at all by the look of it but that's
  the problem, I'm going to be very – I'm probably paranoid about
  this.
SCILLA.
  Leave the country. / Are you serious?
JAKE.
  They've taken my passport. I just wanted to let you know in case
  anything –. I haven't mentioned any of this to Dad / but when the
  shit hits –
SCILLA.
  No, don't get Dad started. Can I do anything?
JAKE.
  No, it's all under control. I feel better talking to you. I didn't go to
  bed, you know how you get in the night. / If anything happens to
  me –

SCILLA.
  Have some more coffee.
  What? Like what?

JAKE.
  Shall I get you another croissant?

SCILLA.
  So what have they found out?

JAKE.
  Jam with it?

SCILLA.
  If you've been making a fortune, I think it's very unfair of you not
  to have let me in on it.

JAKE.
  Forget it.

SCILLA.
  So you haven't got Aids. That's great.

  SCILLA *and* ZAC *continue.*

SCILLA.
  So clearly he was frightened because he'd agreed to tell the DTI
    who else was involved
      (and they'd want to shut him up).
  If I can find out who they are, the murder's halfway solved.
  There's plenty of names and numbers here in his diary
  So I'll start by contacting anyone who looks interesting and making
    my own inquiry.

ZAC.
  Are you OK?

SCILLA.
                    Yes, I feel terrific.

ZAC.
  You'll just find out a whole lot of colleagues' numbers, that won't
    tell you anything specific.
  My number's probably there for God's sake.

SCILLA.
  I'm going to find out who killed Jake.

ZAC.
  Take a sedative, have a sleep, and then see how you feel.

SCILLA.
  Nobody sleeps in the middle of a deal.

ZAC.
You've always been lucky, Scilla, don't abuse it.
  (I mean, these guys, whoever they are, they could be dangerous.)
You're crazy at the moment, / you're in shock.

SCILLA.
                              / I'm in shock, I might as well use it.
(I'll let you know what happens.)

ZAC.
Jake's death was a shock for me too, and I kept thinking about a
  friend of his I'd just met.
She was called Jacinta Condor and we'd all been doing business
  together and I knew she'd be quite upset.

  ZAC *phones.*

ZAC.
I want to order a number of tropical birds . . .
Maybe twenty? . . .
Don't tell me what kinds because I won't have heard . . .
Yeah, parrots, cockatoos, marmosets (no, is that a monkey?)
  lovebirds, sure, stick in some lovebirds, an assortment in good
  bright colours, I don't care the exact number but plenty . . .
No not a cage so much as a small aviary . . .
Deliver it gift wrapped to Jacinta Condor, at the Savoy and the
  card should read, 'From Zac, as a small tribute to your beauty
  and bravery.'

  SCILLA *and* GREVILLE *at* GREVILLE'*s house.*

SCILLA.
Pull yourself together, Daddy.
What does it matter if Jake was a baddy?

GREVILLE.
Poor boy. Who would have thought? I'd rather he'd been a failure.
He used to want to emigrate and sheepfarm in Australia.
He always would rush in. He had no sense of balance.
He could have done anything, you know, he had so many talents.
Musician. Politician. No obstacles in his way.
If he'd done something else, he'd be alive today.

SCILLA.
What was he up to, Daddy?
If it was just insider dealing,
It's not a proper crime like stealing.
They say it's a crime without a victim.
He'd hardly kill himself just because the DTI nicked him.

GREVILLE.
Dammit, why should he die for something that's not a crime?
> (It's not illegal in America, Switzerland, Japan, it's only been illegal here the last few years.)

You have to use what you know. You do it all the time.
That used to be the way you made a reputation.
By having first class contacts, and first class information.
One or two greedy people attracted attention to it.
Suddenly we all pretend Englishmen don't do it.

SCILLA.
So what was he up to, Daddy?

GREVILLE.
> I've simply no idea.

SCILLA.
Do you know who these people are? I've got Jake's diary here.
Marylou Baines.

GREVILLE.
Marylou Baines
Was originally a poor girl from the plains.
She set out to make whatever she wanted hers
And now she's one of America's top arbitrageurs
> (second only to Boesky).

SCILLA.
Condor, Jacinta.

GREVILLE.
A very smart lady from South America who comes here every winter.
Europe sends aid, her family says thanks
And buys Eurobonds in Swiss banks.

SCILLA.
Corman.

GREVILLE.
Billy Corman,
William the Conqueror, the great invader,
A very highly successful dawn raider.
I don't want to hear any more. Did Jake have friends like this?
I wish he was still a baby and giving daddy a kiss.

SCILLA.
Pull yourself together, daddy.
Did he give you information?

GREVILLE.
> Absolutely not.

SCILLA.
I thought you might be in on it.
GREVILLE.

                    In on what?

SCILLA.
Then aren't you annoyed he kept it secret from you and didn't
    share what he'd got?
GREVILLE.
Scilla –
SCILLA.
Jake had powerful friends, that's clear from what you said.
And that means powerful enemies who'd like to see him dead. /
    (He wasn't brave enough to kill himself.)
GREVILLE.
Absolute nonsense.
SCILLA.
I'll start by calling on Corman.
GREVILLE.
                    Security's terribly tight /
He'll never agree to see you.
SCILLA.
Don't worry. I'll get in somehow and see if it gives him a fright.
GREVILLE.
Scilla, you don't seem to realise. Newspapers across the nation.
I could easily lose my job if I lose my reputation.
You and the yobs you work with are hardly worth a mention
    (no one expects them to have any standards),
But I have to keep very quiet, and not attract attention.
Until it's all blown over I think I'll stay in bed.
SCILLA.
You never liked me, Daddy. Jake was always your favourite.
GREVILLE.
I don't like the louts you work with.
SCILLA.
                    And now you've got to pay for it.
GREVILLE.
Poor Scilla, are you suffering from feelings of rejection?
SCILLA.
If I find out you were in on it, you're not getting my protection.
GREVILLE.
        (In on killing Jakey?)

SCILLA.

    (In on anything.)

GREVILLE.

  Darling, don't be difficult when I'm so awfully sad.

  I think Jakey was playing in a bigger league than Dad.

SCILLA.

  I've always been ashamed of you. Your drink and your pomposity.

GREVILLE.

  Scilla, the oiks you work with have made you a monstrosity.

SCILLA.

  If I find you're implicated in my investigation / the *News of the
  World* can have you.

GREVILLE.

  Darling, you always did have a vivid imagination
    (like poor Mummy).

ZAC.

  When I left Scilla I rushed back to work because Corman's bid for
    Albion was just reaching its peak.

  He'd been spending the night in the office the whole of that week.

  We'd been building to this since the day a few months ago

  When Albion started, just one of several deals, easy and slow.

  It started like this:

CORMAN *a corporate raider*. BROWN *and* SMITH, *industrial spies.*
ZAC. MRS ETHERINGTON, *a stockbroker.*

CORMAN.

  The analysts' reports are satisfactory,

  Predicting high industrial synergy.

  I'll have to close the chocolate biscuit factory.

  The management lacks drive and energy.

  Tell me what you learnt about the company.

BROWN.

  I spent a week posing as a secretary.

  The working atmosphere is very pleasant.

  A shock to the chairman would be salutary,

  His presence at his desk is just symbolic,

  He disappears to fish and shoot pheasant.

  The managing director's alcoholic,

  But still he's everybody's favourite,

  His drink 'n' driving ends him up in court,

  He gets the company to pay for it.

  The middle management are sound but lazy,

The details will be found in my report.
The chief of marketing is going crazy.

CORMAN.
Excellent, they'll put up no resistance.
I'll sack them all, put in new staff, maybe promote a few of their
    assistants.
Too late for them to make the company over,
Because I am going to take the company over.
Now to the larger and still more inviting
Albion Products. Fuck the analysts,
What do they know? It's that much more exciting.
Is their chairman gaga too and their managing director always
    pissed?

SMITH.
No, he's sober and quite competent.
Duckett runs a rather happy ship.
I hear the head of sales is impotent,
A very old director broke his hip,
Apart from that they all seem quite efficient.
Employees feel considerable loyalty.
The factory has been visited by royalty.

CORMAN.
Albion is obviously deficient
In management. Old-fashioned and paternal.
These figures stink. I can make it earn a l-
ot more for its shareholders, who are
The owners after all. It will be far
Better run, streamlined, rationalised,
When it forms part of Corman Enterprise.
        (And anyway I want it.)
Right. Both targets will be hit.
Now summon my war cabinet.

CORMAN.
Zac, I really like this company.

ZAC.
It'll take some stalking. It's a big confident beast.

CORMAN.
But I'm told you're a takeover artiste.
Can you get it for me?

ZAC.
Corman, you're the buyer. /
I pride myself I can acquire any company the client

CORMAN.

Anyway, if it was easy it'd bore me.

ZAC.

may desire.

(If I was defending Albion you wouldn't stand a chance.)

We're going to need a whole lot of finance from somewhere.

CORMAN.

Zackerman, that's your ride on the funfair.

Now Etherington. I want you to start a stealthy
Purchase of Albion stock. Don't frighten them.
The price must hardly move, just look quite healthy.
We'll put nooses round their necks and suddenly tighten them.

ETHERINGTON.

Albion's price is three hundred and ten.
I shall acquire twenty million ordinary
Shares on your behalf, imperceptibly.
And I shall let you know of any change.

ZAC.

We've got to get out here and ride the range.

ETHERINGTON.

I don't think you'll find me lacking in assiduity.

CORMAN.

I'm a great admirer of Etherington's ingenuity.

(Top brokers for fuck's sake, what do you think I am? Brokers
to royalty.)

When we tell Duckett I own five per cent

(plus what else I'll control by then)

He'll suddenly wonder where his company went.

DUCKETT.

DUCKETT.

I'm Duckett. I enjoy the *Financial Times*.
It's fun reading about other people's crimes.
My company Albion's price is looking perky.
I think I'll buy that villa in the south of Turkey.

CORMAN, ETHERINGTON, ZAC.

CORMAN.

So what's on the agenda today?
Let's get all the rubbish out of the way.

ETHERINGTON.

We're failing to acquire Mayfield.

CORMAN.
                    Except I never fail.
  Why don't I suggest we'll leave them alone, provided they pay us
    greenmail?
        (American term, greenbacks, blackmail, everybody happy?)

ZAC.
  If they really want to defend themselves they'll do a leveraged
    management buyout to get back their shares.

ETHERINGTON.
  So we make a hundred million.

CORMAN.
                              And the lousy company's still theirs.

ZAC.
  (Plus a whole lot of debt.
  In the US there's an oil company borrowed four billion dollars to
  fight off T. Boone Pickens and now they're paying three million a
  day interest.)

CORMAN.
  So that money goes to improving our position
  With Albion, my favourite acquisition.
  How we doing?

ETHERINGTON.
  The Albion share is up to three fifteen
  And you now own 4.9% /
  Not 5%, so no need to disclose.

CORMAN.
  Excellent.
  So now?

ETHERINGTON.
            Now we contact institutions,
  The pension fund managers who hold
  Millions of Corman shares and indicate
  It would be wise to lend us their support.

ZAC.
  Can we rely on them?

ETHERINGTON.
            They won't say no,
  For otherwise a succulent new issue
  Next time we have one might not come their way.

CORMAN.
It's their duty to keep our price up after all.
The poor old pensioners won't want it to fall.
ETHERINGTON.
We also intimate it's in their interest
To buy up Albion so that more and more
Albion shares belong to friends of ours. /
A fan club and not a concert party.
ZAC.
A concert party.
CORMAN.
                  Come on, don't fart
About, it's a concert party.
ETHERINGTON.
A fan club (of disinterested supporters) is respectable and legal.
A concert party (of people you've induced to support you)
   reprehensible.
This is a line you may trust us to tread /
(as long as necessary)
CORMAN.
Tread in the shit. Tread where you need to tread.
Now purchases must also be made by Metgee, Upkate,
Battershot, Mountainring
ZAC.
                and Stoneark.
CORMAN.
Five nominee companies registered in the Turks and Caicos Islands,
   Panama and Sark.
They can each acquire 4.9%.
ZACKERMAN.
               And one of our problems is solved.
You'll acquire a huge share in Albion without anyone suspecting
   you're involved.
ETHERINGTON.
We're still left with a cashflow problem.
Albion's more than three times as big as Corman.
CORMAN.
Zac, you understand how a buyer works.
Time you stepped in and showed us a few fireworks.
ZAC.
The last couple of years in the United States it's been takeover
   mania

And I guess the deals there have gotten somewhat zanier.
Junk bonds are a quick way of raising cash, but it's kind of a hit 'n' run method, which doesn't go down too well in Britain.
You don't have millions of private investors crazy to gamble on
  debt.

ETHERINGTON.
  No, you wouldn't succeed with junk bonds here just yet.
    But the British public's financial education
  Is going in leaps and bounds with privatisation.
  Sid will buy junk soon. / Just wait.

ZAC.
  Great.

CORMAN.
  So no junk. How do we stand with the loan?
  Can you show us some tricks?

ZAC.
  The money can be supplied from a number of banks here and in the
    United States led by our own.
  I got the rate of interest down a couple of ticks.
  In return they want us to mortgage Upkate, Battershot and
    Stoneark, and form five new nominee companies so we can wind
    up Albion and redistribute its assets,
  Which gives us tax neutral benefits.
  We repay the loan and the interest by selling off certain sections of
    Albion after it's been acquired.

CORMAN.
  Some people might think I'm a touch overgeared.
  Our ratio of debt to equity is – ?

ETHERINGTON.
                         Four hundred per cent.

CORMAN.
  Taking into account the billion and a half you've lent.
    (But being in debt is the best way to be rich.)

ZAC.
        (America's national debt is over a trillion dollars.)

CORMAN.
  So we've got the money. (*To* ETHERINGTON.) Get out there and
    spend it.
  We've got Albion.

ZAC.
            No, let's wait and see how Duckett's going to defend it.
  (Poison pills? shark repellent?)

ETHERINGTON.
  If Albion's shares should fall some of our friends would be in for a
  shock.
ZAC.
  A deposit with us could provide a guarantee.
CORMAN.
  And then there's the question of buying Corman stock.
  To buy your own shares is illegal and cannot be.
ZAC.
  But the bank can buy them, no problem and we'll let you know
  later about our fee.
CORMAN.
  Zackerman, my very sincere thanks.
  This is the kind of service I expect from our banks.
  Etherington, I'm sure you've plenty to do.
  I'll join you later for a glass of poo.

  ETHERINGTON *goes.*

  We don't breathe a word of this to anyone.
  But someone could breathe a word to Marylou.
  I think she could step in here and have some fun.
  But I don't want direct contact and nor should you.
ZAC.
  No problem.

  CORMAN *goes.*

  So I called Jake Todd.

  ZAC *and* JAKE *drinking in champagne bar. Late night. Both
  drunk.*
JAKE.
  What did you think of the family?
ZAC.
  Quite a mansion.
JAKE.
  You could buy yourself something equally handsome.
      (Or three.)
ZAC.
  Why do the British always want land?
      (In Paris or New York you live in an apartment, why do the
      English need gardens?)
JAKE.
  You're not upper class without it, you're too American to
  understand.

ZAC.
You don't make money out of land, you make money out of money.

JAKE.
It's a dream. Woods. Springtime. Owning the spring.
What's so funny?

ZAC.
Is that your dream?

JAKE.
I never dream. / (I never sleep)

ZAC.
Because it's come to an end.
Young kids like you making money now – and I mean the ones who've never had it, not like you – they're going to come up with new ways to spend
Because they're going to come up with new dreams.

JAKE.
I'll tell you, Zac, sometimes it seems . . .

ZAC.
What?

JAKE.
I don't know, what were we saying?

ZAC.
When?

JAKE.
Forget it.

ZAC.
Tell you something, Jake. Give Albion some attention.

JAKE.
I could get on the blower to Marylou / and just give it a mention.

ZAC.
Don't tell me.

JAKE.
Tell you something. I fancy the ocean.
Instead of land. I'd like to own a big cube of sea, right down to the bottom, all the fish, weeds, the lot.
There'd be takers for that.

ZAC.
Sure, it's a great notion.

JAKE.
Or air. Space. A square metre going straight up into infinity.

ZAC.
And a section of God at the top.

JAKE.
                        Oh yes, I'll make you a market in divinity (any day).

MARYLOU BAINES *and* TK *in New York.*

TK.
There's a message from Jake Todd in London.
He recommends buying shares in Albion.

MARYLOU.
Can I take it this is so far completely secret?

TK.
Yes, when it gets out it'll really move the market.

MARYLOU.
Are you trading in this stock on your own account?

TK.
Not for a very considerable amount.

MARYLOU.
You'll soon be setting up your own show.

TK.
No, Ms Baines, I wouldn't go, you taught me everything I know.
I really admire your style, Miss Baines.
      (You're a great American.)

MARYLOU.
Sure, arbitrage is a service to the community,
And it's too bad they're prosecuting people you'd have thought
    would have had immunity.
By buying and selling large amounts of stock we ensure the
    market's liquidity –
I work twenty-four hours a day and take pills for stomach acidity –
So companies can be taken over easy,
Which means discharging superfluous workers, discontinuing
    unprofitable lines, the kind of stuff that makes your lazy
    inefficient management queasy.
So considering the good we do the US economy,
I reckon we should be treated with a little more respect and
    bonhomie.

I have a hundred and fifty telephone lines because I depend on
    information.

TK.
(What's the least a person could start with?

MARYLOU.
I started small – say twenty?)
You need to know what's going on in businesses all over the nation,

TK.
(And Britain)

MARYLOU.
You take a lot of gambles, / which keeps the adrenalin flowing and is why it's known as risk arbitrage,

TK.
(Ms Baines, I admire your guts)

MARYLOU.
Though if you know how to get the right information the risk isn't all that large.

TK.
But since Boesky was caught out –

MARYLOU.
Sure, some of our informants are more cautious,
But information's what it's all about,
So I reckon it's business as usual and only now and then does nervousness make me nauseous.
You and I both know what it's like to have other guys stepping on your head,
And you can't get on when you're dead.

TK.
So you think it's worth me giving it a shot?

MARYLOU.
Get out, TK, and give it all you've got.
After all, what happens if you fail?

TK.
I end up broke and in jail.

MARYLOU.
Look, with his own collapse Boesky did the biggest insider deal of all:
The SEC let him unload over a billion dollars worth of shares ahead of announcing his fall.
So paying a hundred million dollar fine was pretty minimal.
Which is great, because he overstepped some regulations, sure, but the guy's no criminal.

Like he said about his own amazing wealth.
'Greed is all right. Greed is healthy. You can be greedy and still
  feel good about yourself.'

Buy twenty million shares in Albion today.
  (That's in addition to what you've bought.)
In a few weeks when Corman announces the bid and the price
  shoots up, we sell quick, take the profit, and on our way.

DUCKETT, *chairman of* ALBION, *and* MS BIDDULPH, *a white
knight. Both from the north.*

DUCKETT.
Biddulph, I'm desperate. Corman's going to take over Albion. Shall
I pay him greenmail and take on half a million debt? Shall I do one
of those American things, poison pills, shark repellent, make some
arrangement so the company comes to bits if he gets hold of it?
Shall I cash in my Eurobond and emigrate?

BIDDULPH.
Now Duckett, you're under quite serious attack.
It's time to fight back.

DUCKETT.
                         I'd like to fight back.

BIDDULPH.
I know you'd give Corman a terrible fright
If you had a white knight.

DUCKETT.
                         I'd like a white knight.

BIDDULPH.
Now Corman will throw the top management out
But I'd guarantee that your job would remain.

DUCKETT.
Say it again?

BIDDULPH.
                  Your job would remain.
But Corman would throw the top management out.
That's what it's about.

DUCKETT.
                     That's what it's about.
But you'd guarantee that my job would remain.

BIDDULPH.
So if I should step in would I have your support?

DUCKETT.
Would you have my support!

BIDDULPH.
                    That's just what I thought.

DUCKETT.
It's very unfair to be attacked like this. I run a highly efficient
company. I've sacked the finance director and the chief of
marketing who'd both been with the company ten years. I've closed
two factories and made five hundred people redundant. No one can
say I'm not a hardhitting management.

BIDDULPH.
Hold on, Duckett, you've got it all wrong. Think of it from the PR
angle. You're an old-fashioned firm. A good old English firm that
has the loyalty of its employees and the support of the local
community. You spend a lot of money on research and
development.

DUCKETT.
I spend some, I suppose, but I always consider the shareholders'
dividend and the short-term –

BIDDULPH.
No no no, you consider the long term. You're the kind of company
the CBI likes. Corman means short-term profit. You mean industrial
development. Think of Pilkington, Duckett. You're loved locally.
Children like you. Dogs.

DUCKETT.
What I dream of you know is cornering the coffee market. Brazil
needs to be hammered into the ground and the price kept right
down low and –

BIDDULPH.
No, Duckett, not at the moment.

You're a sweet English maiden, all shining and bright.
And Corman's the villain intent upon rape
And I'm the white knight

DUCKETT.
                    You're the white knight

BIDDULPH.
And the knight has a fight and the maiden escapes
And when I'm in charge I'll put everything right.
    (We can talk about closing Scunthorpe later.)

ZAC.

ZAC.

Jake couldn't have picked a worse time to die if he hated my guts.
Corman hadn't slept for forty-eight hours and was driving
himself and everyone else nuts.
Jake was my one real friend over here. It's not that I don't care,
But the deal could get clinched today and I just don't have the
attention to spare.

(If he's put me in the shit with the DTI I'll worry about
that later.)

CORMAN, ZAC, ETHERINGTON *and others of* CORMAN's *team.*

CORMAN.

Right, you all know the position,
Biddulph's stepped in as a white knight to stop us making the
acquisition.
Don't worry, she hasn't a chance, it's just a try on.
We've 15% of Albion stock plus 20% fan club holdings whose
votes we can rely on.
Two aims:
One. Boost our own share price by getting anyone at all to buy
Corman stock to increase the value of our offer. Two. Get
anyone at all who'll vote for us to buy up Albion shares.
So in a word, get anyone you can by any means you can to buy
both our stock and theirs.
From today we're coming to the crunch.
Nobody's going out any more to lunch.

(You can cancel dinner too.)

From today, we're going for the gold.
Put your family life and your sex life on hold.
A deal like this, at the start you gently woo it.
There comes a time when you get in there and screw it.
So you get the stock. And I don't care how you do it.

ETHERINGTON.

My reputation for integrity
Compels me to suggest you should take care.
No point succeeding if that same success
Destroys you and your company forever.
Remember Guinness.

CORMAN.

Thank you, Etherington. Some of us have work to do here.

ZAC.

There's no question there are thin lines and this is definitely a grey
area.

And since Guinness it's a whole lot scarier.
You can't play ball if you keep off the grass.
So promise whatever you have to. Peddle your ass.
Let's give it all we've got and worry later.

CORMAN (*to* ETHERINGTON).
Are you standing there as some kind of arbitrator?
You can piss off, I'll get another broker.
The last thing I need in my pack is some tight-arsed joker.
(I thought you were good at this.)

ETHERINGTON.
My duty has been done in speaking out.
And now I'll help in every way I can.
My reputation for integrity
Will reassure our colleagues of their safety
In making any purchase we advise.

CORMAN.
Then let's get on / with it.

ZAC.
Let's get on with it, guys.

OTHERS *on phones.*

This works as a round, i.e. each starts at slash in previous speech and continues with all speeches as long as required. At end of each speech, each shouts out the amount of stock the person at the other end of the phone has agreed to buy, e.g. twenty thousand, a hundred thousand.

1. If you were interested in acquiring some Corman stock / there is a considerable sum on deposit with Klein Merrick so in the event of any subsequent fall in the share price you would be guaranteed against loss – 20,000

2. If you were interested in buying some Albion stock / there would be no question of being unable to dispose of them at a price at least equal to what you gave – 100,000

3. If you were able to see your way to supporting the bid / the new Albion under Corman management would naturally look favourably at any tenders for office cleaning that compared favourably with our present arrangements –

4. If you should be interested in following our recommendations to acquire Corman stock, an interest-free loan could be arranged at once with which the purchase could be made –

Meanwhile:

ZAC (*on phone*).
Remember me to Vanessa and the boys.
Listen, Corman, this may just be a rumour,
But if it's true it doesn't appeal to my sense of humour,
I've just had a word with a colleague in Atlanta & Gulf.
Marylou's been dealing with Biddulph.
I think it's time you spoke to her yourself.

CORMAN.
Dealing with Biddulph? I just sent her some flowers.
What the fuck does she think − ? She's meant to be one of
   ours.
I tried to call her this morning but I got the machine.
Leave a message after the tone? I'll leave something obscene.

CORMAN *phones* MARYLOU.

CORMAN.
Marylou? You got the flowers? A tragic bereavement.

MARYLOU.
Yes, TK made a real pretty arrangement.

CORMAN.
And our pretty arrangement's still OK?

MARYLOU.
I did dispose of a large holding today.

CORMAN.
You what? Disposed? A large Albion holding?
I gave you that on the clear understanding −

MARYLOU.
No, Corman, don't pursue it.
Anything I do I just happen to do because I want to do it.

CORMAN.
You owe me, Marylou.

MARYLOU.
                    I owe you?
I'm not even certain that I know you.

CORMAN.
How much Albion did you have?

MARYLOU.
                              15%.

CORMAN.
Can I just ask you where the hell it went?

MARYLOU.
   Don't be slow, Bill. That's quite upsetting,
   I like to think I'm dealing with an equal.

CORMAN.
   Marylou, it's not that I'm not smart.
   It's just hard to believe you'd break my heart.
   Biddulph? Biddulph? what? you knew you were getting
   Information from me / via Zackerman via Jake Todd.

MARYLOU.
                    You can't predict the sequel.

   SCILLA *arrives unnoticed by* ZAC *or* CORMAN.

CORMAN.
   But you knew Jake Todd was one of mine.

MARYLOU.
   You are slow, / Bill.

CORMAN.
                    Because he's dead? you didn't want to be connected
   With Jake now he's dead in case someone suspected – /
   So that's why you sold to Biddulph.

MARYLOU.
   I hope these phones are adequately scrambled.

CORMAN.
   I don't give a fuck who else is on the line.
   You cheated me. / I hate you. I'll fucking annihilate you.

MARYLOU.
                    Corman, you'll get rumbled
   If you don't keep your temper. Be glad you're alive
      (as my very irritating old aunty used to say).
   Don't worry about it. What's 15%? Get after the other 85.

   MARYLOU *hangs up.*

ZAC.
   We need her.

   Pause during which SCILLA *explains herself quietly to one of*
   CORMAN's *team.*

SCILLA.
   Kissogram for Mr Corman.

   CORMAN *calls* MARYLOU *back.*

CORMAN.
   Marylou? You know how it is. You say things in haste.
   Our friendship's far too important / to waste

MARYLOU.

> What do you want, Bill?

CORMAN.

Can you see your way to going back into Albion?
Will you buy Corman and support our price?
Smashing Biddulph would be very nice /
If you've anything –

MARYLOU.

Bill, I'd be glad to do something for you / but

CORMAN.

I understand your problem, how can I reassure you?

MARYLOU.

I'm playing with about a billion
But most of that's occupied over here.
If I had another hundred million
In my investment fund,
Then I guess / I'd have a freer hand.

CORMAN.

I think I can probably see my way clear.
This is hardly the moment with so much else on our minds.
But I had been meaning for some time to approach you with a view
to becoming a contributor to your investment fund because I
have of course the greatest admiration / for your wide experience
and market timing.

MARYLOU.

I could have my people send you some documentation.

MARYLOU *hangs up.*

SCILLA *approaches* CORMAN *and sings.*

SCILLA.

Happy takeover day.
Take Albion away.
Happy takeover, Corman.
Happy takeover day.

CORMAN.

What the hell?

SCILLA.

Kissogram from Marylou Baines.

CORMAN.

From Marylou Baines? I'll kill her.

SCILLA.

I'm not really. I'm Jake Todd's sister, Scilla.

ZAC.
  What the —
CORMAN.
  What? Is this a terrorist a- /
  ttack?
SCILLA.
  I heard you. 'Jake Todd was one of mine.'
  Tell me what it's all about. /
  Did someone kill Jake?
CORMAN.
  Will someone please get this lunatic out?
ZAC.
  Hold it, hold it, everything's fine.
  I know her, it's OK, she's not insane, she won't be armed, don't
    press
  The security button, we'll be held up for hours with water
    sprinklers and the SAS. /
      (Let's get on with the job here.)
SCILLA.
  You killed my brother.
CORMAN.
  Zac.
ZAC.
  He didn't / he really didn't. I'm certain he didn't.
CORMAN.
  Do you work for Marylou Baines?
      (Because you can tell her from me –)
SCILLA.
  No, that was a trick to get in. / Now will you explain
CORMAN.
  (Don't work for her.)
SCILLA.
  what 'one of mine' means. One of your what?
  He did something illegal. You were frightened of what he'd say
  To the DTI and you wanted him out of the way.
  Tell me what's going on or I'll tell the press
  My brother was acting for you the night he was shot.
  Did you kill him yourself or get your broker to pull the trigger?
CORMAN.
  After the deal, after the deal I'll confess
  To murdering anyone just let me get on with the deal.

SCILLA.
You and Zac got Jake into some mess.
He did little fiddles but this must have been much bigger.
You and Zac got him involved in some corrupt / ring

CORMAN.
Suppose I had killed Jake, his ghost would have had more sense
than walk in here today and interrupt. /

ZAC.
Can you spare me for five minutes?

CORMAN.
He got on because he knew what was a priority / and he'd have
reckoned

SCILLA.
He got on. Doing what exactly?

CORMAN.
That matters of life and death came a poor second.

ZAC.
Can you spare me for five minutes?

CORMAN.
No, not for two. / Go on.

SCILLA.
I'm not leaving here / until you –

ZAC.
I'll tell you. / I'll tell you.

SCILLA.
You will.

CORMAN.
You'll what?

ZAC.
Can I handle this? Can I just handle this please?

ZAC and SCILLA *outside* CORMAN's *office.*

SCILLA.
So tell me.

ZAC.
Marylou Baines – we'll make it quick, OK? /
Needs inside information and she's willing to pay.

SCILLA.
You knew all this this morning and you didn't say.

ZAC.
So anyone in London with news would give it to Jake,
And he'd get half a percent / on whatever she'd make.

SCILLA.
Half a percent?
That meant . . .

ZAC.
If she made fifty million –

SCILLA.
                    He got two hundred and fifty thousand.
If she made two hundred million / – he never told me.

ZAC.
I think little Jakey could have bought and sold me.
So now you know, OK? And now you drop it.

SCILLA.
What do you mean? / I'm just getting started.

ZAC.
I've got work to do.

CORMAN.
Who killed him? Corman? You?

ZAC.
                        I'm too tenderhearted
And Corman's too busy. Scilla, stop it.
We have to keep this quiet now. Face the facts.
You're never going to find out all Jake's contacts.
Let it go. I've got work to do. Don't get in a state.

SCILLA.
You knew all along. He never told me. Wait.

ZAC *goes*.

He was making serious money.

So Zac went back to Corman and I thought I'd better go to work
despite Jake being dead because Chicago comes in at one twenty
and I hate to miss it. I work on the floor of Liffe, the London
International Financial Futures Exchange.

Trading options and futures looks tricky if you don't understand it.
But if you're good at market timing you can make out like a bandit.
    (It's the most fun I've had since playing cops and robbers with
    Jake when we were children.)
A simple way of looking at futures is take a commodity,
Coffee, cocoa, sugar, zinc, pork bellies, copper, aluminium, oil –

I always think pork bellies is an oddity. ·
(They could just as well have a future in chicken wings.)
Suppose you're a coffee trader and there's a drought in Brazil like last year or suppose there's a good harvest, either way you might lose out,
So you can buy a futures contract that works in the opposite direction so you're covered against loss, and that's what futures are basically about.
But of course you don't have to take delivery of anything at all.
You can buy and sell futures contracts without any danger of ending up with ten tons of pork bellies in the hall.
On the floor of Liffe the commodity is money.
You can buy and sell money, you can buy and sell absence of money, debt, which used to strike me as funny.
For some it's hedging, for most it's speculation.
In New York they've just introduced a futures contract in inflation.
(Pity it's not Bolivian inflation, which hit forty thousand per cent.)
I was terrified when I started because there aren't many girls and they line up to watch you walk,
And every time I opened my mouth I felt self-conscious because of the way I talk.
I found O levels weren't much use, the best qualified people are street traders.
But I love it because it's like playing a cross between roulette and space invaders.

LIFFE canteen.

SCILLA. JOANNE *a runner.* KATHY *a trader.*

JOANNE.
I said I'm not going to work down there.
It's like animals in a zoo. / So then I thought I'll have a bash.
KATHY.
When you start they really stare.
SCILLA.
Don't let them see you care.
JOANNE.
I'll never learn what to do. / I'll never learn hand signals.
SCILLA.
I couldn't walk across the floor / my first day.
KATHY.
This morning's really a bore, / there's nothing happening.

JOANNE.
I answered a telephone / for the first time.

KATHY.
You really feel on your own.

SCILLA.
Never say hold on / because they don't hold on.

KATHY.
I can manage two phones at once but not three.

SCILLA.
Sometimes I've put the phone down because I don't know what they're saying.

JOANNE.
You do get used to the noise. I nearly fainted the first day.

KATHY.
I can deal without shouting, most of them like shouting.

SCILLA.
Men are just little boys. / Dave had lost twenty slips at the end of yesterday and muggins finds them for him.

JOANNE.
Terry asked me out this morning. He was the first person who spoke to me on my first day, he was really friendly.
Is it all right going out? / Do they talk about you?

SCILLA.
You do get talked about, / I hear so and so's knocking off so and so.

KATHY.
Just go out for lunch, / then nothing can happen after.

SCILLA.
They're a very chauvinist bunch.

KATHY.
We've all been out with Terry.

SCILLA.
Anyway they're all too knackered / by the end of the day.

KATHY.
It's true, they're all frustrated / because they never have time to do it.

JOANNE.
I'm completely exhausted.
At midnight I'm washing my knickers / because I'm too speedy to sleep.

KATHY.
  I get up at half-past five and have a good breakfast.
SCILLA.
  Mind you, I like Terry.

  TERRY, DAVE, MARTIN, BRIAN *and* VINCE, *traders, arrive.*

KATHY.
  Hello, Terry.
TERRY.
  What about Saturday?
JOANNE.
  I don't know.
TERRY.
  Think about it.
KATHY.
  Better be getting back.
MARTIN.
  Time we did some work. Nearly time for Chicago.
VINCE.
  Coming out with me tonight?
SCILLA.
  Leave it out, Vince.
DAVE.
  Leave the lady alone.
VINCE (*to* JOANNE).
  Coming out with me tonight?
KATHY.
  Leave it out, Vince.

*Floor of LIFFE. Four separate companies each with their phones, and
a trading pit.*
*Klein Merrick has SCILLA on the phone, TERRY and DAVE on the
floor, MANDY as runner.*
*2 – has SHERILL on the phone, MARTIN and KATHY on the floor,
PETE as runner.*
*3 – has DICK on the phone, BRIAN and JILL on the floor, JOANNE
as runner.*
*4 – has MARY on the phone, VINCE and JOHN on the floor,
ANNIE as runner.*
*They all start going to their places. As ANNIE, who is new, walks
down the lads cheer and jeer.*

TERRY.
　You're in late.
SCILLA.
　Trouble at home. My brother's been shot.
TERRY.
　You what?
SCILLA.
　There's going to be a scandal.
TERRY.
　Another one? / Did you say your brother?
SCILLA.
　Bigger.
TERRY.
　Is it worth trading on?
SCILLA.
　There might be a run on sterling if you're lucky.
KATHY.
　Ere come the c'nardlies.
BRIAN.
　Fuck off, sweaty git.
DICK.
　Fuck off, dogbreath.
BRIAN.
　Yeh, lovely. I'll feel better when I get rid of these oysters.
SCILLA.
　Dave! Dave!
BRIAN.
　And how are you this morning?
JILL.
　Don't talk to me, I'm all fucked up.
JOANNE.
　Do you call him Dick because he's got spots?
JILL.
　No, I call him Spot because he's a dick.
VINCE.
　Annie, if you sell the front and buy the back, / you'll be short of
　front and long of back.
BRIAN.
　Muff city, no pity.

SCILLA.

Dave, Grimes says Zac's got a ten million rollover for March so sell 10 at 9. If you can't get it he'll go to 8. And 15 June at your best price.

TERRY.

Are you Annie? Can you find this guy and give him a message?

ANNIE.

Mike who?

TERRY.

Hunt.

KATHY.

I'm tired of making money for other people. I'd like to be a local.

SCILLA.

Oi! Dave! You can't signal with a pencil in your hand.

DAVE.

Just fuckin have, haven't I.

KATHY.

The theoretical spread is too large.[1]

JOANNE.

Did you see that actor from the Bill who was in here yesterday?

KATHY.

I saw him first.

JOANNE.

I saw him first.

KATHY.

I wonder if he'll come back.

JOANNE.

I wonder if he's married.

Trading is now getting going.

JOANNE.

What do you want this morning?

PETE.

She wants 18 at 15.

JOANNE.

All I want is a bacon roll.

PETE (*sings*).

All I want is a bacon roll.

Meanwhile:

DAVE.
[1]Red June is showing 4 bid for 5.

TERRY.
Sterling showing 5 at 3.

DICK (*phone*).
March showing 9.
(*To* BRIAN *on floor.*) 5 at 9. 5 at 9.
(*Another phone call.*) Is that another 5 or the same 5?
(*To* BRIAN.) 5 more at 9. 5 more. 10 at 9. 10 at 9.

BRIAN.
5 at 9 filled.[2]

DICK (*phone*).
Your first 5 at 9 filled.

SHERILL.
We want 20 out of Footsie and into gilts.[3]
(*To* MARTIN.) Sell 20 at 1. 20 at 1.
(*To* KATHY.) Bid 9 for 20, 9 for 20.

MARTIN.
20 at 1.

KATHY.
9 for 20.

MARY.
[2]March gilts 8 rising fast. Do you want to sell now or wait? They might go another two ticks if you're lucky. (*To floor.*) 5 at 9. 5 at 9.

BRIAN.
[3]Where we going tonight?

TERRY.
The old Chinese?

BRIAN.
Dragon city, no pity.

DAVE.
I'll tell Vince.

BRIAN.
Oi, we're 18 for 15.

TERRY.
18 for 15. Working 20.

DAVE.
Table for 15 please.

JOHN.
10 at 19. 10 at 19.

VINCE.
  John John John – just 5 at 19.
  You can't trust John's bids.
MARY.
  He's had too many beers.
DAVE.
  I've got a certain winner for the 3.30 if anyone's interested.[4]
BRIAN.
  You haven't paid us yesterday's winnings yet.
DAVE.
  Leave it out, Brian, I always pay you.
KATHY.
  [4]Come on gilts. 2 at 4 the gilts.
MARTIN.
  Sterling showing 5 at 3.
TERRY.
  Euro 4 bid now.
SCILLA.
  Dave, you're supposed to be looking at me right?
DAVE.
  Am I in or am I out?[5]
MANDY.
  You gotta listen. If you don't listen we can't get in touch with you.
DAVE.
  What?
SCILLA.
  If you look at me I won't give you stick.
VINCE.
  [5]10 bid for 70. Let's get some stock away.
MARTIN.
  Where the fuck have you been?
PETE.
  Oh I see, you're not even allowed to crap.
MARTIN.
  If Tony rings tell him I can't get out.
BRIAN.
  I'm long on Footsie.
DAVE.
  Don't know why I bothered coming in today.
MARTIN.
  It's really flying. / It's really going somewhere.

SCILLA (*to* MANDY).
  Find out if Brian bought 20 off Dave at 6.

  MANDY *goes to* BRIAN.

MANDY.
  Did you buy 20 off Dave at 6?[6]

BRIAN.
  Going to the Greenhouse tonight?

DICK (*to* BRIAN).
  [5]5 at 9. Have you got that second 5 at 9 filled?

JILL (*to* BRIAN).
  Have you got that second 5 at 9 filled?

BRIAN.
  Leave me alone, I'm talking to the young lady.[7]

  ANNIE *comes up to* BRIAN.

ANNIE.
  I'm looking for Mike Hunt.

BRIAN.
  She's looking for her cunt.

  ANNIE *realises and starts to cry.* MANDY *takes her back to her trading booth.*

MANDY.
  Don't worry, they do it to everyone when they're new.

SHERILL.
  OUT OUT OUT!
  [7]John, phone for you.

MARTIN.
  My car keeps getting stolen.

SAM.
  Don't leave it outside your house.

PETE.
  Then they won't know it's yours.

VINCE.
  Terry! It's a doddle, four-hour drive at most.

TERRY.
  It's four hundred, five, it's five hundred miles.

BRIAN.
  I'm not doing that / on a Sunday.

DICK.
  Check your oil the night before and leave at five.

TERRY.
  What's he doing living in a castle?

VINCE.
  He's a fucking iron.

ALL FOUR.
  Iron 'oof! /

SCILLA.
  Chicago two minutes. Footsie's going to move.

DAVE.
  No, he showed me a picture of his girlfriend once with a carrot in her mouth right up to the green bit.

BRIAN.
  Veg city, no pity.

JOHN.
  Dave, the horse! It won!

  DAVE and JOHN embrace and jump up and down.

DAVE.
  I fucking won two thousand pounds!

KATHY.
  Chicago, Chicago.

  Everyone is suddenly quiet, watching the boards, waiting for Chicago to come in. All burst out at once, furious trading, everyone flat out. Among the things we hear:

VINCE.
  6 for 10. 6 for 10.

JOHN.
  10 at 6. 10 at 6.

VINCE.
  I'm buying at 6, you cunt.

SHERILL (*on phone*).
  11 coming 10, 11 coming 10, 11 10 11 10, 10! 10 10 10 10 coming 9, 10 coming 9, etc.

BRIAN.
  What's your fucking game?

MARTIN.
  Oh fuck off.

BRIAN.
  I'll fucking break your leg, you fucking cunt.

SCILLA (*to DAVE*).
  You'll have to shout louder if you can't signal better.

BRIAN (*to* DAVE). You're trading like a cunt.

Out of furious trading emerges the song:

FUTURES SONG

Out you cunt, out in oh fuck it
I've dealt the gelt below the belt and I'm jacking up the ackers
My front's gone short, fuck off old sport, you're standing on my
    knackers
I've spilt my guts, long gilt's gone nuts and I think I'm going
    crackers
So full of poo I couldn't screw, I fucked it with my backers
                I fucked it with my backers
                I fucked it with my backers

Backups: Out! Buy buy buy! Leave it!
       No! Yes! Cunt!
       4! 5! Sell!
       Quick! Prick! Yes! No! Cunt!

How hard I dredge to earn my wedge, I'm sharper than a knife
Don't fucking cry get out and buy, Chicago's going rife
You're back to front come on you cunt don't give me any strife
You in or out? Don't hang about, you're on the floor of Liffe!

They call me a tart who can hardly fart when it's bedlam in the pit
I'm the local tootsie playing footsie but I don't mind a bit
Cos my future trusts my money lusts as far as it can spit
And my sterling works on mouthy jerks whose bids are full of shit

I'm a Romford scholar in eurodollars and June is showing four
Botham out nineteen on the Reuters screen is the very latest score
I fucked that runner she's a right little stunner so I pulled her off
    the floor
I was bidding straight till my interest rate jumped up and asked for
    more

Money-making money-making money-making money-making
Money-making money-making money-making caper
Do the fucking business do the fucking business do the fucking
    business
And bang it down on paper.

So L.I.F.F.E. is the life for me and I'll burn out when I'm dead
And this fair exchange is like a rifle range what's the price of flying
    lead?
When you soil your jeans on soya beans shove some cocoa up your
head
You can never hide if your spread's too wide, you'll just fuck
    yourself instead.

ACT TWO

JACINTA CONDOR *flying first class.*

JACINTA.

Flight to England that little grey island in the clouds where
governments don't fall overnight and children don't sell themselves
in the street and my money is safe. I'll buy a raincoat. I'll meet Jake
Todd, I'll stay at the Savoy by the stream they call a river with its
Bloody Tower and dead queens, a river is too wide to bridge. The
unfinished bridge across the canyon where the road ends in the air,
waiting for dollars. The office blocks father started, imagining glass,
leather, green screens, the city rising high into the sky, but the
towers stopped short, cement, wires, the city spreading wider
instead with a blur of shacks, miners coming down from the
mountains as the mines close. The International Tin Council, what
a scandal, thank God I wasn't in tin, the price of copper ruined by
the frozen exchange rate, the two rates, and the government will
not let us mining companies exchange enough dollars at the better
rate, they insist we help the country in this crisis, I do not want to
help, I want to be rich, I close my mines and sell my copper on the
London Metal Exchange. It is all because of the debt that will never
be paid because we have to borrow more and more to pay the
interest on the money that came from oil when OPEC had too
much money and your western banks wanted to lend it to us
because who else would pay such high interest, needing it so badly?
Father got his hands on enough of it but what happened, massive
inflation, lucky he'd put the money somewhere safe, the Swiss
mountains so white from the air like our mountains but the people
rich with cattle and clocks and secrets, the American plains yellow
with wheat, the green English fields where lords still live in grey
stone, all with such safe banks and good bonds and exciting
gambles, so as soon as any dollars or pounds come, don't let them
go into our mines or our coffee or look for a sea of oil under the
jungle, no get it out quickly to the western banks (a little money in
cocaine, that's different). Peru leads the way resisting the IMF,
refusing to pay the interest, but I don't want to make things
difficult for the banks, I prefer to support them, why should my

money stay in Peru and suffer? The official closing price yesterday
for grade A copper was 878-8.5, three months 900.5–1, final kerb
close 901-2. Why bother to send aid so many miles, put it straight
into my eurobonds.

*Meanwhile the London metal exchange starts quietly trading
copper. When* JACINTA *finishes speaking the trading reaches its
noisy climax.*

ZAC.
There's some enterprising guys around and here's an example.
You know how if you want to get a job in the States you have to
   give a urine sample?
      (this is to show you're not on drugs).
There's a company now for a fifty dollar fee
They'll provide you with a guaranteed pure, donated by a
   churchgoer, bottle of pee.
      (They also plan to market it dehydrated in a packet and you
      just add water.)
And Aids is making advertisers perplexed
Because it's no longer too good to have your product associated
   with sex.
But it's a great marketing opportunity.
Like the guys opening up blood banks where you pay to store your
   own blood in case of an accident and so be guaranteed immunity.
      (It's also a great time to buy into rubber.)
Anyone who can buy oranges for ten and sell at eleven in a souk or
   bazaar
Has the same human nature and can go equally far.
The so-called third world doesn't want our charity or aid.
All they need is the chance to sit down in front of some green
   screens and trade.
      (They don't have the money, sure, but just so long as they have
      freedom from communism so they can do it when they do have
      the money.)
Pictures of starving babies are misleading and patronising.
Because there's plenty of rich people in those countries, it's just the
   masses that's poor, and Jacinta Condor flew into London and
   was quite enterprising.
It was the day before Jake Todd was found dead
And the deal was really coming to a head.
Jake was helping us find punters because anyone with too much
   money and Jake would know them.
You'd just say, Jake, who's in town, what have you got, and he'd
   bring them in and show them.

ZAC and JAKE.

JAKE.
Señora Condor has plenty of cash in her coffer.
She owns mountains and her garden's twice
The size of Wales. What's Corman going to offer?

ZAC.
He hopes she'll be able to help support his price.

JAKE.
She's going to need some kind of incentive.

ZAC.
I think she'll find Corman quite inventive.

JAKE.
Zac, while we're alone.
I didn't want to say this on the phone.
I had a visit from a DTI inspector.

ZAC.
Have you done something not quite correct or / what?

JAKE.
Zac, it's no joke. They didn't say too much /
But once they –

ZAC.
Did they mention me?

JAKE.
                    I can't say I don't know
You. / (That doesn't tell them anything, knowing you.)

ZAC.
Great.
Sure, no, of course not.

JAKE.
                    Don't let's pay too much
Attention to it. OK? / If you like I'll go.

ZAC.
                    It could be quite a smash. /
Not just for you.

JAKE.
I have been making quite a lot of cash.
When they take your passport you feel surprisingly trapped.
I didn't know I was so fond of travel.

ZAC.
You're the kind of loose thread, Jake, that when they pull you the
    whole fucking City could unravel.

JAKE.
Shall we cancel Condor in case it makes things worse?
ZAC.
Just don't give them the whole thing giftwrapped.
JAKE.
I can walk out the door now.
ZAC.
                    OK.
JAKE.
                              I feel –
JAKE.
What shall I do?
ZAC.
              Jake, I'm not your nurse.
JAKE.
Tell me to walk / and I'll walk.
ZAC.
                    And fuck up the deal?
JAKE.
There might be a bug on the light.
ZAC.
                                      Jake, what the hell.
There might be a microphone under your lapel.
The City's greed or fear, you've got to choose.
JAKE.
Greed's been good to me. Fear's a bitch.
ZAC.
Then be greedy, guy, and let's get this payload home without a
    hitch.
JAKE.
I can always hit the straight and narrow tomorrow.

JACINTA CONDOR arrives.

This is Zac Zackerman you've heard so much about.
The guy who always knows the latest shout.
ZAC.
How are you enjoying your stay in London, Señora Condor?
JACINTA.
I have been for a walk
In your little saint's park

Where the pelicans eat the pigeons (but I didn't see it).
I have been to the opera (very nice).
I have sold all my copper
For a rather small number of millions.

ZAC.
This is no time to sell copper, the price is lousy.

JAKE.
And when's it ever in season?
She's selling copper she's got to have a reason.

JACINTA.
I lose every quarter,
The cash goes like water,
Is better to close the mine.
I chose very well
The moment to sell,
I benefit from the closures in Surinam because of guerrilla activity
and also I leak the news I am closing my mines, which puts the
price up a little, so it is fine.

JAKE.
So you've wiped out your mines? That's telling them who's master.
You must feel like a natural disaster.

ZAC.
Hurricane Jacinta.

JACINTA.
If I keep them Jake I have to be derange.
The Minister of Energy says 'Mining is not dead' –
It brings 45% of our foreign exchange
But a pound of copper won't buy a loaf of bread.
(Our mining companies lost a hundred million dollars last year,
it is the fault of IMF. I don't like to suffer.)

JAKE.
The dagos always like to blame the gringos.
I suppose the miners want a revolution.
The most amazing lake full of flamingos –
(I think that was Peru.)

JACINTA.
How can I support ten thousand people?
When I did they weren't even grateful.
The miners all strike
And do what they like,
They want subsidised food, I say get on your bike.

JAKE.
  I didn't know they had bikes, I thought they had llamas, /
  And woolly hats and trousers like pyjamas.

ZAC.
  (So are the miners bothering you?

JACINTA.
  You come and protect me?)
  It's really a pity,
  They go to the city (where there's no work)
  Or they sit down outside the mine.
  Growing coca is nice,
  A very good price
      (Ten to thirty times as much as tea or coffee or cocoa)
  So I think that's going to be fine.

JAKE.
  Great product to grow.
  Peru with its mountains covered in snow.
  You're not giving up all your Peruvian interests?

JACINTA.
  Europe is more interesting. Mr Corman is fascinating.
  Jake, I have asked a friend to this meeting.

ZAC.
  I'm not sure a –

JACINTA.
  You've heard of Nigel Ajibala?

ZAC.
  I can't say I have.

JAKE.
  Listen, don't cross the señora.

JACINTA.
  I tell you I've caught a
  Big cocoa importer,
  Your deal goes without a hitch.
  His school was at Eton
  Where children are beaten,
  He's a prince and exceedingly rich.

JAKE.
  Any friend of Jacinta
  Will be a good punter.

ZAC.
  So where does he operate?

JACINTA.
He has connections in
Ghana and Zambia
Zaire and Gambia
But it's here that he likes to invest.
His enemies are jealous
Because he's so zealous (and makes so much money) /
And at home he faces arrest
    (like the man they tried to kidnap in the trunk?)

JAKE.
You see, I told you, it's great.

JACINTA.
Here he comes now. Be cunning.

ZAC.
I suppose Corman can always meet him.

    NIGEL AJIBALA *arrives*.

JACINTA.
My friend, Jake Todd, and Mr Zackerman,
A very considerable American.

JAKE.
You spend much time in Zambia and Zaire?

NIGEL.
Yes, but one's mostly based over here.
Africa induces mild hysteria.
Terrible situation in Nigeria.
    (oil earnings down from twenty-five billion dollars to five this
    year so they're refusing to make their interest payments.)
And Zaire
Pays the west a hundred and ninety million more than it receives
    each year.
So as the last of several last resorts
It's cutting its payments to 10% of exports.

JACINTA.
So the IMF
Will turn a deaf
Ear.

NIGEL.
They've just cut off their payments to Zambia.

ZAC.
The IMF is not a charity.
It has to insist on absolute austerity.

NIGEL.
Absolutely. It can't be namby pamby.
These countries must accept restricted diets.
The governments must explain, if there are food riots,
That paying the western banks is the priority.

JAKE.
Bob Geldof was a silly cunt.
He did his charity back to front.
They should have had the concerts in Zaire
And shipped the money to banks over here.

ZAC.
So you're better off out of Africa, I guess.

NIGEL.
The continent is such a frightful mess.
One's based in London so one's operation
Is on the right side of exploitation.
One thing one learned from one's colonial masters,
One makes money from other people's disasters.

ZAC.
Señora Condor tells me you might be interested in Corman
Enterprise.

ZAC takes NIGEL *aside.*

JAKE.
You can't completely pull out of Peru.

JACINTA.
Don't worry, Jake, I don't pull out on you.
I give up all my interests – except the cocaine.
And I keep the houses of course and the aeroplane.
My country is beautiful, Jake, white mountains, jungle greenery.
My people will starve to death among the scenery.
    (Let them rot. I'm sick of it.)

JAKE.
So what's the story?

JACINTA.
The airstrip's rebuilt –
The government feels guilt
So it's always trying to bomb it.
    (also they try to destroy my processing plants which is deceitful
    because they dare not confront the peasants and stop them
    growing it.)
And they don't really want
To destroy all the plants.

They are making billions from it (more than all the rest of our
    exports).
To keep Reagan our friend
We have to pretend,
But the US pretends and we know it.
Who likes a coke buzz?
America does.
They stop using it, we won't grow it.

JAKE.
So when can we see some action? Let's get going.

JACINTA.
I have to get a little cash flowing.
Maybe Mr Corman?

JAKE.
I'm curious to see Corman, we've never met,
I'm just a secret compartment in his desk.
He's very bright so be on your best behaviour.
He's obsessed with the bid and he'll look on you as a saviour.
You can push him quite hard, he likes a risk.
So have you decided what to ask for yet?

JACINTA.
If I buy or sell
I always do well
So don't worry about it, my pet.
Whatever I get
I look after you
And Corman will too
I expect.
Don't be embarrassed, Jake, you're young and greedy, I like to see
    it.

    ZAC *and* NIGEL *rejoin them.*

JAKE.
I was at Eton myself. This is rather a different ballgame.

NIGEL.
Oh not at all. Did you ever play the wall game?

    JAKE *and* NIGEL *talk apart.*

ZAC.
It would be great to see you while you're over here.

JACINTA.
Maybe we could drink some English beer.
I have a meeting at eight,

It won't go on late.
Maybe at half-past nine?

ZAC.
No, I don't think . . .
I'll be stuck with Corman, I can't get out for a drink.
Eleven's probably fine.

JACINTA.
I'm having late supper
With terribly upper-
class people who buy my plantation.

ZAC.
And after that?

JACINTA.
Unfortunately they live in Edinburgh.

ZAC.
How you getting there?

JACINTA.
By helicopter.

ZAC.
I'm beginning to run out of inspiration.

JACINTA.
Breakfast?

ZAC.
Would be great except I have to have breakfast with Corman till
    this deal goes through.
I suppose I might get away for a minute or two.

JACINTA.
That would be heaven.

ZAC.
Maybe eleven?

JACINTA.
Eleven I see my lawyer.
At twelve –

ZAC.
No, please.

JACINTA.
I see some Japanese,
Just briefly in the hotel foyer.
So we meet for lunch?

ZAC.
I have to be in Paris for lunch. I'll be back by four.
JACINTA.
That's good!
ZAC.
But I have to go straight to Corman.
JACINTA.

What a bore.

ZAC.
Maybe we could . . .
JACINTA.
Dinner tomorrow
Much to my sorrow
I have with some eurobond dealers.
ZAC.
Cancel it.
JACINTA.
Business.
ZAC.
Shit.
JACINTA.
Afterward?
ZAC.
Bliss.
No, hang on a minute.
I have as a guest a
Major investor,
I have to put out some feelers.
(The only time he can meet me is after a show.)
I guess I might be through by 1 a.m.
JACINTA.
Zac, I could cry,
There's a nightclub I buy,
And really I must talk to them.
So maybe next morning
You give me a ring?
ZAC.
Maybe I can get out of breakfast with Corman, I'll call you first
thing.
JACINTA.
Which day?

ZAC.
  Tomorrow.

  NIGEL *and* JAKE.

NIGEL.
  If you fancy a wolfhound I'll let you have a pup.

JAKE.
  If I'm down in Wiltshire I'll certainly look you up.

  ZAC *takes* JAKE *aside.*

JACINTA (*to* NIGEL).
  That went very well.
  They can't possibly tell
  You live in one room in a rundown hotel.
  I'll buy you a silk shirt in Jermyn Street.

  ZAC *and* JAKE.

ZAC.
  You've not met Corman before, had you better split?
  There may be a good time to meet him but is this it?
  If you've actually spoken it gets us in more deep –

JAKE.
  What the hell, Zac. Hang for a sheep.

  ZAC *joins* CORMAN *and* ETHERINGTON *in* CORMAN's *office.*

CORMAN.
  Cup of coffee someone. I'm going mental.
  So we get these people involved in distribution,
  Or supply, whatever, and they make a contribution?

ZAC.
  Their involvement should look kind of coincidental.

CORMAN.
  Look what? Zac, don't you start talking sin,
  It'll look terrific. Show the buggers in.

  NIGEL, JACINTA *and* JAKE *come into* CORMAN's *office.*

ZAC.
  Señora Condor. Mr Ajibala.

CORMAN.
  And this must be the infamous Jake Todd.
  I'd begun to think you were a bit like God –
  You make things happen but you don't exist.
  Etherington, don't look as if you smell something burning.
  This is Jake Todd, our invisible earning.

ETHERINGTON.
  How do you do, Mr Todd. Extremely glad.
JAKE.
  You're really so looked up to by my dad.
CORMAN.
  OK, let's skip the introductions.
  How do you do. Let's get on with the ructions.
  What's the idea?
NIGEL.
  Albion seems an excellent investment
  Especially under your expert control.
  I assure you that the stag is not my role.
  I'm talking about a long term commitment.
CORMAN.
  So you'd have the company's interests at heart?
NIGEL.
  I'd certainly be glad to play my part.
  I can't imagine why anyone bothers with water
  When Albion produces so many delicious drinks.
  Orange, coffee, chocolate / with cream –
CORMAN.
  I think the product stinks.
  Cocoa? you're a cocoa importer?
  I know fuckall about the cocoa bean.
  Buy the company first and run it later.
NIGEL.
  The London market suits the speculator.
  You really have to know your way around.
  And excellent bargains can be made.
CORMAN.
  You've wide experience have you in the trade?
NIGEL.
  The only job I haven't done is peasant
  Who grows the stuff, which wouldn't be so pleasant.
CORMAN.
  So what's the story with cocoa –
  Anyone know?
  Are Albion having to pay through the nose?
NIGEL.
  There's mistrust between the countries where it grows
  And countries like this where we consume.

Cocoa is very far from having a boom.
A new agreement has just been implemented.

ZAC.
(Hell of a lot of wrangling about the buffer stock.)

NIGEL.
This has driven the price up a little but it's well below the price at
    which buffer stock buying is permitted,
And 18% down on a year ago.
We consumers are holding the price low.

CORMAN.
So how can you give me a better price than your rivals?

NIGEL.
Because options and futures are more important than physicals.
    (In today's market following an unchanged opening futures
    rallied £15 during the afternoon before trade profit taking
    pared the gains on the closing call. With producers withdrawn
    physical interest was restricted to forward/consumer offtake –)

JAKE.
He buys a forward contract, sells it later,
And every time he's making money off it.

ZAC.
And you get the benefit of the profit.

JACINTA.
It's thrilling to watch such a skilful operator.

CORMAN.
And funny business with import licences, Mr Ajibala? Don't answer
    that.
Right Zac, let's put cocoa on the back burner.
It looks as if it's a nice little earner.
And you Señora? Are you full of beans?
I suppose you want to sell me some caffeine?

JACINTA.
Coffee's no joke,
It makes me go broke,
No, my interest is distribution –

CORMAN.
I spent a good weekend once in Caracas.
You don't by any chance play the maracas?

JACINTA.
I'm here to do business, Mr Corman.
I wish to obtain an exclusive franchise.

CORMAN.
  Señoritas in Brazil have beautiful eyes.

ZAC.
  Cut it out, Corman.

JACINTA.
  Mr Corman, you appreciate my country's spirit.
  I appreciate your company's products and I wish to sell it in Peru,
    Brazil, Argentina, Venezuela and Chile.

ZAC.
  This could very probably be arranged.

CORMAN.
  Zackerman, I hope you haven't changed.

ZAC.
  The proposal has considerable merit.

CORMAN.
  You wouldn't be suggesting something silly?
  Can't you tell me anything good the present distributors did?

ZAC.
  No, they've shown no interest at all in your bid.

CORMAN.
  That's too bad.
  I think we may be in business, Señora.

JACINTA.
  If you want to set up
  Debt for equity swap
  And have Albion plants in Peru
  It's a way that we get
  To sell some of our debt.
  I ask you, what else can we do?
  Better than selling copper.

CORMAN.
  Zac, do I want to invest in South America?

ZAC.
  South American companies will swap their debt
  For dollars you invest in their country, which means you get
  Say a hundred million dollars of equity
  Paid by the government in local currency
  And you've only got to hand over seventy.
  It gives you a great advantage over the locals.

JACINTA.
    Also you could help to build my hospitals.
    I have one for sick and hungry men and women,
    One for poor drug-addicted children.
    I visit and hold the hands of the poor people.

CORMAN.
    This is all extremely admirable,
    Don't you think so, Etherington? (*To* JACINTA.) If you'll excuse
        us.

    CORMAN *takes* ZAC *and* ETHERINGTON *aside.*

    Is this wise?
    Hospitals, she's simply trying to use us.
    Every penny would go in her own pocket.
    Everything she looks at I want to lock it.
    You can't help admiring the way she tries.
    Etherington?

ETHERINGTON.
                    I'm afraid I can't advise.
    Questions of supply and distribution
    For Albion after you make the acquisition
    Are matters of internal management,
    So naturally, I haven't liked to listen. /
    I really don't feel qualified to comment.

CORMAN.
    Do you want the money for the deal or not?
    Zac?

ZAC.
    Swapping debt might come in handy later.
    I agree the hospitals / are just a scam.

CORMAN.
    Hospitals! what does she think I am?

ZAC.
    So we buy his cocoa, give her the franchise and get out the
        calculator.

CORMAN.
    They have got serious money?

ZAC.
                        Jake recommends / them.

CORMAN.
    That boy's got very interesting friends.
    Let's keep them sweet.

CORMAN *returns to others.*

I'd be delighted to make a small contribution
To your hospital, Señora. The distribution
Franchise would of course be contingent
On my acquiring Albion.

JACINTA.
                    I know the arrangement.
If you get it, I get it. I help you get it.

CORMAN.
   And Mr Ajibala.
   I'm most impressed. As Albion's sole supplier /
   Of cocoa?

NIGEL.
   I would feel it my duty to acquire /
   An interest in the company.

CORMAN.
   I think a change of supplier is probably indicated,
   Don't you, Zac?
   Right, you can both discuss the exact sum
   With my banker here, Mr Zackerman.

NIGEL.
   There's a small problem.
   I was hoping to buy five-million poundsworth of Albion stock but I
      have a holdup in cash liquidity.

CORMAN.
   That is a problem.

NIGEL.
   I suppose it is a matter of some urgency?
   If my involvement could be postponed, ten days, or eight?

CORMAN.
   That's too late.

NIGEL.
   If I had an extra two million now a five million purchase could be
      made by several small companies under various names registered
      in various places not traceable to anyone alive.

ZAC.
   Maybe if he buys three million now / and two –

CORMAN.
                              Zac, I want five. Five!

NIGEL.
I don't have five at my immediate disposal.

CORMAN.
Mr Ajibala, if you're happy with my proposal / about the cocoa

NIGEL.
Perfectly.

CORMAN.
I could make a downpayment of two million in advance.
    (We're going to need a hell of a lot of cocoa beans.)

NIGEL.
That way nothing would be left to chance.

CORMAN.
Zackerman will write a cheque.
And Señora Condor, if you see my lawyer.

JACINTA.
The deal is exciting,
I get it in writing?

CORMAN.
I can't be bothered with all these trivialities.
We've got the money. Fuck the personalities.
Etherington will see you all right for stock.

    CORMAN *and* ETHERINGTON *leave, followed by* ZAC.

ZAC (*to* JACINTA).
I'll call you first thing.

JACINTA, NIGEL *and* JAKE *alone.*

NIGEL.
I've got the money! / Two million!

JACINTA.
For Albion?

NIGEL.
I want a better return,
Albion won't earn,

JACINTA.
Put up your stake,
Get it doubled / by Jake.

NIGEL.
Doubled?

JACINTA.
He's a good dealer, let him play with it.

JAKE.
  No problem. Give me a week.

NIGEL.
  I'll go and get the cheque from Zackerman.

  NIGEL *goes*.

JACINTA.
  Two million? What are you going to do?

JAKE.
  I thought I might invest it in Peru.

  JACINTA *phones* MARYLOU BAINES.

JACINTA.
  Hello? Marylou?
  Four million, repeat four,
  Arrives Thursday, the usual way.

MARYLOU.
  But the CIA
  Won't help it through
  Unless we agree to give /
    another 10% to the Contras.

JACINTA.
  But Marylou, already we pay –

MARYLOU.
  I don't think we have an alternative.

JACINTA.
  I expect an increase in what I get from you.

MARYLOU.
  No problem. The guys who use it can easily meet
  A rise in the street price because the street is Wall Street.

JACINTA.
  So how's the weather?

MARYLOU.
  I haven't looked.

  During the above, ZAC *looks in just for this exchange with* JAKE.

ZAC.
  Good work, Jake.

JAKE.
  I'd be OK if my hands didn't shake.

  JACINTA *comes off the phone*.

JACINTA.
Good work, Jake. The franchise I got from Corman – what a pig –
I sell of course to some American.
You will arrange it, no wonder I am so fond,
And I put the money in a delicious Eurobond,
Yumyum.
I think that is all.
One more phone call,
Then I go see Biddulph, the white knight –
But you don't mention this to Zac, all right?

JAKE.
This deal's not enough?

JACINTA.
                    What is enough?
Don't worry, Jake, you're making it.
Just keep on, taking and taking and taking it.

JAKE.
I do.

JACINTA *phones a shop.*

JACINTA.
I like to order a tree. Maybe twenty feet tall. Fig, walnut, banyan?
    Lemon, yes that's sweet.
Send it please to Zac Zackerman, Klein Merrick, and a card saying
    'to Zac with love from Jacinta until we meet'.

DUCKETT *and* BIDDULPH. BIDDULPH *has a newspaper.*

BIDDULPH.
Now Duckett, your image gets better and better.
Have you seen this letter?

DUCKETT.
                    No, show me the letter.

BIDDULPH.
MPs of all parties and union leaders,
Teachers and lawyers and ordinary readers
All hope you'll succeed

DUCKETT.
                    Oh let's have a read.

BIDDULPH.
In stopping the raider who just wants a profit.

DUCKETT.
But we want a profit.

BIDDULPH.
                    We will make a profit.
  But at the right time and in the right place,
  With a smile on our very acceptable face.
  You do so much good, you give so much enjoyment –
DUCKETT.
  Youth unemployment.
BIDDULPH.
                      Yes, youth unemployment,
  Swimming pools, pensioners, toy libraries, art –
DUCKETT.
  What's this about art?
BIDDULPH.
                    You don't give a fart,
  I know it, they know it, you just mustn't show it,
  We're doing so well, Duckett, don't you dare blow it.
  You've commissioned a mural called Urban and Rural,
  It's sixty feet high –
DUCKETT.
                    I've commissioned a mural?
BIDDULPH.
  And tomorrow you're joining the scouts for a hike.
DUCKETT.
  I'm not sure I like –
BIDDULPH.
                    You go for a hike.
  Your picture will be on the front of the *Mail*.
  And we really can't fail.
DUCKETT.
                      You're sure we can't fail?
  Sometimes I dream that I'll end up in jail.
BIDDULPH.
  But you've done nothing wrong, you're an innocent victim,
  Corman's the villain, you'll see when we've licked him.
  He's sure to be up to some terrible schemes.
DUCKETT.
  I just have bad dreams.
BIDDULPH.
                    Well don't have bad dreams.

DUCKETT.
I've done nothing wrong, I'm an innocent victim.

BIDDULPH.
And Corman will lose because we have tricked him.
Now we're meeting Señora Condor.
What the hell's she want I wonder.

JACINTA CONDOR *arrives.*

JACINTA.
Mr Duckett. Miss Biddulph. As a major shareholder I have been
wondering whether I should accept Corman's offer.

BIDDULPH.
You don't want to do that, Señora Condor.

JACINTA.
I was hoping you could help me to make up my mind. I don't know
how much you know about my country.

BIDDULPH.
It's really absurd, from what I have heard,
You bear an intolerable burden of debt.

JACINTA.
My country is poor, it can't stand much more,
I really can see no solution just yet.
When I wish to borrow, much to my sorrow,
The banks here in Britain are overextended.

BIDDULPH.
I think they might lend a small sum to a friend,
And we hope this sad period is very soon ended.

JACINTA.
You think your bank will lend me money?

BIDDULPH.
I think if I explain the special circumstances it could probably be
arranged.

JACINTA.
Señora Biddulph
You are pleased with yourself
And certainly so you ought.
And ah Señor Duckett
You don't know your luck, it
Is now my decision you get my support.

DUCKETT.
We get her support?

BIDDULPH.

                Just as we ought.

DUCKETT.

  I sometimes have dreams that I'll end up in court.

JACINTA.

  And now do you think it is time for a drink?

BIDDULPH.

  Time for a drink!

DUCKETT.

               What do you think, Biddulph?

BIDDULPH.

  I'm telling you, Duckett.
  I begin to think fuck it.
  Pull yourself together.

MERRISON *and* MARYLOU BAINES *at* MARYLOU's *office in New York.*

MERRISON.

  So I've had three years pretty much in the wilderness.
  I've had a great time skiing with my kids.
  I've bred Tennessee walking horses. But I guess
  Banking's in my blood. I miss the bids,
  I miss the late nights, I miss the gambles.
  So now I've gotten my own operation.
  I can't forgive Durkfeld for the shambles
  He's made of Klein Merrick. A great nation
  Needs great enterprises, not black plastic
  And grey lino and guys in polyester.
      (I just bought a Matisse for seven million dollars, could have
      hung in the boardroom.)

MARYLOU.

  I guess the old wound's beginning to fester.
  It's about time you did something drastic.
  Go for it, Jack. Why don't you sabotage
  Durkfeld's deals? I've got a lot of stocks
  Coming and going here in arbitrage
  Should enable you to give him a few knocks.

MERRISON.

  He's got his fingers in a lot of pies.

MARYLOU.

  In the UK there's Corman Enterprise.

MERRISON.
  You think I should step in as a white knight?

MARYLOU.
  No, that's already happening all right.
  Wouldn't it be far wittier to make
  Corman himself a target?

MERRISON.
                    I'll buy a stake
  In Corman straight away. I'll get some little
  Nogood company run by a real punk
  To take it over with a lot of junk.
  I'd really like to see Durkfeld in the hospital.
  Do you happen to have any Corman stock available?

MARYLOU.
  Yes, I kind of thought it might be saleable.
  How much do you want?

MERRISON.
  How much have you got?

MARYLOU.
  Let's talk to TK.

  MERRISON *goes*.

  TK? Sell Mr Merrison all the Corman we've got.
  And buy all you can get straight away.
  He'll give us a good price and take the lot.

TK.
  OK.

SCILLA *and* GRIMES *playing Pass the Pigs*.

SCILLA.
  Grimes and I were having a glass of poo and playing Pass the Pig,
  Where you throw little pigs like dice. It's a good way to unwind
  Because when trading stops you don't know what to do with your
    mind.

GRIMES.
  Trotter!

SCILLA.
  Except my mind was also full of Jake and how he'd been up to
    something big.

GRIMES.
  Razorback, snouter. Fucking pig out.

    I knew Jake was up to something but I'd never have guessed that
      was what it was about.

SCILLA.

He might have made a million. Trotter. Razorback.

GRIMES.

Marylou Baines! And he's in on it somehow, Zac.
Did he leave a will?

SCILLA.

                I don't know.

GRIMES.

                           Trotter, snouter.

Fucking nuisance if he's died without a
Will, / fucking lawyers

SCILLA.

         Daddy and I are next of kin.

GRIMES.

Will you marry me?

SCILLA.

                 Leave it out Grimes.

GRIMES.

Double snouter. I think I'm going to win.
I once threw double snouter three times.

SCILLA.

Are we playing a pound a point?

GRIMES.

                       Snouter, trotter.

There's the money he's made already. There's a lot o'
Money still owing him, bound to be,
And why can't that be collected by you and me?
It's just a matter of tracing his contacts, innit.
They'll want him replacing. / Snouter!

SCILLA.

                  You'll pig out in a minute.

There's someone who killed him.

GRIMES.

                Risks are there to be taken.

Trotter, jowler. Fuckit, makin' bacon.
Do I lose all my points for the whole game?

SCILLA.

Yes, Grimes, isn't it a shame.

And I've got forty-five. Trotter, fifty. / Snouter, sixty. Double
   razorback, eighty. Hell, I've pigged out. Back to forty-five.

GRIMES.
   I'd have some questions for Jake if he was alive.
   What about your old man?

SCILLA.
                         Denies he got a single tip.

GRIMES.
   I bet he knows more / than he lets on.

SCILLA.
              He'll be so pissed by now he might let something slip.

GRIMES.
   He may know where Jake stashed the loot.

SCILLA.
   Let's go round there now and put in the boot.
   Really, this morning he couldn't have been fouler.
   Let's drive / there now.

GRIMES.
              Double leaning jowler!
   Double leaning jowler as I live and breathe!

SCILLA.
   He's so two-faced you don't know what to believe.
   We'll make him talk.

GRIMES.
   I'm winning! Double fucking leaning jowler!

SCILLA.
   Bring the pigs.

GREVILLE *and* FROSBY *at* GREVILLE's *house. Drinking.*

GREVILLE.
   It's times like this you need an old friend.
   We haven't seen each other for a while,
   I blame myself but know that in the end
   It's only you that travels that last mile.
   It helps so much to have someone I'm fond
   Of here to sit and drink and share my grief.
   There's no one else I'm sure his word's his bond.
   Talking things over gives me such relief.

FROSBY.
   Greville, there's something –

GREVILLE.
   Poor Jake. You knew him as a little lad.
   Remember the wooden soldier you once made him?

FROSBY.
   Greville, there's something –

GREVILLE.
                              He wasn't really bad.
   Some bastard whizzkid probably betrayed him.
   Poor Jakey, how could anybody sell you?

FROSBY.
   Greville, there's something that I ought to tell you.

   SCILLA *and* GRIMES *arrive*.

SCILLA.
   Daddy!

GREVILLE.
   Scilla!

SCILLA.
   Grimes, a colleague. My dad. Mr Frosby.

GRIMES.
   Nice place you've got. High ceilings. Plenty of headroom.
   Room for a chandelier. How many bedrooms?

GREVILLE.
   Six, actually, now that you come to mention –

GRIMES.
   That's all right. I could always build an extension.

GREVILLE.
   It's not for sale.

GRIMES.
                    No, I was just thinking.
   I'd give you half a million.

GREVILLE.
                              What are you drinking?

SCILLA.
   Daddy. Tell me the truth if you're sober en –
   ough to talk properly. About Jake.

GRIMES.
   I'd get an alsatian and a doberman.

GREVILLE.
   Darling, I think you're making a mistake.

SCILLA.
Do I know more than you? Marylou Baines.
Yes?

GREVILLE.
Now Scilla –

SCILLA.
Don't think you can smile a
Lot and not tell me. Ill gotten gains,
Right? Millions!

GRIMES.
I'll get a rottweiler.

SCILLA.
And nobody told me.

GREVILLE.
I know nothing about –

SCILLA.
Nothing?

GREVILLE.
Scilla, there's no need to shout.
Of course my son would make the odd suggestion –

SCILLA.
Where's his money?

GREVILLE.
But there's no question –
Marylou Baines?

GRIMES.
A rottweiler's a killer.

SCILLA.
What about me?

GREVILLE.
I protected you, Scilla.
It's bad enough to see a woman get work
Without her being part of an old boy network.

SCILLA.
Fuck off. I want my share.

GREVILLE.
Your share of what?
Daddy's always given you all he's got.
My little girl! Jake seems to have been much bigger
Than poor old daddy knew. If it's as you say,

If we're really dealing with a six nought figure.
Where the hell's he hidden it away?

GRIMES.

Don't piss about. We haven't got all day.
Who's his solicitor?

GREVILLE.

               I'm afraid I don't –

GRIMES.

Who's his accountant?

GREVILLE.

              In any case I won't –

FROSBY.

Who is this? An awful lout.

GRIMES.

If he really don't know we should get back.

FROSBY.

Ordering everyone about.

GRIMES.

It might be more use talking to Zac.

SCILLA.

If you're holding out on me daddy you'll be sorry.

GRIMES.

We'll have your feet run over by a lorry.

FROSBY.

Who is this horrible young vandal?
I don't need to know his name.
Responsible for all the scandal.
He's the one you ought to blame.

GRIMES.

You've all been coining it for years.

FROSBY.

My lovely city's sadly changed.
Sic transit gloria! Glory passes!
Any wonder I'm deranged,
Surrounded by the criminal classes.

GRIMES.

You've all been coining it for years.
All you fuckwits in the City.
It just don't look quite so pretty,

All the cunning little jobs,
When you see them done by yobs.

FROSBY.
He's the one you ought to blame.

GRIMES.
We're only doing just the same
All you bastards always done.
New faces in your old square mile,
Making money with a smile,
Just as clever, just as vile.

GREVILLE.
No, he's right, you killed my son.

GRIMES.
All your lives you've been in clover,
Fucking everybody over,
You just don't like to see us at it.

GREVILLE.
Scilla, I forbid you to associate with this oik.

SCILLA.
Daddy, you're trading like a cunt.
This is a waste of time. I'm going to see Corman again.

GREVILLE.
Scilla, wait, if you find out about Jake's money –

SCILLA.
Don't worry, I won't tell you, I'll protect you.

GREVILLE.
Scilla –

GRIMES.
If you want to sell the house I can pay cash.

SCILLA *and* GRIMES *leave.*

GREVILLE.
Because of yobs like him my Jake was led astray.
If it wasn't for that bastard he'd be alive today.
It's times like this you need an old friend –

FROSBY.
Greville.
It's me that told the DTI.
I can't quite remember why.
It didn't occur to me he'd die.

ZAC.

ZAC.

That afternoon things were going from bad to worse.

Jake was dead and I'd just as soon it was me they'd taken off in a hearse.

I'd just discovered Jacinta and Ajibala were no fucking help at all,

And I find Scilla hanging about in the hall.

ZAC *and* SCILLA *outside* CORMAN's *office.*

SCILLA.

Zac, I want to see Corman. Get me in.

ZAC.

Don't talk to me. We may not even win.

Jacinta Condor's supporting Biddulph which may wreck

The whole deal, and Nigel Ajibala's done god knows what with a two million pound cheque.

SCILLA.

Jacinta Condor? Nigel Ajibala?

ZAC.

I've got to get this sorted / before Corman finds out.

SCILLA.

But they were in Jake's diary.

ZAC.

                              Scilla, don't shout.

SCILLA.

Would either of them be likely to kill

Jake? Or more important still

Could they tell me about his bank account?

Which bank is it in? / And what's the total amount?

ZAC.

They've kicked this dog of a deal when I hoped they'd pat it. /
I've got to find them.

SCILLA.

And if it's in a numbered Swiss account, Zac, how do I get at it?

ZAC *goes.* MELISSA, *a model, enters.*

SCILLA.

Are you going to see Mr Corman?

MELISSA.

                              I don't know his name.

I'm having a picture taken. The PR

Consultant is in there with him, she's called Dolcie Starr.

Last time I did a job like this the bastard put his hand on my
   crutch.
I was ready to walk out, I said, 'What's your game?'
I hope nothing like that –

SCILLA.
   Can I go instead of you?

MELISSA.
                        How much?

CORMAN *and* DOLCIE STARR, *a PR consultant.*

CORMAN.
   My image is atrocious. 'Profiteering.'
   'Decline of British Industry.' 'Robber gangs.'
   There's even a cartoon here where I'm leering
   At an innocent girl called Albion and I've got fangs.
   I want to be seen as Albion's Mr Right.
   I need to be transformed overnight.
   Can you make me look as good as Duckett?

STARR.
   No, I'm afraid he's completely cornered the market
   In fatherly, blue-eyed, babies, workers' friend,
   Someone on whom the CBI can depend –

CORMAN.
   I'm all that.

STARR.
           No, you're none of that.

CORMAN.
                                Shit.

STARR.
   Cheer up, Corman, you're the opposite.

CORMAN.
   Then what am I paying you good money for?

STARR.
   Let Duckett be good. And a bore.
   Then you can be bad. And glamorous.
   You'll have top billing by tonight.
   Everyone loves a villain if he's handled right. /
   Bad has connotations of amorous.

CORMAN.
   Bad and glamorous?

STARR.
Two dimensions, spiritual and physical. First, spiritual.

CORMAN.
That's Duckett's area. He's a lay preacher. /
You don't want me to be a Moslem?

STARR.
No, secular spiritual. Arts. For you to reach a
Wide audience it's absolutely essential /
You sponsor –

CORMAN.
Duckett sponsors arts.

STARR.
                              He sponsors provincial
Orchestras. You need the National
Theatre for power, opera for decadence,
String quartets bearing your name for sensitivity and elegance,
And a fringe show with bad language for a thrill.
That should take care of the spiritual.
Now the physical. It's a pity you haven't a yacht.

CORMAN.
I'll buy one now.

STARR.
                        No, we'll work with what we've got.
I do recommend a sex scandal.

CORMAN.
Sex scandal? / That's the last thing –

STARR.
Will you let me handle this?
You think because you're already scandalous /
In the financial –

CORMAN.
I don't want –

STARR.
But that's the point. Fight scandal with scandal.
We provide a young girl who'll say you did it eight times a night.
Your wife is standing by you, so that's all right. /

CORMAN.
(I'm not married.)

STARR.
There could be a suggestion the girl might take her life –
If necessary we provide the wife.

CORMAN.
  I'm not sure –

STARR.
  There's ugly greedy and sexy greedy, you dope.
  At the moment you're ugly which is no hope.
  If you stay ugly, god knows what your fate is.
  But sexy greedy *is* the late eighties.

CORMAN.
  What about Aids? I thought sexy was out.

STARR.
  The more you don't do it, the more it's fun to read about.
  We might have made you make a statement about taking care.
  Wicked and responsible, the perfect chair / man.

CORMAN.
  I don't think I –

STARR.
  We can take the pictures straightaway. / Melissa!

CORMAN.
  Pictures?

STARR.
  You don't have to do a thing, not even kiss her.

  SCILLA *comes in.*

SCILLA.
  Melissa's ill. I'm Scilla, the replacement.

STARR.
  Mr Corman, you need to stand more adjacent.

CORMAN.
  I can't stop working while you take pictures. Zac!
  Where the fuck's he gone and why isn't he back?

  He recognises SCILLA.

  You again?

  SCILLA *and* CORMAN *talk while* STARR *takes photographs.*

SCILLA.
  I've important news for you about Albion,
  If you'll tell me more about Jake.

CORMAN.
  What news?

SCILLA.
  Jacinta Condor?

CORMAN.
What about her?

SCILLA.
How much did he make?

STARR.
Please look fonder.

SCILLA.
How much did you pay him?

CORMAN.
Two hundred grand.

SCILLA.
What did he do with it?

STARR.
If you took her hand.

CORMAN.
What about the señora?

SCILLA.
She's supporting Biddulph's bid.

STARR.
Could you be more a-
ffectionate – keep still please. Please smile. Smile, kid.

CORMAN.
I'll kill the bitch. /
I knew there was something funny.

SCILLA.
He was so fucking rich.
Who else gave him money?

CORMAN.
What else? Is that the lot?

SCILLA.
Ajibala.

CORMAN.
            What? what?

SCILLA.
More about Jake, or I won't say a word.

CORMAN.
I could name six companies he's dealt with, four merchant banks
    and two MPs and that's only what I've heard.
Your brother was widely respected in the City.
Now what about Ajibala? have some pity.

SCILLA.
  I'll tell you about him for a small fee.
  Three companies, two banks and one MP.
  CORMAN *whispers to* SCILLA. STARR *snaps enthusiastically.*

STARR.
  That's the way. That's what we like to see.
  Look as if you're having a lot of fun.
  We'll have the front page story of the *Sun*.

SCILLA.
  Ajibala's gone off with the two million you gave him.

CORMAN.
  Not bought my stock? There's nothing going to save him, Zac!
  He realises about the pictures.

CORMAN.
  Hang on a minute, you can't use these, this girl is the sister of the
    dead whizzkid in today's papers.

STARR.
  And that's a scandal with which you've got no connection?

CORMAN.
  No, that's the scandal where there is a connection but I don't want
    it known, I just want to be connected with the fictitious scandal
    where I've got a permanent erection.
      (Eight times a night? Maybe four, let's be plausible.)

STARR.
  But we can't let the whole story escape us.
  This other scandal's a high-profile thriller.
  Terrific pictures. / What's your name? Scilla?

CORMAN.
  No, please –

SCILLA.
  What's this about eight times a night?

STARR.
  You make a statement to the press saying –

SCILLA.
  Right. Keep paying or I'll agree.
  Three companies.
  CORMAN *whispers to* SCILLA.
  Two banks.
  CORMAN *whispers.*
  One MP.

CORMAN *whispers.*

SCILLA.
I've never seen Mr Corman before.
From what I do see he's an awful bore.

CORMAN.
Great! More! more! Don't skimp.

SCILLA.
He's physically repellent. What a wimp.

STARR.
Ok Ok, I get it. What duplicity.
Why don't you people appreciate publicity?
You've wasted a lot of film. Where's Melissa?

STARR *leaves.*

CORMAN.
Do you want a job? Most of the people who work for me are
mentally defective.

SCILLA.
Maybe later when I've finished being a detective.

CORMAN.
Zac! Etherington!
I want blood. What the fuck's going on?

ZAC *comes in followed by* NIGEL AJIBALA.

ZAC.
Hold on, I've got Ajibala right here.

CORMAN. Where's my money? You'd better start talking fast.
You can stick your cocoa beans up your arse.
Where's my two million pounds?

NIGEL.
I'm delighted to have this opportunity
Of explaining how by judicious speculation
I plan to increase the sum that you gave me so that I can buy even
    more shares in support of your acquisition.
I think I may certainly say with impunity /
That when you –

ETHERINGTON *comes in with* GREVETT, *a DTI inspector.*

CORMAN.
Ajibala, I've been tricked.

I gave you two million pounds / on the strict
Understanding that you'd –

ETHERINGTON.
Mr Corman. Mr Corman. Mr Corman.

GREVETT.
Do finish your sentence, Mr Corman.

CORMAN.
What's going on? Who the hell's this?
Who let him in? Sack the receptionist.

GREVETT.
I identified myself to your receptionist
As Grevett from the Department of Trade and Industry. /
People don't usually refuse to see me.

CORMAN.
Very nice to meet you, Mr Grevett.

ETHERINGTON.
I assured Mr Grevett we'd be delighted to assist
With his inquiries in any way we could. /
We know the DTI is a force for good.

CORMAN.
Delighted.

GREVETT.
What was that about two million pounds?

ETHERINGTON.
I thought it might interest you, because it sounds /
Unusual, but in fact –

CORMAN.
What was it, Zac?

ZAC.
Mr Corman is paying Klein Merrick, the bank I work for, two
    million pounds for advisory /
Services.

ETHERINGTON.
The sum's derisory /
Considering the immense –

GREVETT.
I believed he was addressing this gentleman?

ETHERINGTON.
                                        By no means.

CORMAN.
  Mr Ajibala, who supplies our cocoa beans.

GREVETT.
  So the sum in question was to do with the cocoa trade?

ZAC *and* ETHERINGTON.
  No.

CORMAN (*simultaneously*).
  Yes. That is no, but we have made
  Some arrangements to do with cocoa which were being discussed.

ETHERINGTON.
  But the two million pounds was a payment to Klein.

ZAC.
  Yes, that side of the business is all mine.

GREVETT.
  Mr Ajibala, you can confirm I trust
  That you never received the sum of two million?

NIGEL.
  I only wish I had.

  All laugh except GREVETT.

GREVETT.
  The suggestion seems to cause you some amusement.
  I have to establish you see that no inducement
  Financial or otherwise was offered by Mr Corman
  To buy stock to help support his price.

NIGEL.
  Two million pounds would be extremely nice.
  But no, Mr Grevett, I assure you.
  An account of the cocoa trade would only bore you.

GREVETT.
  And you Mr Corman would confirm – ?

CORMAN. Absolutely.

GREVETT.
  It sounded as if you were asking him to return
  Two million pounds. I must have misunderstood.
  You weren't asking – ?

CORMAN.
                              No, no no, why should I?
  I never gave him a two million pound cheque.

NIGEL.
  So naturally he can't ask for it back.

I must be going. I've meetings to attend.
Good afternoon, Mr Corman.

CORMAN.
  Wait.

GREVETT.
  What?

CORMAN.
  Nothing.

  SCILLA *waylays* NIGEL *on his way out.*

SCILLA.
  I've got to talk to you. You were a friend
  Of my brother Jake.

NIGEL.
                    Who? I never met him.

SCILLA.
  It seems to be very easy to forget him.
  Do you owe him money?

NIGEL.
                    This is crazier and crazier.
  If you'll excuse me I have a very important meeting about cocoa
    stocks in Malaysia.

  NIGEL AJIBALA *leaves.*

GREVETT.
  Does the name Jake Todd ring a bell?

CORMAN.
  No. Oh yes, in the paper. Most unfortunate.
      (I hope the stupid bastard rots in hell.)

GREVETT.
  Not someone with whom you were personally acquainted?

CORMAN.
  No, not at all. He seems to have been tainted /
  By allegations of –

GREVETT.
  I don't wish to be importunate,
  But I was wondering if it would be possible for me to cast an eye
  Over any papers relating to your interest in Albion, just a formality.

CORMAN.
  This way.

GREVETT.
   Your involvement, Mrs Etherington, naturally goes a long way to reassure us of the transaction's total legality.

ETHERINGTON.
   There could of course be aspects of which I wasn't aware because my participation wasn't required.

CORMAN.
   Etherington, you're fired.

   GREVETT *and* ETHERINGTON *leave.*

CORMAN.
   We'll give him a pile of papers ten feet high
   And keep him busy till after the deal's completed.
   Fuck the DTI, Zac, I refuse to be defeated.
   I don't care if I go to jail, I'll win whatever the cost.
   They may say I'm a bastard but they'll never say I lost.

ZAC.
   Corman, there's one thing.
   Gleason called and said he's seeing Lear at the National.
   Could you meet him and have a word at the interval.
   I don't know why you're being asked to meet a cabinet minister,
   I hope it's nothing sinister.
   But when the government asks you for a date, you don't stand them up.

CORMAN.
   Fuck.

   CORMAN *leaves.* ZAC *and* SCILLA *alone.*

ZAC.
   Whether we'll get away with this is anybody's guess.
      (My guess is no.)
   And to think Jacinta Condor – / god, what an awful mess.

SCILLA.
   She knew Jake, didn't she? Ajibala denied it.

ZAC.
   He's the key to all the deals, of course they're going to hide it.

SCILLA.
   I want to meet them.

ZAC.
                      Scilla, we all have to lie low.

SCILLA.
   I want to meet all his contacts because someone's going to know where / his money is.

ZAC.

It'll be in a nominee company, and god knows where, no one
    except maybe Marylou Baines might know.

SCILLA.

Then I'll go and see Marylou Baines. / She's the one who made him.

ZAC.

No Scilla, I didn't mean –

SCILLA.

Yes, she'll know where his money is because she'll know how she
    paid him.

Do you think she owes him money? / Maybe I could collect.

ZAC.

Scilla –

SCILLA.

I'll go to New York / tonight.

ZAC.

                              Scilla, we must keep out of the news.
If you're going to be stupid I'll call Marylou and warn her and
    she'll refuse –

SCILLA.

How much does Mr Grevett of the DTI suspect?
I could go and have a word / with him

ZAC.

Scilla, don't be absurd.

SCILLA.

I could have my picture in the papers
With Corman alleging all kinds of capers /
And linking him publicly with bad Jake Todd.

ZAC.

Scilla, you wouldn't. God.

SCILLA.

So call Marylou Baines and tell her I'm on my way to Heathrow
    and she's to see me. Do it.

ZAC.

At least you'll be out of England.

SCILLA.

I'll send you a postcard.

ZAC.

Scilla, I thought you were some kind of English rose.

SCILLA.

Go stick the thorns up your nose, bozo.

SCILLA *goes.*

ZAC.

Somewhere along the line I really blew it.

MERRISON *and* SOAT, *President of Missouri Gumballs, at a drugstore in Missouri.*

MERRISON.

So how would you like to acquire a multinational?

SOAT.

Mr Merrison, this hardly seems rational.

My company is really extremely small.

You realise our only product is those little balls

Of gum you buy in the street out of machines?

If Corman took me over, I'd understand it.

But I'm really not cut out for a corporate bandit.

I've hardly got out from under my last creditor

And now you're trying to turn me into a predator.

MERRISON.

The smaller you are, the bigger the triumph for me.

I can raise four billion dollars of junk.

SOAT.

Mr Merrison. I'm afraid I'm in a funk.

I don't know what to say. What're you doin'?

MERRISON.

I'm using you, Mr Soat, to humiliate

Somebody I have good reason to hate.

SOAT.

I'm not sure –

MERRISON.

I wouldn't like to ruin

Missouri Gumballs, it seems kind of dumb.

SOAT.

No no. No no no no. Don't take my gum.

I'll think about it. I've thought about it. Great.

CORMAN, GLEASON, *a cabinet minister, in the interval at the National Theatre.*

GLEASON.

Enjoying the show?

CORMAN.
               I'm not watching it.

GLEASON.
   It's excellent of course, they're not botching it.
   But after a hard day's work my eyes keep closing.
   I keep jerking awake when they shout.

CORMAN.
   It's hard to follow the plot if you keep dozing. /
   What exactly is this meeting all about?

GLEASON.
   Yes, Goneril and Reagan and Ophelia –
   Good of you to come.
   We have here two conflicting interests.
   On the one hand it's natural the investor
   Wants to make all the profit that he can,
   And institutions' duty to the pensioners
   Does put the onus on the short-term plan.
   On the other hand one can't but help mention
   The problems this creates for industry,
   Who needs long-term research and development
   In order to create more employment.
   It's hard to reconcile but we must try.

CORMAN.
   I totally agree with the CBI.
   Long-term issues mustn't be neglected.
   The responsibility of management –

GLEASON.
   We – by which I mean of course the government –
   Recognise that alas nothing's perfect.
   That's something you learn in politics.
   We want to cut the top rate of tax,
   And profit related pay's a good incentive.
   But we do think things have gone too far
   In the quick-profit short-term direction.
   We wouldn't interfere in a free market.
   But we are of course approaching an election.

CORMAN.
   Absolutely and I hope to give
   More than moral support to the party.
   I've always been a staunch Conservative.

GLEASON.
   My dear fellow, nobody doubts your loyalty.

That's why I have so little hesitation
In asking this small service to the nation.
Drop your bid. Give up. Leave it alone.

CORMAN.

Out of the question. Sorry. Out of the question.

GLEASON.

I absolutely appreciate the problem –

CORMAN.

Leave me alone will you to do my job.

GLEASON.

I'm sorry, Corman, but I must forbid it.
A takeover like this in the present climate
Makes you, and the City, and us look greedy.
Help us be seen to care about the needy.
Help us to counteract the effect of Tebbit.

CORMAN.

What if I say no?

GLEASON.

I wouldn't like to dwell on the unsavoury
Story of that young man's suicide –

CORMAN.

Are you threatening me?

GLEASON.

                        I do admire your bravery.
No, but my colleagues in the DTI
Did, I believe, call on you today.

CORMAN.

Leave it out, Gleason, I've had enough.
DTI? I'm going to call your bluff.
If my takeover's going to hurt your image
Another scandal would do far more damage

GLEASON.

Mr Corman, I'll be brutally frank.
A scandal would not be welcomed by the Bank
Nor will it be tolerated by the Tories.
Whenever you businessmen do something shitty
Some of it gets wiped off on the City,
And the government's smelly from the nasty stories.

Meanwhile, 'Ladies and gentlemen take your seats' etc.

CORMAN.

Us businessmen? / The banks are full of crap.

GLEASON.
    So if you persist and make a nasty mess
    Not a single bank will handle your business.

CORMAN.
    You can't do that, Gleason, don't make me laugh.

GLEASON.
    Corman, please, don't make my patience snap.
    I wouldn't want to miss the second half.
    You drop your bid. We stop the DTI.

CORMAN.
    You'd stop the scandal breaking anyway.
    Are you telling me you can't control the press?

GLEASON.
    Yes, but we'd break you. Do you want to try?
    You drop the bid. We stop the DTI.

CORMAN.
    Why pick on me? Everyone's the same.
    I'm just good at playing a rough game.

GLEASON.
    Exactly, and the game must be protected.
    You can go on playing after we're elected.
    Five more glorious years free enterprise,
    And your services to industry will be recognised.

    GLEASON *goes.*

CORMAN.
    Cunt. Right. Good.
    At least a knighthood.

ZAC *and* JACINTA, *exhausted, in the foyer of the Savoy.*

ZAC.
    So he cancelled the deal.

JACINTA.
    And how do you feel?

ZAC.
    Exhausted.

JACINTA.
                I get you a drink.
    At least we can meet,
    You're not rushed off your feet,
    It's better like this I think.

ZAC.

Jacinta, I still can't forgive you for going to Biddulph, the whole deal could have been wrecked.

JACINTA.

But I get more money that way, Zac, really what do you expect?
I can't do bad business just because I feel romantic.

ZAC.

The way you do business, Jacinta, drives me completely frantic.

JACINTA.

I love the way you are so obsessed when you're thinking about your bids.

ZAC.

I love that terrible hospital scam / and the drug addicted kids.

JACINTA.

(That's true, Zac!)
I love the way you never stop work, I hate a man who's lazy.

ZAC.

The way you unloaded your copper mines drove me completely crazy.

JACINTA.

Zac, you're so charming, I'm almost as fond
Of you as I am of a eurobond.

ZAC.

I thought we'd never manage to make a date.
You're more of a thrill than a changing interest rate.

JACINTA.

This is a very public place to meet.

ZAC.

Maybe we ought to go up to your suite.

They get up to go.

ZAC.

Did you ever play with a hoop when you were a child and when it stops turning it falls down flat?
I feel kind of like that.

JACINTA.

I am very happy. My feeling for you is deep.
But will you mind very much if we go to sleep?

GREVILLE, *drunk.*

GREVILLE.

Maybe I should retire while my career is at its pinnacle.

Working in the City can make one rather cynical.

When an oil tanker sank with a hundred men the lads cheered
because they'd make a million.

When Sadat was shot I was rather chuffed because I was long of
gold bullion.

Life's been very good to me. I think I'll work for Oxfam.

FROSBY, *with a gun.*

FROSBY.

I thought the sun would never set.

I thought I'd be extremely rich.

You can't be certain what you'll get.

I've heard the young say Life's a bitch.

I betrayed my oldest friend.

It didn't give me too much fun.

My way of life is at an end.

At least I have a friendly gun.

My word is my junk bond.

DAVE *and* MARTIN *have just come out of a Chinese restaurant. Late
night.*

DAVE.

I've eaten too many crab claws.

MARTIN.

You'll be sick in the cab again.

DAVE.

You'll get stick from your wife again.

MARTIN.

She don't care if I'm late.

DAVE.

What's she up to then?

MARTIN.

Watch it.

DAVE.

Late city, no pity.

BRIAN, TERRY *and* VINCE *follow.*

BRIAN.

Guy meets a guy and he says what do you do for a living and he
says I hurt people. / He says you hurt people,

TERRY.
Sounds like my girlfriend.

BRIAN.
he says yes I hurt people for money. / I'm a hitman.*

TERRY.
Sounds like a trader.

MARTIN.
How much was it?

DAVE.
Bet it was two fifty.

MARTIN.
Bet it was three hundred.

DAVE.
How much?

MARTIN.
Ten.

VINCE.
Two eighty five.

MARTIN.
Told you. All that crab.

DAVE *gives* MARTIN *ten pounds.*

BRIAN.
*Break a leg, five hundred pounds, break a back, a thousand /

DAVE.
I know him, he works for Liffe.

BRIAN.
And he says I'm glad I met you because my neighbour's carrying on
    with my wife.
So he takes him home and says see that lighted window, that's
    where they are, I want her dead,
How much would it cost to shoot her through the head?*

TERRY. You can't get rid of your money in Crete.
    Hire every speedboat, drink till you pass out, eat
    Till you puke and you're still loaded with drachs.

MARTIN. } Drach attack! drach attack!
DAVE.

VINCE.
Why's a clitoris like a filofax?

DAVE *and* OTHERS.
Every cunt's got one.

BRIAN.
  *And he says five grand.
  And he says, now my neighbour what would it cost if you shot off
    his prick and his balls.
  And he says that's five grand and all.
  So he says ten grand! Yes all right, it's worth it, go on, so the
    hitman's stood there by the garden gate
  And he points his gun at the window, and he's stood there and
    stood there, and he says get on with it, and the hitman says Wait.
  Time it right / and I'll save you five grand.

DAVE.
  I'll save you five grand.

MARTIN.
  Two eurobond dealers walking through Trafalgar Square, one of
    them said what would you do if a bird shat on your head?
  And he said /
  I don't think I'd ask her out again.

DAVE.
  I don't think I'd ask her out again.

SCILLA *at* MARYLOU BAINES' *office in New York.*
SCILLA, TK.

TK.
  Hi, I'm TK, Marylou Baines' personal assistant.

SCILLA.
  Tell Marylou Baines
  I've just flown in from London, I've come here straight off the
    plane.
  I'm Jake Todd's sister and I've got some information
  That I didn't want to trust to the telephone so I've brought it
    myself personally to its destination.

TK.
  Ms Baines won't see you I'm afraid but if you like to give me the
    information instead,
  I'm setting up in business myself and can guarantee you'd receive
    service second to none because it's always those who are starting
    up who work hardest because they want to get ahead.
  So can I help you?

SCILLA.
  I didn't spend six hours crossing the Atlantic
  To be fobbed off by a personal assistant.

TK.

I'm sorry about this but it is part of my job description to be resistant.

SCILLA.

I warn you, I'm very tired and I'm getting frantic,
And Marylou will get a terrible fright
Tomorrow morning if she doesn't see me tonight.

TK.

If you just give me some indication of what your problem's about –

SCILLA.

Get out of my way. OUT OUT OUT.

MARYLOU *comes in.*

MARYLOU.

So. Todd's sister. You've come flying
From London with information?

SCILLA.

No, I was lying.
You don't get information this time, Marylou.
I want to know things from you.

MARYLOU.

You can ask.

SCILLA.

I had been wondering if you killed Jake, but now I hardly care.
It's not going to bring him alive again, and the main thing's to get my share.
They left me out because I'm a girl and it's terribly unfair.
You were Jake's main employer so tell me please
How did you pay him his enormous fees?
Did somebody pass a briefcase of notes at a station under a clock?
Or did you make over a whole lot of stock?
Did he have a company and what's its name?
And how can I get in on the game?
You'll need a replacement in London who knows their way round the businesses and banks.
Can I suggest somebody?

MARYLOU.

No thanks.

SCILLA.

If you don't help me I'll go to the authorities and tell them –

MARYLOU.

Is this blackmail?

SCILLA.
  Yes, of course. I can put you in jail.

MARYLOU.
  I'll take the risk. I'm a risk arbitrageur.
  So run off home.

TK.
  And nobody in America runs better risks than her.

SCILLA.
  You can stick your arbitrage up your arse.
  If you don't tell me about his company
  You'll find me quite a dangerous enemy.
  I'm greedy and completely amoral.
  I've the cunning and connections of the middle class
  And I'm tough as a yob.

MARYLOU.
  Scilla, don't let's quarrel.
  My personal assistant's leaving. Do you want a job?

TK.
  Right now?

MARYLOU.
  Sure, TK, you said you wanted out,
  Scilla wants in. So don't let's hang about.

  MARYLOU *and* SCILLA *go.*

TK.
  One thing I've learned from working for Marylou:
  Do others before they can do you.

ZAC.

ZAC.
  So Scilla never came back.
  She sent me a postcard of the Statue of Liberty saying Bye bye Zac.
  She never did find out who killed her brother but I'm sure it wasn't
    Corman or Jacinta or Marylou or any of us.
  Who didn't want Jake to talk to the DTI? Who wanted him out of
    the way?
  The British government, because another scandal just before the
    election would have been too much fuss.
  So I reckon it was MI5 or the CIA.
      (Or he could even have shot himself, the kid wasn't stable.)
  There's bound to be endless scandals in the city but really it's
    incidental.

It can be a nuisance because it gives the wrong impression
And if people lose confidence in us there could be a big recession.
Sure this is a dangerous system and it could crash any minute and I
    sometimes wake up in bed
And think is Armageddon Aids, nuclear war or a crash, and how
    will I end up dead?
        (But that's just before breakfast.)
What really matters is the massive sums of money being passed
    round the world, and trying to appreciate their size can drive you
    mental.
There haven't been a million days since Christ died.
So think a billion, that's a thousand million, and have you ever tried
To think a trillion? Think a trillion dollars a day.
That's the gross national product of the USA.
There's people who say the American eagle is more like a vulture.
I say don't piss on your own culture.
Naturally there's a whole lot of greed and
That's no problem because money buys freedom.
So the Tories kept the scandal to the minimum. Greville Todd was
    arrested and put in prison to show the government was serious
    about keeping the city clean and nobody shed any tears.
And the Conservatives romped home with a landslide victory for
    five more glorious years.
        (Which was handy though not essential because it would take
        far more than Labour to stop us.)

I've been having a great time raising sixteen billion dollars to build
    a satellite,
And I reckon I can wrap it up tonight.

EVERYBODY

SCILLA.
    Scilla's been named by Business Week as Wall Street's rising star.
GREVILLE.
    Greville walked out of the open prison but didn't get very far.
GRIMES.
    Grimes does insider dealing for Scilla and Marylou (and he bought
    Greville's house).
JAKE.
    Jake's ghost appeared to Jacinta one midnight in Peru.
JACINTA.
    Jacinta marries Zac next week and they honeymoon in Shanghai.
        (Good business to be done in China now.)

NIGEL.
Nigel Ajibala's doing something in Dubai.

CORMAN.
Lord Corman's helping organise the tunnel under the channel.
(He's also chairman of the board of the National Theatre.)

ETHERINGTON.
Etherington runs the City's new disciplinary panel.

DUCKETT.
Duckett had a breakdown and was given ECT.

BIDDULPH.
Biddulph's running Albion and is big in ITV.

TK.
TK ended up in jail because of some funny tricks.

MARYLOU.
Marylou Baines ran for president in 1996.

MERRISON.
Merrison's been ambassador to London, Paris, Rome.

DURKFELD.
Durkfeld had a heart attack one quiet Sunday at home.

SOAT.
Soat acquired Corman Enterprise and a dangerous reputation.

STARR.
Dolcie Starr does his PR so he's loved by the whole nation.

TERRY.
Terry went to Chicago and did a lot of coke.

VINCE.
Vince spent every penny he earned and thought it was a joke.

KATHY.
Kathy's got a telly spot, advice on buying shares.

JOANNE.
Joanne became a trader and soon she moved upstairs.

MARTIN.
Martin moved to eurobonds.

BRIAN.
                              Brian bought a deer park.

DAVE.
Dave went to Australia and was eaten by a shark.

FROSBY.
Frosby was forgotten.

FIVE MORE GLORIOUS YEARS

Wa-doooo do-ya-doody, wa-doooo do-ya-do
These are the best years of our lives, let wealth and favour be our guide
We can expect another five, join hands across the great divide
BACK UP: wa-doooo do-ya-doody, wa-doooo do-ya-doody
         Say-wa   do-ya-doody, wa-doooo do-ya-do

So raise your oysters and champagne, and as we toast the blushing bride
Pon crystal mountains of cocaine, our nostrils flare and open wide
B/U: tippy-tum-tee-tippy-tum-tum, tippy-tippy tum-tum
     tippy-tum-tee-tippy-tum-tum, tippy-tippy tum-tum
     say-wa   tippy-tippy tum-tum
     tippy-tum-tee-tippy-tum-tum, tippy-tippy tum-tum.

Chorus:
Five more glorious years, five more glorious years
B/U: we're saved from the valley of tears for five more glorious years
     pissed and promiscuous the money's ridiculous
     send her victorious for five fucking morious
     Five more glorious years

These are the best years of our lives, with information from inside
My new Ferrari has just arrived, these pleasures stay unqualified
B/U: Fiddle diddle iddle fiddle diddle, fiddle diddle iddle
     Fiddle diddle iddle fiddle diddle, fiddle diddle iddle
     Say-wa   fiddle diddle iddle
     Fiddle-diddle-iddle-fiddle-diddle-fiddle-diddle-iddle

Chorus:
Five more glorious years, five more glorious years
B/U: we're crossing forbidden frontiers, we're sniding beneath our veneer
     pissed and promiscuous, the money's ridiculous
     send her victorious for five fucking morious
     five more glorious years
Five more glorious years, five more glorious years
     we're saved from the valley of tears for five more glorious years
     pissed and promiscuous, the money's ridiculous
     send her victorious for five fucking morious
     five more glorious years

A capella:
These are the best years of our lives, these are the best years of our lives
These are the best years of our lives, these are the best years of our lives
B/U: wa-doooo do-ya-doody, wa-doooo do-ya-doody
     Say-wa   do-ya-doody, wa-doooo do-ya-do

These are the best years of our lives, and as we toast the blushing bride
My Maserati has arrived, join hands across the great divide

B/U: fiddle diddle iddle fiddle diddle, fiddle diddle iddle
      fiddle diddle iddle fiddle diddle, fiddle diddle iddle
      Say-wa   fiddle diddle iddle
      Fiddle diddle iddle- ddle diddle, fiddle diddle iddle

Chorus:
Five more glorious years, five more glorious years
B/U: we're saved from the valley of tears for five more glorious years
      pissed and promiscuous, the money's ridiculous
      send her victorious for five fucking morious
      five more glorious years

Chorus:
Five more glorious years, five more glorious years
B/U: We're crossing forbidden frontiers for five more glorious years
      pissed and promiscuous, the money's ridiculous
      send her victorious for five fucking morious
      five more glorious years

For a complete catalogue of Methuen Drama titles
write to:

Methuen Drama
A & C Black Publishers Limited
38 Soho Square
London
W1D 3HB

or you can visit our website at:

www.acblack.com